Also by Sarah Knott

Sensibility and the American Revolution
Women, Gender and Enlightenment (coeditor)

MOTHER IS A VERB

MOTHER IS A VERB

An
Unconventional
History

SARAH KNOTT

Sarah Crichton Books   Farrar, Straus and Giroux   New York

Sarah Crichton Books
Farrar, Straus and Giroux
175 Varick Street, New York 10014

Printed in the United States of America
Originally published in 2019 by Viking, an imprint of Penguin Random House,
Great Britain, as *Mother: An Unconventional History*
Published in the United States by Sarah Crichton Books / Farrar, Straus and Giroux
First American edition, 2019

Grateful acknowledgment is made for permission to reprint excerpts from the following
previously published material: *Frontispiece*: © 2018 Artists Rights Society (ARS), New York /
DACS, London. *Chapter 2*: Excerpt from "Annus Mirabilis" from *The Complete Poems of Philip
Larkin* by Philip Larkin, edited by Archie Burnett. Copyright © 2012 by the Estate of Philip
Larkin. Reprinted by permission of Farrar, Straus and Giroux. *Chapter 4*: Excerpt of 6 lines
from "Parliament Hill Fields," from *The Collected Poems of Sylvia Plath*, edited by Ted Hughes.
Copyright © 1960, 1965, 1971, 1981 by the Estate of Sylvia Plath. Editorial material copyright
© 1981 by Ted Hughes. Reprinted by permission of HarperCollins Publishers. *Chapter 7*: "This
giving birth, this glistening verb," excerpted from the poem "The Language of the Brag," from
Satan Says, by Sharon Olds, copyright 1980. Reprinted by permission of the University of
Pittsburgh Press. *Chapter 11*: "The Waiting" from *The City in Which I Love You*, copyright
1990 by Li-Young Lee, BOA Editions, Ltd., www.boaeditions.org. *Chapter 13*: Brenda
Shaughnessy, excerpt from "Liquid Flesh" from *Our Andromeda*. Copyright 2012 by Brenda
Shaughnessy. Reprinted by permission of The Permissions Company, Inc., on behalf of
Copper Canyon Press, www.coppercanyonpress.org.

Library of Congress Cataloging-in-Publication Data
Names: Knott, Sarah, 1972– author.
Title: Mother is a verb : an unconventional history / Sarah Knott.
Description: New York : Sarah Crichton Books, Farrar, Straus and Giroux,
    [2019] | Includes bibliographical references.
Identifiers: LCCN 2018047978 | ISBN 9780374213589 (hardcover)
Subjects: LCSH: Motherhood. | Mothers.
Classification: LCC HQ759 .K596 2019 | DDC 306.874/3—dc23
LC record available at https://lccn.loc.gov/2018047978

Designed by Abby Kagan

Our books may be purchased in bulk for promotional, educational, or business use. Please
contact your local bookseller or the Macmillan Corporate and Premium Sales Department at
1-800-221-7945, extension 5442, or by e-mail at MacmillanSpecialMarkets@macmillan.com.

www.fsgbooks.com
www.twitter.com/fsgbooks • www.facebook.com/fsgbooks

1 3 5 7 9 10 8 6 4 2

Frontispiece: Jenny Saville, *Study for Pentimenti III (sinopia)*, 2011 to K, M, and V

Contents

CONTENTS

MOTHER IS A VERB

Prologue

There's a sepia document on the kitchen table, just out of the new baby's reach. My mum brought it the last time she visited us, thinking I'd be interested in her maternity records. The print on the envelope reads "CONFIDENTIAL." "IMPORTANT NOTE" runs along the bottom: "This card must be kept in YOUR POSSESSION." In the 1970s, Britain's National Health Service spoke to its patients in officious tones.

The brown-beige color of the envelope is not unlike the seventeenth- and eighteenth-century manuscripts I usually read in my job as a historian. Paper often starts out almost white, but the centuries bring out the impurities by the time the sheets rest in a contemporary archive.

The NHS envelope is scuffed from use, but in good enough shape to open. On the outside, my mother's London N14 address is crossed through, replaced by the Essex address of my childhood. A small urban flat switched for a tidy three-bedroom house in a village not far from the North Sea.

I'd like to remove the envelope's contents, but the baby keeps moving on my lap, locks eyes and wants distracting, smells good and distracts. Starfish hands bat toward round face, signaling the naptime hour.

What are the many different pasts of becoming a mother? What can we know of what, say, seventeenth-century people called "going with child": carrying and caring for an infant? "Going with child is, as it were, a rough sea on which a big-bellied woman and her infant floats the space of nine months," reckoned an observer in 1688. Then "labour, which is the only port, is so full of dangerous rocks, that very often both the one and the other, after they are arrived . . . have yet need of much help to defend them." A stormy, shape-shifting scene, fraught and rocky, full of drama.[1]

In an hour and a half, there will be a clatter at the front door, and my spouse, K, will arrive with the baby's noisy older sibling. Better put the envelope, and its single homegrown piece of evidence, aside for now.

The baby is asleep, and slanting sunlight falls on the "Mrs." printed by the envelope's first address line. The late-twentieth-century NHS presumed that pregnancy indicated marriage. The everyday phrase "unwed mother" shifted to the less pejorative "single mother" in the 1960s, but a wedding and stay-at-home motherhood were still held out as the family norm.

Inside the envelope is a "Co-operation Record Card for Maternity Patients" with an infant's immunization record stapled on top. What insights might this hold about mothering an infant in 1970s Britain? Antenatal care began at three months, after a test administered by a doctor to confirm the pregnancy. Twelve weeks, reads the record card. Fourteen weeks, eighteen, twenty-two . . .

Other London mothers of the same decade told the sociologist Ann Oakley about attending an prenatal clinic. "Very assembly line," reckoned the twenty-six-year-old illustrator Gillian Hartley about her first visit; "I got up a nervous wreck as usual," though the staff were nice. Nina Brady, a shop assistant who called Oakley "dear," found the encounter with a doctor so embarrassing that she did not want to go again. Brady told one of the nurses about a woman who never attended the clinic because she thought it was all a load of rubbish. Twenty-six weeks, twenty-eight, thirty. My mother, then a shy nurse in her late twenties, attended all her appointments.[2]

"Quickening" gets its own entry on the record card. The first time a person felt their baby move was deemed medically important. The term has a long pedigree. Seventeenth-century Englishwomen took quickening as definitive proof of pregnancy. Ojibwe women native to North America saw this as the moment when a life within became a human being. Familiarity with the term has come and gone. Charlotte Hirsch, a novelist who in 1917 anonymously wrote the first published personal account of being pregnant, had always thought the word meant the baby taking its first breaths of outside air. My English friends and family routinely know the term. The friends and colleagues where I usually reside and work in the United States sometimes do not.[3]

The record card documents the sensations and feelings of pregnancy tersely and at second hand. "Quickening" is recorded by a date, with no other details. "Well" recorded the London doctor at thirty-four weeks. "Feels well" wrote the Essex doctor a little later. "Well" again, at forty. If it's a dilemma figuring out how to recapture experiences from the 1970s, how much greater for the terrain of Britain and North America since the seventeenth century? These places have sometimes been connected—by a colonial past or by changes common to the West—and sometimes not.

"Feels well." The brevity of that tiny phrase is typical of what past experiences of mothering have left behind for us to notice, retrospectively, and to wonder about. Even in the best-lit corners of past and present, caring for an infant interrupts thinking, punctures reflection, or leaves a book half read. The richest records, such as letters and diaries, often stop exactly as they are getting interesting. A piece of correspondence is left off, mid-sentence; the letter writer called away by a cry, or a diary suspends, because both hands are needed to hold the baby.

The political revolutions I more usually research as a historian lend themselves to massive paper trails: declarations of independence, constitutions, newspaper columns, ideological pamphlets, wartime correspondence. When not on maternity leave, I tell my students grand narratives about the late-eighteenth-century transition from kingdoms to republics. Their eyes widen at the less familiar parts: not the doings of a Benjamin Franklin or a Marie Antoinette, but enslaved men and women escaping to freedom, or Native American diplomats forging alliances with France or Spain, Britain or the United States, in an attempt to stop settlers' expansion across the American continent. About mothering an infant, I am on smaller, grittier ground. The drama is piecemeal, and the record is fragmentary.

Some of quickening, or of "feeling well," 1970s-style, is illuminated by contexts immediately beyond the maternity card. Pregnancy should be "healthy and content," according to medical recommendations of the day—a "happy event."

Will it be a *happy* book? my very private mother asks, kindly, tentatively, on the phone, a thread of worry in her voice.

In fact, we know more about experiences of mothering in the 1970s than in any earlier generation, thanks to the women's liberation movement of that decade. When Ann Oakley asked her London interviewees about quickening, they detailed the baby's first movements variously as "like food resting," or "just like fluttering," or a "little butterfly," "a fish swimming—or a very large tadpole." Some writers, mainly white feminists in the United States, published maternal memoirs, as if the fact that having a baby had become optional finally allowed the complexity of maternity to be worthy of interest. Others defiantly wrote poetry. "The Language of the Brag," Sharon Olds titled her poem about giving birth.[4]

But what's left behind from Britain and North America *before* the 1970s is mainly a hundredweight of fragments. A seventeenth-century court record happens to reveal a baby being noisy in church. Or an eighteenth-century traveler describes a Native woman tanning a leather hide and tending to the occupant of a cradleboard. Or a nineteenth-century social reformer notes an infant suspended in an egg box from a factory ceiling, hinting at how working mothers managed. Or a farmer's wife in the 1930s dashes off an account of colic to a government department, requesting the latest medical advice.

These are such small shards of evidence. I've been complaining to K, who is also a historian, that there's not much to work with. At least my mother's life generated a medical record.

Perhaps the best way to explore the pasts of having a baby is to put grand narratives aside, and pay attention to the fragments and the anecdotes. Perhaps the best way to explore mothering's many pasts is to build a trellis of tiny scenes, pursuing the many different actions involved. Conceiving, miscarrying, quickening, carrying, birthing. And then, cleaning, feeding, sleeping, not sleeping, providing, being interrupted, passing back and forth. These make up the visceral ongoingness, the blood and guts of being "with child." The verbs.

"Mother" as a verb.

This evening, K has the radio on and is getting things ready for the baby's bath. The white noise should prevent any conversation from waking the firstborn. Did you know, I say, leaning in the doorframe, that when the British psychoanalyst Donald Winnicott was doing the first radio programs about mothering back in the 1940s, listeners initially thought he was a woman? His high, reedy voice sounded female. Perhaps Winnicott's attitude about infant care helped; unlike so many male experts before and since, he clearly liked and trusted mothers.

On the radio tonight there's discussion of a memoir by a Canadian trans man who nurses his own baby and works as a lactation consultant. Having a baby is such a moving target. Think of all the changes in our twenty-first century, the new figures and styles on the social landscape: the trans man in Winnipeg, queer families with an infant, new fathers staying at home, egalitarian mothering of babies among working parents. Or the rolling back of health services and state support, and the low value assigned to caregiving under capitalism.

K nods and agrees, preoccupied with washing the baby's torso. His New York accent bounces lightly against my English tones, another half conversation in a stream of half conversations.

I take the baby back in my arms. That's exactly what makes the different pasts of mothering so compelling. A changing present calls forth changing histories.

The NHS record I am putting in a safe place under a pile of my diaries presents maternity mainly as a biological affair, a natural process to be monitored. LMP, last menstrual period. EDC, estimated date of confinement, what we now just call birth. But mothering, I am finding out, is more bodily than biological.

The historical fragments are just so various. Carrying and caring for a baby depends richly on time and place, more so than we might ever have guessed. Mothering an infant is not a fixed state. Physical, yes. Visceral, yes, enormously so. Biological, universal, unchanging, merely natural: not so much. If so, grasping what mothering has been means getting plural and specific, exploring its immense variety. To "pluralize and specify" is Eve Kosofsky Sedgwick's beautiful, succinct phrase: a promise to remake understanding, to take nothing physical for granted.[5]

I take endless notes, walking up and down the garden path with the new baby in a naptime sling and an article or book in hand. I read historians, demographers, archaeologists, anthropologists, and sociologists. I read memoirs, letters, diaries; government reports and court records; surveys and interviews—sources that often have little directly to do with pregnancy or infants but reveal something along the way.

The research began when I was initially contemplating motherhood, and kept going during the turmoil of my first child's infancy. A new small detail or a series of details, a flash of empathy, or the challenge of walking for a moment in another's shoes, a sense of familiarity or distance, these were solace and illumination.

Typing and revising in snatches of time, like an evening hour or a half day at work, I aim to hold on to the flavor of the original sets of notes: the sleepless, pell-mell quality, the peculiar interrupted attention, the short sentences, the fretting about sleep or damp cloth, the joy and jaggedness and distaste for sentimentality. Having this second child has returned a sense of urgency to the enquiry.

Next morning, needing to get out after a broken night, I take the bus into town on an errand. Mild rain presses on the umbrella's top, darkens the tip of each shoe. Across a stone courtyard, the revolving door of a museum beckons into the dry. There's no other spot in town to sit with a baby without buying a tea or a coffee.

In the gallery where I head in hazy fatigue, the magenta red of the low stools seems to pull the paintings' Renaissance color into the middle of the room. On the walls, bright doublets pose stiffly and lush skirts swathe. A Madonna and Child hold perfectly still. It's sixteenth-century Florence, or Naples. Then a break in all the crimson calls attention to a thoroughly modern image, a temporary addition to the gallery walls. Plain charcoal lines dart and cluster to shape a woman who holds an infant. Almost all color is gone, but the image pulses with motion. The child's body arches, kicks into hanging air. The mother clasps, steadies, and gazes out.[6]

A museum guard glances at me, not entirely unsympathetically, across the room, filled with Asian tourists and local school groups. Maybe he sees a nursing mother being a nuisance, or a youngish white woman looking damp and preoccupied, or a parent enjoying a child.

"When my first child was born, I felt like flying," explains the artist of the charcoal image in a taped interview. Jenny Saville traded in paint for the quick freedom of wide charcoal strokes. The massive sketch reprises Leonardo's Madonna, reworking her as the contemporary living mother of a living child. The scale is dwarfing. Open lines, rather than hard silhouette, suggest that mothering is made and remade. Saville's present enlivens the gallery's past, just as the past shapes the present. Joined and contrasted, each appears richer and more kinetic.

Historical curiosity lets us fly, I am reckoning, allows us to get free of ourselves. To doubt, and to reimagine. To own more fully our own times, discerning in the contours what they are or might become. The past can burden us or the past can release.

1

Mothering by Numbers

Back to the beginning, before there is any child on hand, just as research is under way. Mothering is only an abstract prospect.[1]

The clock tower outside the window shows ten to the hour. University students hurry to late-summer classes, their feet flattening pathways across the parched grass. I'm in a heated conversation with a colleague, a close friend, about life and work.

If I have children, I'm not sure if I'll have one or two, I announce a little too brightly.

This is slightly fraught territory. We both know—or at least I think we both know—that surveys suggest that men with partners and children, like him, progress very well in our workplace. Women with children, not so much. Their success rate slows, falling behind those of childless men and women.

His retort is bemused and a touch impatient: You choose to have *one* first.

How did people in the past act about how many children to have, and what did they assume about family size? What might a person have seen, of mothering and numbers, in their own time and place?

The Miami and the Potawatomi people who once moved across the hilly Midwestern landscape beyond the window, traveling between large summer agricultural settlements and smaller winter villages, cared little for singletons. The women who processed furs and cultivated corn, pumpkin, and kidney beans had multiple children apiece and cared for them communally. Children were cautiously spaced three to four years apart by the use of local abortifacient herbs, sexual abstinence, and late weaning. This was a kin-based world, in which family cooperation was crucial to survival. In Pennsylvania or in Ohio, observers routinely noted that Indian families averaged four to six children.[2]

Farther east in these seventeenth and eighteenth centuries, the settlers edging onto the vast North American continent had more children than the Native peoples they sought to displace and the Old Worlders they had left behind. The settler women who inhabited former Iroquois or Algonquian lands typically married in their late teens or early twenties and gave birth every eighteen months to two years. This more frequent birthrate was the approved rhythm of reproduction, so usual as to seem natural and God-given, as well as a sign of prosperity. Large families were especially typical among the gentry, in urban Jewish communities, and among German inhabitants, all of whom married young. In the old European societies from which the colonists had migrated, meanwhile, where economic life was often less certain, women married later, if they ever did wed, and gave birth every two to three years. Many never had the material security to marry at all.

Most societies are not interested in keeping collective numerical accounts. I learn about these birthrates mainly thanks to modern demographers working backward.

For a childless person, the numbers can seem terribly cold and out of reach, even off-putting. Modern demographers who count and graph show that the numbers have shifted further over time, from an average of eight or seven children in seventeenth- and eighteenth-century North America, or five or four in Britain, to 2.2 or lower in both places by the later twentieth century. They culled and amassed the numbers mainly from Western sources: local censuses, family histories, wills, church records, and then, since the nineteenth century, from national surveys. I pause, take in a breath over the first North American number: an *average*, nearly, of broad-hipped, thick-shaped 8.[3]

Can the numbers be brought forward into the warm hubbub of daily routine, I wonder? The fertility transition, as the demographers crisply term it, is surely the major shift that has shaped maternity since the seventeenth century. If there *is* an overarching narrative about mothering, the change in likelihood from larger to smaller families is as close as we might get.

The average numbers—from eight or five to 2.2—suggest three broad changes in lived expectations, a trilogy of shifts in what a person might anticipate in their future:

From childbearing . . . to childrearing. Or, less succinctly put, a "before" of bearing many babies and inhabiting a body marked by multiple pregnancies and births, and an "after" of bearing just a few. A "before" of mothering an assemblage of children, maternal attention distracted and divided, and an "after" of the intensive mothering of one child, or half a handful . . . not that I can quite imagine either.

From accepting the fertility mainly handed out by fate . . . to an emphasis on family planning. That shift was driven less by new forms of contraception and more by knowledge and by the arrival of a strong orientation to the future—indeed, of counting more precisely. Plan your children, ran the later logic, consider their spacing, assess what you can afford, act accordingly.

And from the prospect of continual maternity, layered over with grandmothering, to just a handful of years caring for infants. Once, the numbers suggest, mothering lent a permanent and defining adult status.

13

Later, and today, mothering babies became more like a short moment in a life cycle.

"Do not you, my friend," Susanna Hopkins wrote in a letter, "think the person very contracted in his notions"—small-minded—"who would have us [women] to be nothing more than domesticated animals?" The young Marylander was writing at the beginning of these changes, in the late-eighteenth-century United States. She recoiled from older ways that she thought treated women like breeding livestock. The fertility transition began in exactly her generation, around the American Revolution, when some women had the opportunity to apply the radical message of liberty and independence to their personal lives. Sarah Logan Fisher, a Quaker merchant's wife, remarked on a contemporary's "6th child before she is 29": too many, too early, and too fast. The rejection of older ways, the sense of enacting new possibilities, seems as radical and profound as throwing off monarchy.[4]

Frenchwomen's demographic history followed a similarly revolutionary path. Britain followed suit in reducing family size by the later nineteenth century, a change most often associated with industrialization.

Whenever and wherever the transition in family size, women gained in health and in control over their bodies and their time. They came to peg ideal family size to precise and particular numbers. Esther Atlee, an elite Pennsylvanian, might have assessed the shift as an improved lot. In the 1780s she noted her poor mood on being pregnant yet again: "I cannot account for a glooming which too frequently comes over me," she wrote, immediately adding, "if I had some relief in my family affairs . . . I should be much easier." (This pregnancy would nudge the number of her children into two figures.) Looking back from 1855 at the rural life of her grandmother, who had a dozen children, Martha Bowen of Williamsport noted that "having the care of a large family . . . her sphere of operation was limited." The intervening generation had four children. Martha, a minister's wife, had only one.[5]

The altered prospects were typically experienced piecemeal and in local circumstances. Visitors to the small American city of Muncie, Indiana, in the 1920s noted that the obligatory fruitfulness inherited from the 1890s had been "relaxed." Families of six to fourteen children were no longer seen "as 'nice' as families of two, three or four." In 1930s London, a young woman like the sewing machinist Doris Hanslow could associate having fewer children with such other recent domestic improvements as hot running water or electric lighting or municipal housing. Her mother had eight children in turn-of-the-century Bermondsey. Like other working-class London women of her generation, Doris would have fewer, just two. My London grandmother, who scrubbed steps for extra cash, was behind the curve; she had five children, three of whom lived to adulthood. Asked about ideal family size, a woman on the city's streets, just after the Second World War, might answer "one's enough," or maybe two or three. One, because "You've got to bring them up decent, haven't you." Three, because "I'd like to give them all I possibly could and I don't think I could afford more."[6]

In particular communities, the numbers sometimes went the other way. Nineteenth-century Cree women, living on the North American prairies, usually had four children. But the numbers rose in the 1860s, perhaps because of increasingly sedentary lifestyles as the buffalo-hunt years came to an end. Numbers found their way into Cree stories: "'Long ago' we never had more children than we could grab and run with if there was a battle." Ojibwe people living on reservations in 1930s Wisconsin, Michigan, and Minnesota might have agreed that it was better to have fewer children as in the old days. An informant told the Catholic nun and anthropologist Inez Hilger that it was "a disgrace to have children like steps and stairs."[7]

The demands of fruitfulness, the threat of "glooming," the limits placed on a woman's "sphere of operation," emerge rugged and intimidating from times of large families.

The possible pleasures taken in what has been lost are more intangible. Quiet pride in a stout, teeming body, perhaps. Or the pleasing generosity of gathering up a parcel of children. Or the reappearance in a newborn of the looks of a now-grown child. Or the carved documentation on a gravestone of dozens of living descendants. Somewhere between the fecund past and the parsimonious present, mothering as dilemma replaced mothering as destiny.

When I was growing up, it seemed unlikely that I would have children. I wanted an interesting life. I wanted to be independent and to have an equal relationship—aspirations that befitted an English grammar school-girl and a beneficiary of second-wave feminism. Motherhood looked boring, constrained, domestic, and drained of adult conversation. I loved my mum with all the complacency of the well-loved child, but I disliked her deference to my dad, with whom I also closely identified. He did not like small children; nor did I; only in my twenties did I realize that some people were not simply being polite when they cooed over a baby.

When I was in my early thirties, an older friend I greatly admire observed that her life's regret was not having children. I met some independent-minded types who unabashedly adored and enjoyed their kids. Suddenly the matter seemed entirely different. This kind of revelation is not uncommon in the twenty-first century, when, it seems, a person is not having a child, until they are. Deciding for or against is the latest version of mothering by numbers, a very contemporary twist: not just how many children to have, but rather, whether to have a child at all.

Many considerations and many different heritages can shape such a revelation. "Choosing Motherhood After a Lifetime of Ambivalence" reads the subtitle of a memoir by Rebecca Walker, daughter of the black feminist icon Alice Walker. To the Edinburgh writer Chitra Ramaswamy, pregnancy appears as a sudden temptation and a complex riddle: how to cast aside the sentimentality, sanitization, and science; the prescription, self-help, and emotionally manipulative doggerel; the lies, misconceptions, and unwanted advice; the politicking; the never-ending slew of new stories?[8]

The issue of children is already settled for my colleague. His partner radiates competence. When K and I go hiking with them in the local woods, she sends their two small children ahead looking for an oversize mushroom here, or a letter-shaped stick there, spurring them past fatigue. The same competence clings to my colleague and, I notice, to K, who lifts the smaller one onto his shoulders. You choose to have one first.

The demographic graph stays with me, peoples my imagination about former, lost worlds. In most societies before the twentieth century, there must have been crowds and crowds of little children. Infants were visible to all: quite the contrast with our present day, where those who are not mothering are typically sequestered from those who are. My ignorance about babies, the sharp sense of a divide, is a modern invention.[9]

Those little children of former times ran in crowds, despite higher infant mortality. By the middle of the twentieth century, few parents lost a baby, but in all previous centuries infant death was an experience that parents would have been lucky to avoid. Demographers cannot entirely explain the declining mortality rates, though they point to improved standards of living.

My less haunting subject, I determine, will be among those who stayed alive and together: the living mothering of a living child, rather than maternal mortality, infant loss, or forced relinquishment. In the raw unknown of whether a child is in my future, only that mothering is fully bearable to contemplate.

The more ghostly histories I leave to others. The living mothering of a living child, those twinned becomings, takes imagination and research enough.

"How I shall get along when I have got ½ dozen or 10 Children I can't devise," fretted the New Jersey colonist Esther Edwards Burr after her child's birth in 1755. Narcissa Whitman, a pioneer in Oregon a century later, might have recognized these concerns, knowing firsthand the immediate consequences of mothering a large brood. "My Dear Parents," she wrote in a rare but warmly affectionate missive back to New York in 1845, "I have now a family of eleven children. This makes me feel as if I could not write a letter."[10]

I come upon more and more letters or firsthand accounts that contain such chance references, such unintended and on-the-ground dispatches from different points along the fertility transition. The vast majority were penned by the most literate and the more leisured. Here, in these beginnings of research, it proves easiest to turn mothering by numbers into people, to imagine how the changing fertility numbers felt real, for the literate classes of Britain and North America.

It is much harder to bring mothering alive for, say, enslaved women, or for Native peoples, or for the working classes of my own past. Literacy was harshly prohibited among enslaved people, meaning that we have few documents left behind in their own handwriting. North American Native groups of all kinds conveyed their cultures orally rather than in written words that were deposited in archives. The working classes of every race and ethnicity spent most of their waking hours simply getting by. But I can persist. Without them, the view is misleading, truncated, wrong.

My colleague's small children keep growing, and he is sticking with a pair. Nought, one, or two? None or some?

2

Generation

Conceiving takes moments. Repeating moments, perhaps, but moments nonetheless. After so many years of safe sex, a whole adult life of carefully unreproductive and alternate intimacies, there was a certain glimmer of novelty about the whole business. There is surely a history to such moments of coital sex, to the acts associated with what one late-eighteenth-century diarist termed "jumbling up" a child.[1]

·Recent generations are heirs to the sexual revolution and to the story of sex it tells about the past. Famously, as the poet Philip Larkin quipped, sex did not begin until 1963. For the first time, or so it seemed, the Pill separated sex from reproduction, and a racy new world of sexuality was born. Earlier generations were pitied as repressed, unfulfilled, and weighed down with shame and moral anxiety. Women of former times were imagined to have silently lain back and thought about something else.

Now the Pill was commonly seen as a blessing. Modern sensuality meant sexual openness, sex as pleasure, sex for its own sake. Anything else, or anything earlier, was bad or indifferent.[2]

The glimmering novelty I feel, the sheer peculiarity of adding reproduction to sex, procreative hopes to sexual desire, surely makes me an inheritor of this modern story, its fortunate beneficiary. I am the beneficiary, too, of an even newer world, in which sex appears loosed from heterosexuality. Coming of age can routinely mean coming out. "Choice" now concerns both whom you sleep with and whether or not you want to conceive a child, even as such forces as poverty, male rapacity, or die-hard conservatism work to deny that. I may be hoping to conceive, with a man, the old-fashioned way, but I am getting to be choosy, doing so of my own volition.

What of the Dark Ages of sex implied by these recent stories of sexual revolution and of comings out? Was there really only an unrelenting, unchanging, silent world of coital sex before 1963? That seems like a caricature, or perhaps a myth, sex rarely being simply pleasure or simply procreation.

Of course, the history of past sexual activities is almost uniquely hard to know. But we can ask the question. If "mother" is a verb, then procreating is a usual, original activity, babies of any kind—adoptive, surrogate, your "own"—not coming from storks.

Was sex only dreary and silent before the sexual revolution? Occasionally that question has been asked directly of those who knew best. Members of the generations just prior—those who came of age and married in the 1930s and 1940s—are mainly gone now. But before the century's end, some from the English industrial heartlands of Lancashire and the more affluent Home Counties sat down with a pair of researchers. Phyllis, a lower-middle-class woman born in Blackburn in 1921, who ran a small grocery business with her husband, was among them. She remembered the topic of sex as decidedly off-limits. "It wasn't discussed at school; it wasn't discussed at home" with her parents. She hadn't liked boys who were "pushy." Most young women, wanting to preserve their respectability, were encouraged to steer clear of any discussion of sex, even in confiding relationships with a mother or friends. They grew up carefully trained to be private and hygienic with their bodies, discreetly covering themselves from view on family wash night, and avoiding wandering hands on the way home from a dance hall.[3]

Doreen, a churchgoer and builder's wife, awkwardly recalled her wedding night. The pair lay there, one on each side of the bed, "thick as two planks." Asked what sort of kisses she had, she answered, "Not sloppy ones." "I wouldn't tolerate that." "I've had plenty of kisses but they've had to be proper ones." These women voiced concerns about passing on germs, and hinted at strong taboos against experimentation. Surely this made for unsatisfactory or dreary sex? Doreen, for one, never really liked that marital obligation. At first glance, drear and silence seem exactly right. Dreary ignorance, dreary duty.

Yet not entirely so. Some of these same ways showed themselves, perhaps surprisingly, as a foundation for meaningful sex. That same privacy, or the prizing of cleanliness, could be hallmarks of loving sex, dimensions of sexiness. Phyllis and her husband did find it impossible to undress in front of each other. "I mean we'd never get in bed naked or get undressed, you know, in front of people"—that is, each other. But did she enjoy sex? "Yes, I suppose so, yes." Her husband would deliberately "hold back" for her pleasure. Dora, a dressmaker who married a car mechanic in 1945, remarked with implicit relish, "He built me a gorgeous bathroom. It was as big as that . . . it took two years to build. He was a devil really, honestly." Penny "didn't ever undress" for sex, but she saw "it" as natural, enjoyable, and easy. On courting with her "country boy" and later husband, they'd go walking and "sort of lay down and have a kiss and a cuddle." She added, "I think it just goes on from there . . . it just led up to that and then you know it automatically . . . it automatically came to you that something was going to happen."

Perhaps most striking, these women did not link sexual duty in marriage to sexual misery. For them, dutiful sex might also be pleasurable. Phyllis's tentative affirmation that she liked sex—"Yes, I suppose so, yes"— came with an explanation: "It's a, to me it was just a way of saying 'I love you,' you, er, showing your" (coughs) "showing your affection for each other really." What did Eleanor, a former weaver, actually enjoy about it? "Well the actual thing, you know" (pause) "yeah the actual thing . . . it's nice for a woman to enjoy sex because a man likes you to enjoy it, doesn't he?" The remark teetered between her pleasure and his, between marital expectation and her enjoyment.

In the wake of the sexual revolution, engaging in sex as a form of obligation is seen as unpleasurable almost by definition, as clear evidence that a relationship is in crisis. These women recalled good sex, and bad sex, rather differently. If they guessed, correctly, that later generations thought their ethos of privacy "silly" or "stupid"—all that never seeing each other "in the nuddie" and the scrupulous bath taking—they also thought their younger, modern critics did not take proper care of themselves.

Most touching, looking back from now, is the absence of fretting about the curve of a thigh or the depth of a cleavage. Shining hair, a clean complexion, and trim clothes seem to have mattered to sexual attractiveness, but not much else. Most strange and distancing, retrospectively, and most confirming of later assumptions, is the absence of words, the lack of language to accompany the gestures and touch and feelings between two people.

The women spoke to their interviewers in fumbling, unrehearsed stories, as if sexual intimacy was being described aloud for the first time, as if marital sex was a silent, interior experience. The women did not merely "sit back and then settle back," as one middle-class woman wryly put it, but sex was certainly shrouded in silence, left largely undiscussed, undescribed, unspoken. The signs of a husband being interested might simply be "the usual, two arms around me instead of one." Or a wife might cue, "Go and have a bath upstairs."

Obligation hovers, sometimes duels with spontaneity. I count out the fertile days, lightly, discreetly. I tell K about the bathrooms, the silences.

If not always dreary and indifferent, was silence invariably a feature of coital moments before the revolution of 1963? The silence of the 1930s and 1940s generation seems confirmed by the mainstream dictionaries of the twentieth century, where words for sex appeared only with the advent of the sexual revolution. Nor do sex words appear in the lexicographical tomes of the nineteenth century, their absence fitting the general stereotype that procreative sex among British and American Victorians was short, prudish, and unhappy. Nor, to keep going backward, can sex words be found in Samuel Johnson's famous mid-eighteenth-century *Dictionary of the English Language*. A lexicographical investigation seems to end in a quiet cul-de-sac.[4]

Yet head back considerably further, and the arrival of sex words in the 1960s turns out to be merely a reappearance. They *are* there in the English dictionaries of the seventeenth century and even earlier. Of what do they speak?[5]

Sitting on a dictionary page, seventeenth-century sex words look earthy, vigorous, often big on metaphor or on body parts, and sometimes baffling. Yielding. Sporting. Tumbling. Clipping. Clapping. There's a way to reread such words now that can slip between shame and prurience, and reveal something of past sexual moments, even at great distance. (No oral interviewers were on hand in the seventeenth century, and no direct traces of sexual moments were left behind in a woman's own handwriting.) We can think of the dictionary words as offstage actions turned into vibrant, lively language—a glimpse of acts at one remove. If so, having sex in that century made for the following verbs and phrases for sex in general: lusting; being lewd or lascivious, or wanton or bawdy; having carnal knowledge or congress; enacting the rite of love. Some of these terms sound passionate or wild, others exploratory or possessive, others loving.

Coital sex between men and women, my particular concern, suggested such verbs as fornicating, copulating, consummating, lying with, and swiving—rhymes with jiving. (Below the radar, seventeenth-century pornography portrayed procreative sex as especially sexy.) The moving body parts during such acts forged a massive array of nouns, of one thing fitting into another thing. Arranged in pairings of female and male, the reproductive parts were bit and bit, box and bauble, cony and pintle, fig and pizzle, purse and yard. Some of the accompanying acts and gestures, meanwhile, invoked wooing, chin chucking (a facial caress), patting fondly, fondling, and firking like a flounder (a way of arousing someone, though quite how is elusive).

The tumble of words sounds faintly Shakespearean, like attending a play and waiting for your ear to attune to a different vocabulary. That's an appropriate scene to reimagine. The audience at one early modern theatrical performance heard a character remark, playing the line for laughs: talk about sex straight out and stop tiptoeing about with "your 'rope in the ring,' your 'obelisk in the Coliseum,' your 'leek in the garden,' your 'key in the lock,' your 'bolt in the door' . . . not to mention . . . your 'little monkey,' your 'this,' your 'that,' your 'him' and your 'her.'" The character, a courtesan, had metaphors aplenty: pestle in the mortar, sword in the scabbard.

I don't know if those seventeenth-century Englishwomen who consulted dictionaries or attended plays experienced these acts and words as belonging fully to them as well as to men. Certainly there were women of all kinds in the audiences of seventeenth-century theaters. Workingwomen, gentry, aristocrats, prostitutes, and mistresses jostled shoulders.[6] Some surely expected to get a funny line by a courtesan about a rope in the ring or an obelisk in a garden. Others surely carefully adjusted their faces. The metaphors for coital sex usually assumed that men took charge of the action—picking a lock, pounding an anvil, piercing a bodkin, jousting with a lance, stealing the treasure, laying siege—but women may have preferred to think of a "bit" fitting with a "bit" over being pierced or besieged, over gardens and obelisks, locks and keys, sheaths and scabbards.

Not being able to describe sex was typically seen as virtuous. But in seventeenth-century England, women were generally seen as the lustier sex, their passions readily able to overwhelm.

So moments of coital sex in seventeenth-century England, by this evidence, were unlikely to have been as silent as versions in 1930s and 1940s Lancashire. That particular society, from among those of the Dark Ages of sex, could be relatively unskittish about sex talk. In the world of the lexicographers and the theatergoers, the bawdy wordiness lasted at least until the later part of the century, when a rising puritan propriety tamped down sex talk. The evidence suggests a kind of sexual revolution in reverse, as brisk as the changes of the 1960s. The lexicographers and playwrights heard people stop talking publicly about chin chucking or firking like flounders, and we no longer have such phrases in our stock.

Conceiving does indeed take repeating moments, and weeks turn into months. The clarity of wanting to get pregnant wears away.

Things won't change between us, will they? I ask of K. There'll just be an addition, something new in our lives, but not something altered between you and me?

I locate a recording of Philip Larkin reading his poem about the sexual revolution. His tone is offhand and deadpan, his voice faintly proper. In 1967, the year the poem was composed, the Family Planning Act was making oral contraception easily accessible to unmarried as well as to married British women. Similar changes occurred in France in 1967, and the United States in 1972. It must have seemed as if the whole world, whether unmarried, married, or never married, was changing overnight. I'm not surprised that the story that emerged was so confident about a singularly bad past.[7]

"Until then," Larkin reads with flat disdain, "there'd only been" the tussle between men and women over sex and marriage. Bargaining. The threat of shame. A "wrangle" over a wedding ring. British women of his youth had a whole, worried vocabulary for premarital sex: "losing one's head," "giving in," "giving way." Sheila Walker was among the unlucky bargainers. At age nineteen she had fallen for the father of her child "hook, line and sinker": "I saw marriage on the horizon with him so I thought that it was probably okay. I was quite safe, and he would take good care of me if anything happened . . ." But he "just went completely cold on me. He changed and that was it, that was the end." She ended up in a Mother and Baby Home.[8]

If the singular drear and silence of the Dark Ages of sex is overstated, Larkin's "there'd only been" is understatement, too. I think of the bald fact of male privilege, and the coercive forms it could take. In rural Essex, some three hundred years before I was raised there, notions of sexual property posed a dilemma for ordinary young women. Most worked as farm servants: tending cows, pulling weeds, caring for chickens. But such women had long been seen as the sexual property of their masters. A majority of illegitimate births were among farm servants, more than half of whom had become pregnant by the men who hired them. That a master of a family "had to do with me" was a baleful and frequent remark in the church courts. City life was no better. As Robert Parker told Alice Ashmore in 1606 London, "Thou art my servant and I may do with thee what I please." Such humiliating phrases got recorded in courts set up to enforce marital morality.[9]

Being treated as sexual property was the dilemma, too, of enslaved women in North America. During the centuries of American slavery, the rapacity of overseers and slaveholders revealed itself through children perceived to have a distinctive hue, or through the existence of entire "shadow" families. In the 1930s, a formerly enslaved man recalled the tactics of a South Carolinian master before the Civil War. He would instruct a young woman to "go shell corn in the crib": the granary. "He's the master so she had to go. Then he sent the others to work some other place." The story continued: "Then he went to the crib. He did this to my very aunt and she had a mulatto boy."[10]

In a rare and famous firsthand account, the abolitionist Harriet Jacobs explained these ordinary facts of life. Her North Carolina slave master was already the father of eleven slaves. James Norcom "told me," she recounted in 1861, that "I was his property; that I must be subject to his will in all things." He whispered and threatened and harassed. He was violent. Such stories were news neither to Southern slaves nor to white slave mistresses, who routinely loathed their husbands' "concubines" and "fancy maids." Under a pseudonym, Harriet Jacobs explained to the white women readers of the free North her calculation: to form a relationship with an unmarried white man who might better protect the resulting children. Her involvement with a town lawyer was, as she cast it, "a perilous passage." Perhaps James Norcom would back off, perhaps the Edenton lawyer might purchase and free the two children she eventually bore.[11]

Still not pregnant. What's missing in the story that the sexual revolution of the sixties wanted to tell, I now notice—and there's no reason it should have wanted otherwise—is the desire for a begotten child, the fleshy history of hopes to conceive. In 1776, the wife of a Scottish linen draper was impregnated with the aid of a warm syringe, a rare and daring—and successful—early attempt at artificial insemination. (The advising physician dared to publish his notes only many years later.) For the first century thereafter, in medical fit to marital expectations, only a husband's sperm was used.[12]

The giving and receiving of "seed," where it got named aloud, was called ecstasy, epilepsy, cough, spilling, dousing, purging, or flowing forth. The longest-standing historical answer to how to conceive held that a woman, as well as a man, must experience something like this, something like what we now call orgasm. This understanding, popularly held among white American settlers and their descendants, and by English people, derived from a certain logic of sexual sameness. People were thought to have roughly the same sex organs, just differently located. To paraphrase one medical student, turn the scrotum, testicles, and penis inside out and you get a woman's genitalia. An early bishop put the same idea more gently: "Women have the same genitals as men, except that theirs are inside the body and not outside it."[13]

A seventeenth-century treatise on midwifery in the Lilly Library, five minutes from my office, displays an anatomical engraving that looks at first glance like a slightly unattractive, hairy penis with a thick-rimmed head. But the image is of internal female anatomy. The tiny crouched fetus-in-a-womb displayed at the organ's top makes the point unmissable. The logic of sameness had the sometimes happy, sometimes terrible effect of suggesting that *both* a woman and a man had to "orgasm" for conception to occur. The "emissions" were mutual: a man emitted, a woman emitted and received.[14]

Intuitive ideas often take a long time to die. As late as the 1860s, one urban doctor sniffily complained that it was still "the vulgar opinion" that "to ensure conception, sexual intercourse should be performed with a certain degree of completeness, that would give an exhaustive satisfaction to both parties at the same moment." A social scientist interviewing poor American farm women in the 1930s noted a "belief indirectly alluded to but only once expressly stated is that a woman conceives when she has an orgasm."[15]

Licit and deliberately procreative sex has been encouraged in many different ways. Recommendations included eating and drinking moderately, being in a peaceful frame of mind, and enjoying foreplay and the "warming" of the woman's parts. Margaret Godolphin, then a young bride, heard from a male mentor in 1676 that the avoidance of female orgasm during intercourse was "not only impossible, but a stupidity, and an impediment to the chief End." (His explanation switched the usual seventeenth-century emphasis on male action: a husband might be "perpetually ravished with her Love.") Take warming herbs, such as rocket, pepper, ginger, and cinnamon, or make a syrup from sea holly. Separate slowly and carefully afterward—and avoid coughing or sneezing. Have sex once a week (handed down from Plato), or perhaps three or four times a week (a physician named Willich)—but not too much, as too frequent intercourse is debilitating.[16]

What about the act of generation since 1963? Bonnie Pereira, who was a young lesbian in 1970s America, remarked that she "wanted to be a mother" and had sex with a man exclusively to do so. Her contemporary Michelle O'Neill, who spoke to the same researcher, explained that she had "always loved children, particularly babies" and had conceived her son through artificial insemination. Turkey-baster babies, they were initially called.[17] It's not just that sex can be separated from reproduction, it's also that both have been released from heterosexual relations. The twenty-first century is a world of proliferating identities and forms of family-making. Across the street from my house, a lesbian couple has two children, one by each mother. Karen tells me about being the surrogate, too, for close straight friends—the legalities, the medical interviews to check her suitability.

I replay Larkin's recording for a final time, drawn back to its particular datedness. The simple equation on which it is based sounds quaint and narrow: a straight man and a straight woman equals sexual attraction. This formulation was archetypal of the twentieth century in which Larkin was born, lived, and died. Being a heterosexual—having heterosexuality as a full-on identity, excluding all others, seeing coitus as "it"—properly came with stringent naming and normalization in the later nineteenth century. The word entered vernacular use via marriage guides and advice columns in the 1920s.[18] Isn't heterosexual identity fading in our twenty-first century?

This changing present calls forth changing histories. What if the ways that individual societies and particular people knitted together intimacy, desire, and identity—and baby-making—have differed quite considerably? Discrete moments of coital sex may have occurred alongside and around a range of experiences, that is, were experienced in relation to varieties of desire previously unacknowledged. The seventeenth-century dictionaries certainly suggest a great range of visceral acts and bedmates. Boy love, male-mingled love. Sodomitesse, fricatrice. Many of the English dictionary sex words had little to do with coition. A great many failed to presume that sex occurs between a man and a woman.[19]

And elsewhere? One historical alternative to heterosexuality existed among seventeenth-century Native Miami peoples. Here were men who dressed in women's clothing and took on the ostensibly female roles of tending the fields, cooking, and making clothing, behavior that astonished early French observers. Another historical alternative occurred in the eighteenth and nineteenth centuries, when "female husbands" appeared in the English popular press on both sides of the Atlantic, a familiar if often mocking byword for same-sex unions. The Scottish-born Charles Hamilton, married to a Mary Price, was reckoned by a doctor in 1752 to be "a Woman in Men's Clothes." A hundred years later, an infant was born to a person who lived most of their life as Joseph Lobdell. The surviving records document Lobdell's intent "to dress in men's attire to seek labor," being "used to men's work," and marriage to a Marie Louise Perry in 1862 Pennsylvania. Laws against cross-dressing were adopted only in the last few decades of the nineteenth century.[20]

Or warm sensuality between women may have characterized straight-married lives. In the nineteenth century, middle-class married women's letters to their female friends could breathe with an erotic intimacy we would now relabel, and re-steer, as distinctly lesbian or queer. The New Yorker Jeannie Fisher ended a missive to her former boarding school friend Sarah Wister in 1861: "I will go to bed . . . [though] I could write all night—A thousand kisses—I love you with my whole soul—Your Angelina." Age twenty-nine and married, she declared in another letter, "I shall be entirely alone [this coming week]. I can give you no idea how desperately I shall want you." These female friends were not straining at convention. They saw themselves as entirely respectable, living at ease in a world that highly segregated women and men. Aside from sharing sensual love, the main activities of such middle-class matrons were confined to being domestic and attending church, visiting female friends and family, and having children.[21]

A thousand kisses, wrote Jeannie Fisher. Moments of coital sex happened in and around other intimacies. There have been many ways to be sensual or intimate or sexy: many life contexts for moments of procreation. Pluralize and specify, I think to myself. Take nothing bodily for granted, nothing visceral as self-evident. That's exhilarating.

Past experiences of desire reach us only in the form of words, echoes, or little translations of feelings and sensations that often went unspoken and even unnamed.

Silent or not, moments of sex can be neither fully represented in words nor contained by myths. That's true of then, and of now. "Letting your husband having it after you" (Mrs. E. E. Coley, 1918, Eckerty, Indiana). "We just sort of fiddled around till we found something . . . this is the way it was" (Sue Baxter, early-twentieth-century Lambeth, London). "I always say that when you chew tobacco, it don't make so much mess if you spit it out the window" (1930s Appalachia). "Extraordinary delight," a kind of yawning and stretching all over, some shivering and quaking, and eventually a chill between the shoulders (1612, of conception). A thousand kisses.[22]

3

Finding Out

Today, sex happens all over the place: in bedrooms and hotel rooms, under burning sun or faint moonlight, on top of sheets and mats and grass. Finding out you are pregnant, however, is more a business of the bathroom. Peeing on a stick—they call it, more elegantly, a "wand"—occurs in public lavatories or in the bathrooms of friends or in workplaces or, most usually, at home. Whatever the mode of reproducing, your annunciation usually comes down to a toilet and a stick.

I stand by an unfamiliar sink, hard white tiles beneath my feet, waiting for a line to appear. It is the end of a holiday with friends, a beachside week laced with milky coffees and late suppers. My period is latish. Maybe by three days, maybe four? Earlier, I drove with one of the friends to one of those large pharmacies that sell everything from sunglasses to bread. The woman at the cash register greeted our nervy cool with an uninterested smile, shunting the box, along with unnecessary tissues and lip salve, past the scanner. No, the "home" test has not made finding out a private matter.

The bathroom floor is not entirely clean in the corners. Cat hair is balled up against one baseboard. A recent magazine, wet at the edges, is curled limply around the lowest bar of a towel rack. Unfolded instructions flutter to the floor. It is still not time to check for the line.

It is still not quite time, but I do. And there it is. Unmistakably a line, which is still getting darker. Linear. Reaching across from one side of the oval window to the other. I blink. Here it is, then: the crossing of a line from not being pregnant to being pregnant, the moment of finding out. The hormones say so. They have said so, by different ways and means, since they were named in the 1890s, or more properly since the "A–Z" test was devised in 1927. Aschheim and Zondek injected a woman's urine into a rat or a mouse, which then went into heat if the woman was pregnant. In the Roaring Twenties, rats and mice were forced to say so. Rabbits came next, and then, in the 1950s, toads.[1]

Several hours later, after a celebratory supper ("Can she eat shellfish?") and the cooling of my reddened face, K and I take a walk. I am eerily content. So I really *did* want to be pregnant, and now, abruptly, I am.

Before the A–Z test mapped hormonal change like a fork in the road, pregnancy was apprehended later and more gradually. *Aristotle's Masterpiece*, the favored health handbook of English speakers for some centuries, used biblical lines hinting that being pregnant was a bit like cheese curdling: "Have you not poured me out as milk, and curdled me as Cheese? You have clothed me with Skin and Flesh, and have fenced me with Bones and Sinews." In rural societies, making butter, cream, and cheese was central to most women's work. Imagining being pregnant as curdling may have given the inchoate processes of early pregnancy a marvelous lucidity. Being pregnant was fluid and gradual, the matter that would become a child being shaped by slow, turning, churning coagulation.[2]

Uncertainty about pregnancy was taken for granted. Women tended to experience a progression of swellings and evacuations throughout their fertile years, not invariably linked to specific pregnancies. And if presumed indeterminacy was the case even for the experienced mothers of living children, it was especially so for those who had never borne a child. As one mid-seventeenth-century midwifery book observed rather tartly, "Young women especially of their first Child, are so ignorant commonly, that they cannot tell whether they have conceived or not." If only they knew better, they would properly anticipate the time of birth "and not so suddenly be surprised as many of them are." Or, as another explained, a person might be as easily mistaken about the length of a pregnancy "as a Woman can mistake one Shoe for another in the dark."[3]

The absence of menstrual periods, such a familiar sign in the present, was not always the first or clear proof of a pregnancy. Malnutrition made some women's periods irregular, and others might simply not have been counting days and weeks. The influential seventeenth-century male midwife Francis Mauriceau warned that "many women are themselves deceived, concluding themselves with child, from the staying of their courses [periods]." The remark correctly indicates that Mauriceau's female contemporaries were used to depending on knowledge of their own bodies: on "themselves," as his form of words tellingly repeated. Pregnancy in the "pre-hormonal" past was determined, slowly, by the woman. Even the most elite did not tend to turn to a physician for diagnosis.[4]

What, then, were the bodily signs? Another seventeenth-century midwife, the plainly named Jane Sharp, listed fourteen. Missed menstruation only came sixth on her list. The others I rearrange for myself in order of familiarity and foreignness. After all, we come to know our bodies only through the means that culture offers. Not all of Sharp's signs can be cleanly translated into contemporary vocabularies, nor yield to modern observation.[5]

Sharp's signs included growing breasts with swollen veins, pains in the abdomen, cravings for things not typically fit to eat or drink, and what we would name mood swings. "For some time she will be merry," the midwife reported, "or sad suddenly upon no manifest cause." It is as brisk and precise a description as one might find of the kinds of feelings now read as "being hormonal."

The signs continue on to an unusually flat belly (because the "womb sinks down to cherish the seed"), reddened nipples, "sour belchings," a discolored face, and more prominent veins around the eyes, especially just below the lids. Altogether these are, Sharp reassured, the "common rules," and if they are too general to appear in all women, nonetheless, "some of them seldom fail in any." Individual eighteenth-century women reported other kinds of signs. One knew she was pregnant from a certain discharge in her nose; another from the blood rising to the left-hand side of her head; another from the beating of a vein in her neck.

There were ancestors to the modern urine test. Readers of the 1639 *An Alphabetical Book of Physical Secrets* learned that if a woman's urine, once boiled, was "red as gold with a watery circle above it," then it "shows she is with child." If she could see her face reflected, this only confirmed the news. If the urine was white, the child was dead, but if there were clear streaks in it, then the "child has life." The late-seventeenth-century Londoner Katherine Boyle wrote down a recipe, in dashing and confident handwriting, in which color was interpreted differently: urine that turned white, this time when boiled with salt, suggested pregnancy, while a red color did not. Other ventures in uroscopy—the long-standing practice of examining pee—suggested that live worms could be found in a pregnant woman's urine after three days, or that a needle placed in it would gather red spots. (Black spots did not count.) *The Expert Midwife* of 1637 required a woman's urine to be "poured over barley seed and if it sprouted after ten days, she had conceived."[6]

Some of these urinary experiments conjure the magical thinking of bygone times: the promise of secrets, the red-golden water, the shimmering face reflected in liquid. But not only that. The last, in which urine was poured over grain, made an unusually direct link between the fertility of women and their agricultural world. Having conceived could be understood not only as akin to the slow curdling of cream and butter. Pregnancy was also thought to be the nurturing of seed.

Plowing and sowing seed were as familiar to almost every rural woman as dairy work, even if the precise process by which seed turned into a plant was entirely mysterious. Human seed was imagined as a kind of guest within the mother's body. She would provide it hospitality just as she would to visitors in her own home. In the womb, the germinating seed was watered and nourished by the blood that was no longer discharged from her body as menses. The author of *The Birth of Mankind: Otherwise Named the Womans Book* described the "blood in the veins as a very natural source, spring, fountain or well evermore ready to arouse, water and nourish the fetus as soon as it shall be conceived." By this reckoning, women's bodies were as naturally welcoming as moist, tilled land. The idea fit as tidily with long-standing notions of female hospitality as with the earthy rhythms of agriculture.[7]

It made sense, then, to pour women's urine onto barley to see if it would grow. The ancient Egyptians would have approved; they too believed that a pregnant woman's urine would cause barley or wheat to germinate and sprout. As it turns out, current experts suggest that such a test is 70 percent reliable.[8]

Creamy pasta, hot toast dripping with butter: my favorite foods now make me nauseated. I am back in the bathroom again. My gaze becomes overly familiar with the tile floors of the bathrooms near my lecture hall, at the supermarket, and opposite my office. The midwife Jane Sharp listed a whole series of similar signs: lack of desire for meat, loathing of food in general, vomiting, "weak stomach." (I feel green at the gills; is this what she meant by a discolored face?) The term "morning sickness" was coined in the 1840s, surely by a half-knowing physician, since there is no restricting the sensation to the first part of the day. Luckily, the mouth-drying adrenaline of lecturing seems to trump the saliva of pregnancy. I find a pocket in my bag for dry biscuits. I don't vomit, which places me in a happy twenty-first-century minority. The nausea may betray our secret, for dutifully we wait until the end of the first trimester to make any announcements. Only the holiday friends know.[9]

"I have a great deal of sick stomach," wrote Ella Clanton Thomas in nineteenth-century Georgia, "and find that I am again destined to become a mother." (She gave birth a scant few months later.) The wife of Charles Lyttelton, as he grumbled three centuries earlier, was "so continually sick

with (I think) breeding, that she can do nothing but puke." Genteel northern Englishwomen of the eighteenth century, by contrast, rarely mentioned nausea during pregnancy. Purging was their general cure-all,
making themselves sick an ordinary way of maintaining health, so vomiting may have been seen as usual and beneath remark.[10]

Only recently has discerning pregnancy been experienced early and
as an event: the distinct crossing of a line from one state to another, seemingly in an instant. More often, such as among the Cree peoples of northern Saskatchewan or the working-class Londoners of the early twentieth
century, a woman did not consider herself definitively pregnant until
quickening, until a baby kicked.[11]

The sharp joy of my holiday's ending, the red-faced confusion of a half-
private and half-public moment, these are distinctly contemporary experiences: commonplace and secular annunciations. I hug the secret to
myself, willing the weeks of nausea on.

4

Week Ten, or Eight Weeks Gone

By week eight, as modern embryologists count it, body parts have formed and the heart is beating. The cells of the embryo have not merely grown and divided—the story of cells in my schoolgirl biology—but as stem cells, they have broken free, sprouted snail-like feet, and migrated to evolve into particular structures and organs. The embryo is the size of a paper clip. A week later, all the organs and body parts are present in a more or less recognizable form, and the embryo has become a fetus. Modern obstetricians count slightly differently: they date pregnancy from the last period. The embryologist's week eight is their week ten.[1]

I have become slower but no less nauseated during these cellular migrations.

What we see on the ultrasound screen is peanut-shaped, a definite small mass. I watch the technician's face, which is expressionless and unchanging as she takes different sets of measurements. By observing the length of the long bones and the size of the head, sonographers calculate conception to within three days and provide a due date. To an untutored gaze, the peanut yields no sign of a spine or legs or skull. The technician communicates nothing more, exiting the room's haze of happy curiosity without a backward glance. She leaves to find a midwife.

Sonar makes pictures of the echoes of the deep. The technology derives from the military equipment used to detect enemy warships in the Second World War. Winston Churchill credited sonar as one of the key factors in the Battle of Britain. Enterprising surgeons came to use the technology to operate in the dark. Now the technique that was used to reveal submarines in the watery depths has been modified to detect and diagnose submerged embryos. Sound waves bumping into something become images of a peanut on a monitor.[2]

There's a long pause before the midwife arrives. Time elongates, curiosity wavers.

The ultrasound revealed an embryo without a heartbeat, she explains. It could have shown a living embryo or an empty embryonic sac or no sac at all. Sorry. There are statistics that stab at reassurance. Losses are very common, the most usually cited figure being 15 to 20 percent of all pregnancies. One miscarriage—is that what is happening, then?—is no predictor of future miscarriages. A single pregnancy loss does not make another.

There has been no blood, no pain, and no mess. Not even a small red seep. This is called a "silent" miscarriage.

Silence. Then the echoes of fond hopes escape the room, pursuing us home.

On February 6, 1763, the dark-haired and affluent Philadelphia Quaker Elizabeth Drinker wrote in her diary: "Afternoon very unwell, Miscarried. [Words crossed out.] Sally, Inoculated." There's a pause, and a paragraph break. Then: "8 Weeks gone, when it happened."

The entry is not unusually terse or reticent. Eighteenth-century journals tended to be records of events that helped jog memory or keep track.

Perhaps in the words written and then scratched out, and in the disorderly return to the timing of the miscarriage, there is some sign of an unsteady emotional state. Or perhaps these are no more than indications of the preoccupying distraction of a vulnerable child—the fifteen-month-old Sally had been inoculated with a smallpox virus—or the time taken to calculate when Drinker's husband, often away on business, had been staying at home some weeks before.[3]

On a February day nearly two centuries later, the poet Sylvia Plath miscarried. Like Drinker, she already had a small daughter. Unlike Drinker, she wrote richly about miscarriage. The early 1960s was the moment of the Beatles and the obscenity trial for *Lady Chatterley's Lover*, and Plath was becoming known as a "confessional" poet. One poem's narrator walks on London's Parliament Hill Fields, her mind running with gulls and with a crocodile of schoolgirls in ill-assorted blue uniforms, and with the meaning of absence:

> Your absence is inconspicuous;
> Nobody can tell what I lack . . .
> I suppose it's pointless to think of you at all.
> Already your doll grip lets go . . .
> Your cry fades like the cry of a gnat.
> I lose sight of you on your blind journey.[4]

We might suppose that miscarrying, like madness, can only be captured by poets. But that's not quite right, for many cultures talk as readily about miscarriage as they do about cabbages and kings. In late-twentieth-century Nepal, women chatted as "easily" and "loudly" about infertility and miscarriages as they did about births. Among their contemporaries in rural Jordan, miscarriage was marked by a ritual meal.

Yet in mid-twentieth-century London, Plath was breaking something of a taboo. Today, the factual ordinariness of miscarrying is built neither into medical culture, where unpleasant topics are not brought up until they must be, nor into consumer culture. The pregnancy home test had made no mention, leaving me faintly deceived. Our discretion, which now feels confusing, meant that almost no one knew.[5]

In Drinker's early modern world, peers certainly talked routinely among themselves about miscarriage. Her diary for these months briefly reports two friends miscarrying: Becky James, the matronly companion of her husband's business partner, and Catty Howell, another merchant's wife, whose pregnancy loss made her "very ill." Perhaps miscarriage was on Drinker's mind; in other years, she did not bother noting similar information. Miscarriages were known between mistresses and servants, and they were discussed among circles of friends. Diaries like Drinker's were read aloud and shared for evening entertainment and reminiscence.[6]

What people said to one another exactly is more elusive. Sometimes there is an oblique glimpse in court records or in doctors' notes. Elizabeth Lewys, in seventeenth-century Somerset, told the widow Margaret Whorewood that she had been exceedingly ill the night before and gave her a "most filthy cloth to wash." She "would have taken anything that had first come to hand, if it had been the best linen she had." Matter continued to flow from her body. The next morning, Elizabeth Bradford was given "a most menstrous cloth to wash," and remarked later that Lewys's "diseases as it seemed by that cloth was far different from the natural disease [menstruation] that women use to have." Another described what Lewys shed as "as much blood (as thick as jelly) as a man could hold in both his hands." Miscarriage was bloody, like menstruation, but thick and heavy, distinctive, jellylike, prodigious.[7]

One unusual eighteenth-century German doctor, Johann Storch, made direct notes of women's own words before making his deductions. The women of Eisenach described evacuating blood curds, burnt-out stuff, and singed blood. They shed things that were leathery or made up of skins, matter that appeared watery and windy, bloody and bubbly, and stony. Even in the first weeks of uncertain pregnancy, an evacuation from the womb was frightening. Women described what they purged as "false conception" or "useless" or wrong "growth." In his own words, Storch noted evil growths, burned stuff, singed skins, and fleshy morsels as well as— in more learned language—mooncalves and moles. Conception, according to the physician, could be "true and real" and lead to the timely appearance of a child, or it could be "wasted, empty and useless." The latter should be expelled through laborlike pains or with the help of expulsive medicines such as red coral powder.[8]

My expulsion is neat and tidy, a half day outsourced to an outpatient clinic of sharp lights, vacuumed carpet, and cold anesthesia snaking up my arm.

Unsure what to make of events, I wonder about infertility. My mind races ahead to childlessness.

Blighted fertility has been more dangerous than shedding blood or having an anesthetic. Fears of damaged fertility were the subject of an act passed against witchcraft by the English Parliament in 1604. The last such statute was revoked only in 1736. Across early modern Europe and the American colonies, fertility was thought to be prey to magical, evil attacks in both the natural and human worlds. An infertile woman might be a witch, or her infertility might be caused by witchcraft. Under conditions of stress, fear of infertility sowed dissension among women, generating the kind of suspicion and hatred that made the Devil and his henchwomen seem at hand. Fecund married women could be envied; and childless women, young and old, could be vulnerable. Witch-hunt crazes depended on the religious armory of inquisitions and inquisitors, but they also depended on women fearfully accusing other women.[9]

Being "barren" is hard wherever childbearing is central to a person's reputation or when childlessness is involuntary. The Londoner who put down her neighbor by saying "I have ten children, and you have never had one" spoke in the seventeenth century, but a jibe of "some" versus "none" worked until deep into the twentieth, and still resonates. Early New England settlers depended on children for many of the common tasks of life, and women saw infertility as a result of God's ill favor. Barrenness threatened both material survival and piety. For the Quaker farmers who settled farther south in the Middle Colonies, children were expenses rather than sources of income, but among them, successful pregnancy was also contrasted with reproductive failure. Fertility and fruitfulness were opposed to barrenness both for women and for farms. Marriage and children went together, and together they comprised women's proper lot.

41

Elizabeth Drinker's older sister Mary, who remained single and childless, was reduced to being her "housekeeper."[10]

Old habits die hard. The last woman to be hunted down as a witch in the Drinkers' Philadelphia died in 1787. Accused of rendering a woman childless, she was "cut in the forehead, according to ancient and immemorial custom," carried through the streets and pelted, and soon after found dead. She was poor, old, perhaps a basketmaker. The newspapers cast these scenes as remnants of earlier, unenlightened times.[11]

Witchcraft has not been the only unwelcome companion to childlessness. In the mid-twentieth-century United States, before the backlash to the baby boom years, childless women were seen as unfeminine, socially maladjusted, and un-American. Personal happiness and patriotism alike were cast as depending on a woman's fertility. Even the screen siren Elizabeth Taylor was "a Woman at last" only once she had a baby. Among modern women, words could be hurtful, if not as dangerous as accusations of witchcraft. Sylvia Plath's "Barren Woman" imagines herself like an empty museum, all pillars, porticoes, and rotundas, but no statuary. The poem may have been directed, a biographer suggests, at Olwyn Hughes, the childless sister-in-law with whom Plath had fallen out.

Nasty meanings have clustered round the term "barren" like wasps to a picnic: unproductive, sterile, stark, deficient, lacking, wanting, destitute, devoid, bare. Some imply failure and incompetence. Others conjure a void.[12]

No wider social world knew of my pregnancy. I have not been a mother in any sense I understand. I am changed, though: I was becoming. Now I am suspended.

Losing a pregnancy is not just inseparable from time and place—an ultrasound in a scrapbook, a bloody cloth, a walk in a London park—but soaks into a broader life. This loss is overridden by family demands. My mother is in a coma after a brain hemorrhage. In Essex, my sister and I share my old bed with her new baby son. We take care of our frail father. My sister leaves, and I continue to play my mother's role. My mother wakens; she draws a picture of an outfit knitted for a friend's baby; she tells me that she dreamed my sister was pregnant again. Across a terrible autumn, my English family is taken apart and, miraculously, put back together.

Childless, for months I am the daughter who cooks and drives and arranges and plays housekeeper. I inhabit my mother's domestic life on her behalf. I am useful. Then my mother can move her legs, next she can speak, and finally she leaves hospital. A miscarriage seems like small fry; it is not to be shared.

When my parents are reunited, I return to my American household. I am suspended.

True to her eighteenth-century times, Elizabeth Drinker went on to have four more living children after Sally. In "Parliament Hill Fields," Plath imagines the miscarrying woman taking joyful comfort in her young daughter. She walks home to a lit house and the glow of an occupied nursery. Unexceptional in her modern fertility, if in little else, Plath went on to have a second child before her suicide thirteen months later.

In the spring, just at the time a baby would have been born, I dream of a tiny child with a shock of hair, staring curiously at me on a garden path. The next month, I am pregnant again.

5

Quickening

The pothole in the road is sharp-edged. I drive straight over the top, thump-thrum, and then clear. My heart leaps into my mouth in momentary fear that the wheel will be ripped off, but something else leaps too, a jolt just marginally out of step.

Five days later, I feel the tiny leaping again. There it is. This is quickening: what once was experienced as the first certain sign of being pregnant, a yeasty term for a baby's movements within. Some have described these movements as like a butterfly or a tiny bird flapping its wings. This captures the fleetness, but imagining a small creature I've never held—switching a fetus for a cabbage white or a hummingbird—does not quite bring the motion alive in my mind. Pops, twitches, taps: these are closer. I'm with the twentieth-century Vancouver writer Gladys Hindmarch: "You kick within, light thumps move out slightly in tiny waves. Where you knock doesn't hurt, is slightly like a blood spurt in one spot of a large vein." That the knocking and spurting does not hurt needs saying: the sensations are initially so strange that I am impressed by their lightness. It is summer. A cotton shirt grazes my stomach from the outside; the baby grazes it from within.[1]

This inner touch is characteristic of pregnancy—perhaps, aside from birth, its most persistent feature. Typically, quickening is felt once the nausea properly fades, at between four and five months. In 1667, the English gentlewoman Alice Thornton recalled, "I was exceedingly sickly in breeding, till I was with quick child; after which I was very strong and healthy." My second pregnancy repeats the nausea of the first, but this time the sickness recedes with time and not with miscarriage. The local midwife laughs at our caution in counting out ten weeks, eleven weeks, twelve weeks.[2]

The interior touch preoccupies me, as if the baby is suddenly let in on my everyday. We go here, we go there. For a few nights, under a whirring fan, sharing a bed feels busy. K shares the bed with me, but I share him with the baby. Or perhaps I am shared between him and the baby. The bustle fades into odd companionship. Without doing anything at all, without thinking or moving, I am toucher and touched.

My mother picks up her knitting needles again.

Touching, seeing, hearing, smelling, tasting. We are used to thinking of five senses, five standard means for taking in the world. Yet elsewhere their number alters. Some Buddhist cultures count six by adding the mind, while the Nigerian Hausa count only two: they have one term for seeing and one for all the other modes of sensing. The most elemental ways in which we sense and apprehend things shift depending on our circumstances.[3]

Once, sensing an interior touch was the first full proof that life grew within. One of the earliest written traces I find comes from the winter of 1662. The London diarist Samuel Pepys recorded that the king's mistress "quickened at my Lord Gerard's at dinner, and cried out that she was undone. And all the lords and men were fain to quit the room, and women called to help her." A movement in the belly changed a royal mistress's status, and she was the one who felt and announced as much. The mistress's testimony of pregnancy was accepted by Gerard's company, among whom the men left and the women stayed. Touching was knowing. Touch held authority.[4]

That compares quite dramatically to the increasingly technocratic modern period. Today, a window on a urine test displays a chemical pregnancy and an ultrasound screen illuminates the physiological developments. Now, seeing is knowing, and sight holds authority. Modern science is said to have dispensed with quickening, and English usage is piecemeal following suit. By now, the triumph of sight over touch is declared more or less complete.[5]

Yet living in a quickened body, week in, week out, dispels my confidence that this is the whole story. The sensations repeat and change. I shift, the baby shifts. The touch remains elusive to a hand on the outside, but insistent and compelling within. When alone, I fall into the habit of sitting with one hand resting absentmindedly on the muscles of my belly, at an exact and vibrant place in that thin wall. What is the tactile history of carrying a quickened infant? Perhaps the brush of enlarged breasts against an inner arm. Feet pressing flatter into familiar shoes until they pinch. The push of a needle into fabric cut unusually small. The stroke or press of another's hand against a tautening belly. Stretchy fabrics, awkward seat belts. If a history could be written of pregnancy and touching, what would it embrace?

It is possible to reimagine the quickening of Lady Castlemaine, the king's mistress, at that dinner in December 1662. It is winter, so the teeth-rattling carriage that conducts her along London's filthy pebbled streets to Lord Gerard's lets in chill air. Close on either side, the coach passes plaster-faced timber houses, their upper stories jutting unevenly forward over the pavement. Signboards for different trades hang low from almost every building. A cradle means a basketmaker. A row of coffins implies a carpenter. Adam and Eve suggest the selling of apples and other fruit. Foul-smelling smog from domestic fireplaces obscures the finer details of other signs, like the elephant indicating such merchandise as ivory combs and other exotic goods.[6] Barbara Castlemaine is twenty-two years old, forceful, gorgeous, and at the height of her powers at the royal court.

The Puritan Commonwealth, with its republican austerity, had been replaced by the Restoration monarchy a few short years earlier. That day, the pugnacious soldier and aristocrat Baron Gerard—Castlemaine's host on the day of her quickening—had ridden at the head of Charles II's guards in their triumphal entry into London. Now the popular new king ritually touches thousands of people, his touch believed by many to have medicinal healing powers. Public bans on dancing and the theater have been lifted, signs of a certain new indulgence in sensory pleasures. These pleasures take their most concentrated form in the unabashed sexuality of the court itself.

A 1662 portrait of Barbara Castlemaine by Peter Lely shows a heavy-lidded, flush-cheeked woman surrounded by rich damasks and textured draperies. She has long, dark unbound hair, a nipped-in waist, and gazes directly and languidly at the viewer. The flowing tresses and saintly pose, resting head in hand, cue her depiction—with breathtaking insouciance— as Mary Magdalene, the Bible's famous harlot and devoted follower of Christ. This was pretty scandalous and witty stuff, celebrating Castlemaine's sex appeal and equating a prince with the Son of God. Samuel Pepys, ever the good civil servant of the former Puritan regime, was appalled and enthralled in equal measure. "I must have a copy," he wrote. The portraitist's and Castlemaine's fortunes rose together. Courtiers bought engraved reproductions to hang in dining rooms and entryways.[7]

So what was Barbara Castlemaine's world of touch? The grasp of a duke's hand at the entrance to a ball. The throw of dice and the shuffling of cards. The weight of a heavy string of pearls around her neck. Oil of almond and tartar to cleanse the skin. Linen petticoats edged with rich lace. Pepys, whose diary often dwelled on the court gossip about Castlemaine, saw her underwear drying in the Privy Garden, as off-limits to his touch as the young woman herself, but it "did me good to look upon them."[8]

And a baby's inner touch. Like most childbearers in history, Castlemaine has left no words describing the sensation. Pepys kept his diary, of course, as did various of his male peers, but among the Englishwomen of his diary-keeping years there are almost no known journals. We rely on his voyeurism and the relaying of court gossip for this singular insight about early modern quickening. Wagging tongues—this time it was his boss's housekeeper—suggested that the tiny movements prompted a loud response on her part: Castlemaine's cry out loud that she was "undone."

Did quickening threaten her fortunes as a mistress, a baby's inner touch ending her erotic appeal? No more nipped-in waist, allure undone? This is my first thought, although it does not square with my own flushed experiences of pregnancy, nor with the coy remarks in more than one recent pregnancy manual that the middle trimester feels "much sexier," the effect of all that extra blood flowing.[9]

At any rate, more gossip, and another portrait, suggest otherwise. For Castlemaine already had two children by Charles, and two more would come. She was pregnant most of the time she was a royal mistress. Pregnancy was shiny coin in Castlemaine's relations with the king, hard currency in her competition with the queen and with the court's other showy beauties. During the previous summer, when she was nearly at full term, Charles ate "every day and night" at Castlemaine's house on King Street, where they had not-so-private jokes about her condition: "The King and she did send for a pair of scales and weighed one another; and she, being with child, was said to be heaviest." In another Lely portrait, this time audaciously mimicking the Madonna and Child, a sleepy-eyed and visibly pregnant Castlemaine holds the king's son with evident satisfaction. (A version of the portrait hung in a French convent, believed to be an orthodox image, until the actual subject was pointed out and the painting quickly removed.)[10]

So the tiny sensing of a baby's first movement may have felt like the rush of power. Given Castlemaine's adroit maneuvering at court, and how she chose to be portrayed, the declaration of being "undone"—ruined—may have been a deliberately stagy gesture toward the biblical teaching about female chastity. The Madonna, after all, had been a virgin. The sexy Mary Magdalene was the *penitent* woman of sin.

Or perhaps Castlemaine's loud response was more spontaneous and more genuine, the effect of doubt over the child's paternity. Like her royal partner, she was a libertine, taking many lovers, and as sexually unfaithful to the king as he was to her. Sympathetic contemporaries associated the sexual freedom of libertines with honesty, good nature, and royalism—a kind of lifestyle that was loyal to the restored monarchy. That winter, rumor held that Castlemaine was sleeping with the womanizing courtier Henry Jermyn, an affair from which she hoped Charles would be distracted by his own latest infatuation.

This rumored quickening of the winter of 1662–63 came to nothing. But by spring, when Castlemaine quickened again, she moved from private lodgings to an apartment in Whitehall that was more luxurious even than the queen's. Catherine of Braganza remained childless. The mistress's apartment surrounded Castlemaine with the touch of dense tapestries, deep velvet and gilt leather, of shiny India silks, oriental carpets, and chimney furniture made of smooth silver. The quickening of the king's mistress knitted a baby's inner touch to the tactile rewards of royal patronage.

Even if quickening happens in every successful pregnancy, I can reconstruct no continuous history. The remaining records do not allow it.

My pregnancy continues. The baby's movements become more solid, more predictable. Feet to the stars, elbows splayed. A foot buries itself under my ribs, poking me upright. I stop leaning forward at my desk or into the sink. Against the cool metal pole in an underground train, the baby pushes in protest before spooling around its own spine. If sight is the master sense, then perhaps pregnancy is a reeducation in tactility. Touch is the Braille of knowledge between the baby and me, the master sense by which the middle and late months of pregnancy are lived and known. The watching for a line on a pregnancy test, the unhappy or happy scanning of a monitor screen, these visual moments in which the baby is represented "out there" are fading before the "in there" insistence of touch. Touch is the vital bond along which emotions thrill and move. The baby feels like an alien, like a companion, like myself.

So what piecemeal history might continue from a woman's loud cry at a court dinner? Is it possible to locate past experiences of pregnancy and touch going forward to other times and places? In politics, Charles II's reign saw the resumption of the English colonization of North America after a thirty-year hiatus. He granted the "restoration colony" of Carolina to loyal supporters of the monarchy. Some of his courtiers were slave traders; Castlemaine's host at the court dinner was a member of the Royal African Company, which enslaved and traded African people. In the 1680s, some five thousand enslaved people were transported every year. By the end of the century, after a ruthless expansion, England led the world in slave trafficking. Some displaced Africans, like a child referred to as Barbara Castlemaine's "little black boy," became servants of the elite in England, while the vast majority ended up enslaved on plantations in the Americas. The touch of silk and pearl enjoyed at Charles II's court depended in part on these ugly entrepreneurial ventures.[11]

In the settlements of Lowcountry Carolina, rice became the staple cash crop within a generation. The fabled Carolina Gold rice converted into massive profits for planters. To produce the small, hard, smooth grains in such volume demanded the importation of more Africans to South Carolina than anywhere else on the North American mainland.[12]

South Carolina: a distinctive climate, people of different descents in a biracial society, the later years of slavery. A nineteenth-century rice plantation that stretched flat and wide across swampy land. There, tides from the sea pushed freshwater upriver, irrigating the fields, feeding the fragile and shallow-rooted rice plants, and drowning weeds. The smell of stagnant water hung in the air before the dam gates were opened at low tide. Dangles of moss swayed from the low-hanging limbs of live oaks. Snakes infested marshy pathways. Weather-darkened slave cabins with cypress-shingled roofs and broad front porches vaguely reminded English visitors of a country village. The cabin interiors were like the two-room Yoruba houses of Nigeria, and dark and stuffy. Field slaves, men and women alike, labored for nine, eleven, fourteen hours a day in rice fields. There was no separate "women's work." Bondwomen worked the soil at a pace dictated to reap the largest harvest for a white master.

The tactile experience of their overworked and malnourished bodies? Material culture, and weather conditions, suggest coarse linen gown against skin, the skirt drawn up with a cord tightened a little above the hips. A bandanna stretched across the brow, often with a thick piece of paper stuffed at the back of the head to look like a comb. Shoes with no left and no right. Scorching sun. Humidity that could be felt but not seen. The familiar rub and weight of that year's hoe: local wood for the handle, burnished smooth from hard use; eight or nine inches of bar iron edged with durable steel at the base. The hoe was raised and lowered according to the rhythm of work songs. Swing above the head, lower to bite into the earth, pull free, and repeat. Women and men worked row by row, side by side.

The calloused hands grasping the hoe may have been stained with black walnut or indigo from dyeing cloth. At day's end, tired fingers might have trailed off the side of a flatboat as rice and slaves were carried back to the plantation barnyard, or reached down to touch a pierced coin or piece of animal bone on an ankle string to ward off ill fortune. These charms were also known as tobies, mojos, jacks.

To cook rice to eat, an enslaved woman rolled up her sleeves as high as she could, took soap and washed her hands clean, washed the pot and filled it with water, put the pot on the fire, waited for the liquid to boil, washed the rice, put salt in the pot, put the rice in when the water was boiling hard, let the rice boil until it swelled, poured off the water, and put the pot back on the stove to steam. There was so much repetition. Hands prepared corn bread, peas, pork, or fish for cooking over open fires, stirring from time to time with cedar paddles. Such a woman knew the feel of sticky molasses and rough-skinned sweet potatoes. Wooden spoon, clamshell, a shard of pottery: these were her utensils.

Feeling a baby's inner touch entails the privilege of relative stillness. At first quickening, a woman on a South Carolina rice plantation was typically around nineteen years of age. The season was most likely late spring or early summer: on such plantations most conceptions occurred in the winter, the grueling tempo of the harvest having given way to the repairing of roads and dikes and the milling of flour. Perhaps such a woman felt the first movements after straightening up next to a wooden washtub, or perhaps as her hands coiled and bound straw to make a wide circular basket for winnowing rice, her fingers following the design of ancestors in Senegambia or Angola. Or perhaps she intuited the movements within as she stood dropping the seed rice into trenches and covering it with her foot, or, later in the summer when the rice heads were nearly ripened, while shooing away the yellow and black bobolinks, also called rice birds, as they began their southward migration. Or perhaps the baby's movement first responded to the ecstatic sounds of divine worship, the alternating call-and-response of slave religion, the drumming on rice mortars covered in animal skin.[13]

Quickening also surely entailed feeling the gaze of a slaveholder determined to protect his interests. Women's distinctive ordeal under slavery was to be reproductive as well as productive. Infertile women were often sold away. "You better have the whitefolks some babies if you didn't want to be sold," recalled Alice Douglass, a former Tennessee slave interviewed in the 1930s. Quickening may have felt like the rush of a new, small security: the greater likelihood of staying in place. Or perhaps the pulsing swell was of pride, for motherhood was revered in African cultures and the forms they took under enslavement in the Americas. Or perhaps the beat and thump was of hatred for a rapacious overseer or master, a reminder and echo of trauma. Maybe it was all those possibilities.[14]

On some South Carolina plantations, quickening led to new physical "privileges," replacing the routine touches of everyday life with novel tools and new surfaces. Pregnant women were assigned the work of a half-hand, like girls or boys, in place of the heavy stooping labor of the field gang; or, eventually, brought into the "Big House," where the slave owners lived, to undertake lighter domestic chores. To a white interviewer, Gracie Gibson later recalled that "women bearing children not yet born, did carding with hand-cards; then some would get at the spinning wheel and spin thread." Quickening might lead to the swapping of sun and wind on skin for the protection of four solid walls, and the exchange of the hoe for the unfamiliar lightness and thin wires of a hand card. The natural grease of the wool had a softening effect on the skin. Carding thread involved using a couple of small paddles with hundreds of little wire spikes. The fibers were stroked to align them in the right direction, and then the thread was ready for spinning. Carding required a new and different kind of dexterity and was carried out under the immediate supervision of the slave mistress.[15]

52

For pregnant enslaved women, quickening and manual labor endlessly reverberated; they did not separate. Evoking the slow creeping of a tiny insect across a reachless expanse, the former slave Hannah Davidson remembered, "I been so exhausted working, I was like an inchworm crawling along a roof. I worked till I thought another lick would kill me."[16]

The nineteenth-century slave mistress, the descendant of European settlers, on the other hand, was raised to despise manual labor. Her touch of wood was not that of a hoe's handle, but of the burnished banisters of a staircase, the carved panel of a veranda, or the curve of a chair from which she dispensed the orders essential for the running of a large household. The touch of iron was not the toe of a field hoe, but the filigree of keys to a storehouse. A feather cut tidily into a quill was her most likely tool. Isolated from former friends and family on plantations throughout the South, slave mistresses confided the latest news in chatty letters and shared diaries. "I think I felt slight indications of a new life tonight," wrote Mahala Roach of her quickening in November 1858, adding a week later that her "signs of 'life' . . . were real, I have felt them ever since." Two decades earlier, Adele Allston's sister advised her to abandon the usual whalebone stays in favor of dressing "loosely" and to leave the plantation's humidity for the cooler breezes of Charleston.[17]

These mistresses' letters suggest that they saw in enslaved women both a source of frustration and faint versions of themselves. Many complained bitterly of recalcitrant slaves who failed to complete tasks or stitch neatly or work readily without a whipping. Some mistresses, in fits of temper, resorted to slapping and hitting enslaved women in the face, pulling their hair, or burning their skin. A few also felt some kind of identification rooted in bodily likeness: "I know that if I had sole management of a plantation, pregnant women would be highly favored," wrote one in self-congratulation. "A woman myself, I can sympathize with my sex whether white or black." The remark is corroborated, very occasionally, in the recollections of enslaved people: "Sometimes the wife of the planter learned the condition of the woman and said to her husband you must cut down her day's work," noted a field hand.[18]

When the bondpeople of South Carolina and the rest of the American South ended chattel slavery during the Civil War, former field slaves put down their hoes and slid into the night. Slavery had endured for two hundred years in the South Carolina rice fields, and even longer in the tobacco plantations of Virginia and Maryland. Tens of thousands of babies had been born to the bondwomen who worked the rice plantations. Some took their former mistresses' finery, donning dresses or tying ribbons in their children's hair as symbols of freedom. Newfound liberty took one form in the grasp of forbidden objects.[19]

"Seeing is believing," runs the proverb. Pregnancy breathes life into the longer original formulation: "Seeing is believing, but feeling's the truth."[20]

When a pregnant person lies down, the baby moves more easily, free of the curve of their lumbar spine. Unborn babies have kicked in the wooden box beds of Carolinian slave quarters, under linen ticks stuffed with straw or broken-up corncobs, in the feather beds of the Big House, in a mistress's apartments in Whitehall, in nearly every bedroom or dwelling place on your street. Given a name, or not, the distinctive inner touch of quickening perseveres across time.

Feeling may be the truth, but touch both disconnects and connects. Sometimes, shared sensations are broken by the distance of history, or by inequalities and coercion. Paper letters, portraits, iron hoes, and keys can endure across time, but flesh decomposes and disappears, going the way of most things. Extremes of fortune and coercion dissolve empathy: the stinging slap of a slave mistress on a bondwoman's face. At other times, shared sensations stir connection, between a person and their baby, between people of the past and the present, then and now: the caress of a swollen belly, an intervention on behalf of a pregnant laborer, an act of imagination to step into unfamiliar shoes.

6

The Rising of the Apron

I wake to a silence. Now the long, quiet mornings and afternoons. K moves up and down the tile of the kitchen floor, preparing breakfast or supper, organizing meals for the week ahead, reorganizing the toolbox after the construction of furniture (a wooden crib, a chest of drawers).

As the eighth month turns into the ninth, I consult the next chapter of the pregnancy manual, gather up notes taken at a birth class, count down the lectures left to teach, pull something from a diminishing array of wearable clothes. In her London almanac of 1659, the medical practitioner Sarah Jinner described late pregnancy as "the rising of the Apron." On a bike, I sit upright like a stately matron, arms straight ahead, knees jutting away from a belly that has risen all the way to my rib cage. A driver tsks. A shopkeeper addresses my stomach rather than my face. Kindly chitchat shifts away from work or the winter cold. Is it a boy or a girl? Take care of yourself! With little direction from me, every conversation is expectant.[1]

"I am as Fleshy and Fresh that you ever saw me," bragged one New Jersey woman in a 1753 correspondence with a close friend. "Like a fighting bird!" described a prairie homesteader in a letter of 1912. "Prodigiously big" ... "ready to get down" ... "still as pregnant as the Trojan Horse" ... tired of "breeding" ... ran other individual remarks.[2] How do people talk when they talk about late pregnancy? Bagged, bound, and heavy were terms the seventeenth century inherited from the fifteenth. The term "pregnant" dates from the same times. Between the sixteenth and eighteenth centuries, a heavily pregnant woman might be teeming, great-wombed, great-bellied, big-bellied, or child-great, all terms marking fecundity and bulk. Or she was brooding, as if tending to an unhatched egg or cherishing a small duck under a wing. Or fruitful. Plentiful. Flourishing. Prolific. Lusty.[3]

For privileged women, such talk changed around the same time that they took charge of the number of children they had and birthrates dropped. Elite nineteenth-century women were newly cast as disembodied, rational creatures. Euphemism became the order of the day. Such women became in the family way, or in the way of becoming a mother, or in a *delicate* state of health. Some took refuge in foreign coinage. British aristocrats may have been Francophobes, despising the French for their godlessness and republican ways, but now they became *enceinte* or endured a *grossesse*. Susan Magoffin, who in 1846 liked to think she was the first "American lady" to travel into Mexico, bringing presumptions of Anglo-American superiority with her, nonetheless described herself using the Spanish *embarazada* (pregnant, or as she wrote it, *em beraso*). When the librarian of the Missouri Historical Society published Magoffin's diary of the Santa Fe Trail in 1926, she indexed the description with the enduringly inoffensive phrase "in delicate condition."[4]

The swollen womb, the big belly that raised the apron, thus disappeared from polite English speech and private letters in the nineteenth century. Being pregnant was no longer a frequent adult state. Childbearing was somehow unnatural, and all too natural. Respectable talk shifted awkwardly from lusty size toward the passively awaited result: the little stranger, or the urchin, or the miscreant, the newcomer, or even the first pledge of matrimonial love. The phrases lurched between prim distance and mawkish sentimentality. Pincushions given to new mothers were decorated with warm but stilted words: welcome little stranger. The irony is poignant. Just as such women were acknowledged to be rational creatures, just as they were reducing family size, so a rich and meaningful vocabulary of bodily experience dipped out of view. "Dear old journal . . . I will have a pledge of love given me," confided Eleanor Cohen from the wealthy Jewish community of mid-nineteenth-century South Carolina. Elizabeth Cabot in Boston reported, vaguely, that a friend had "gone the way of all flesh, [and] expects her finale in August." Cotton-wool euphemism and a commitment to female reason worked to separate minds from physical bodies.[5]

"No one can say 'breeding' or 'with child' or 'lying-in' without being thought indelicate," wrote an elderly aristocrat in 1818, remarking on the changes among the elite of her lifetime. She added that "in the family way" and "confinement" have taken their place. The Gentleman's Magazine of 1791 sarcastically caught the same generational shift in language and attitude among the snobbish classes: "All our mothers and grandmothers, used in due course of time to become *with child* or as Shakespeare has it, *round-wombed* . . . but it is very well known that no female, above the degree of chambermaid or laundress, has been with child these ten years past."[6]

The parlance of working people and nineteenth-century slang were barely more direct. In the pudding club. Up the duff. A bun in the oven. The sticky-sweet euphemisms invoke men and sex. Pudding was low talk for penis or semen. Invoking a duff (an Australian pud) or a bun meant you were up the stick, up the creek, up the spout: in trouble. From the nineteenth century until strikingly modern times, English-speaking pregnant women could take their pick: be respectable or be in trouble, but let euphemism rule. Verbal modesty, and even the complete ignoring of a visible pregnancy, was usual among many large working-class families—in turn-of-the-century London, say, or in rural Nebraska. "A woman in the family way is said to be in the *pudding club*," wrote the authors of an 1889 dictionary of slang, forcing one euphemism to rely on another.[7]

Dictionary makers reckoned that slang was often used for lack of terms sufficiently strong to convey the speaker's feelings. If someone in the nineteenth century was sweet on, or mashed on, or gone on, they were in love. If they had had a lot to drink, they might be kisky, flying high, paralyzed, boozed, or as drunk as a lord, an emperor, or a fish. But in the case of being pregnant, the feeling of occupying a rounded, heavy body was concealed rather than conveyed by words. Great girth was hidden in plain sight.

Is it a boy or a girl? I don't know—I want it to be a surprise.

The query is an ordinary pleasantry, prompted when my silhouette turns sideways, by my bright and risen conspicuousness, and surely well meant. The question also teases, chafes, and tweaks at my feminism. I don't want sex or gender to come crashing in just yet. A black-and-white photograph held at the local Kinsey Institute shows a woman looking down toward the indignant, wailing face of her baby at exactly the moment of birth: head emerged, shoulders and body still within. Mariette Pathy Allen poignantly, fiercely, titled the 1983 image *The Last Gender Free Moment*.

During a routine test, the baby is described as having a "handsome" brain. K notices the unintended slip, but does not mention the remark until much later. Others we know pursue all the medical information they can get: planning ahead, trying a relationship on for size, or clawing back some pleasure from diagnostic worries. On the radio, a discussion about Gallup polls announces that Americans prefer boys to girls in the same way they did in 1941.

Most but not all past societies witnessed a hard-nosed preference for boys. That's patriarchy. That's also seeing bodies as binary, the sorting of the world into people who are one thing or the other, even when some babies decidedly are not. Past workaday predictions to forecast who a baby would be have ranged considerably: warm food at conception favors boys, cold food favors girls. Boys sit higher in the womb than girls. If a woman's right breast is firmer, or her right eye brighter, she will have a boy. If the left, a girl. Younger mothers most frequently have boys, and older mothers most usually have girls.[8]

Gallup pollsters asked random Americans about their preference for boys or girls six times between 1941 and the close of the twentieth century. The numbers stayed remarkably stable: between 36 and 41 percent preferred boys. But large numbers expressed no preference, or uncertainty, or no opinion: 38 percent (1941), 35 percent (1947), 41 percent (1997). I'm not sure what to make of these figures in toto. An individual is always more complex than a society. A random American polled in 1947, wondering about personal preferences, might have been thinking about family members lost in the Second World War or about whom they enjoyed among the children of their best friend.[9]

Meanwhile, the way "a boy or a girl?" gets heard has changed. Feminist and mainstream notions of sex and gender have shifted since the 1940s, often in muddled ways. That there was a sex/gender distinction could be a revelation. The gender to which Pathy Allen referred in 1983 was the changing roles and rights of men and women as distinct from the biology of the two sexes. Like other feminists in that moment, the photographer suggested that gender, and female subordination, was not—should not be—conferred by nature. Mainstream notions of gender after the middle of the twentieth century took several paths. Gender was a social status, imposed on people from the outside by virtue of perceptions of their sex. Or gender was a kind of identity, linked to the sex of a person's brain, which could be freely expressed. The expression of gender was binary, like sex. Or it was nonbinary or fluid.[10]

Gallup's own question became simpler and more precise. There's a hint of recognition, perhaps, of the overall lowering of birthrates, and the choice to have just one or no children at all. "If you could have only one (one more) child, which would you prefer to have—a boy or a girl?" (March 1941). "If you had another child, would you rather have a boy or girl?" (September 1947). More recently: "Suppose you could have only one child. Would you prefer that it be a boy or a girl?" Always binary.[11]

Who recalls what I was eating at the salient hours of conception? Anyway, isn't my brain handsome enough?

Take care of yourself! Take care!

I will. Thanks.

Vulnerability has always attended being pregnant. Projections of vulnerability on the visibly pregnant, too. Misogyny, fears of monstrosity, or merely the small details of nature—landscape, crop, the hue of a bird's egg—have flowed into worries about maternal influence on an unborn child.

Contemporary commentary fixates on diet. Avoid alcohol, coffee, tea, seafood, and soft cheese. The expertise vastly outweighs the evidence. But until well into the twentieth century, the primary concern had more to do with experiences. Certainly some kinds of people were expected to change what they ate. In their genteel *grossesse*, British aristocrats, whose primary role was to produce an heir, were not spared injunctions about diet: eat no meat, less salt, no alcohol, more fiber. American ladies like the *em beraso* Susan Magoffin were encouraged to avoid rich and spicy foods, coffee and liquor, and to use enemas to clear the digestive system. More people worried about getting enough to eat at all. Pregnancy is a hungry business.[12]

More typically, maternal experience mattered because events and emotions could mark an infant inside. Sights, frights, foods, dreams, and strong feelings might have an effect. Stories circulated about strange-shaped marks—mother's marks, they were often called—or monstrous births. At Nett Lake in Minnesota, Native mothers connected seagull eggs with freckles, and warned one another off consuming porcupines, which might make babies headstrong, difficult to train, hateful, and touchy, because the needles of a porcupine are sharp.[13]

Sometimes the idea of mother's marks opened conspicuously pregnant women up to exploitation or to scolding. Early modern Englishwomen might be followed by beggars with sores and deformities who were hoping to be bought off. Unwholesome longings, went one typical medical warning, could make "foul impressions" on the child. Caring too much about fashion might result in children born with growths shaped like the stiff ruffs of Tudor portraits.[14]

At other times, the idea of mother's marks gave individual women negotiating room, even power. A pregnant mistress angered by an apprentice's behavior might take him before the Lord Mayor's Court in London. Husbands who otherwise held patriarchal authority understood that wives' reasonable whims should be indulged. A celebrated botanist was told by his pregnant wife that she had an urge to smash a dozen eggs in his face—which he then endured. Grotesque stories made the moral plain. An eighteenth-century husband who failed to buy a lobster for his wife at Leadenhall Market shocked her when finally bringing one home, but the child born later looked "boiled and red."[15]

When Emma Foster, an enslaved woman, bore a child with six fingers on each hand, she interpreted the extra digits as the result of having rubbed a friend's injured finger. A plantation mistress in the Old South, who had likely broken the racial and sexual taboos of her community, pointed to her fear of local slave rebellion as the reason she gave birth to a dark-skinned child. In 1742, the novelist Henry Fielding distinguished one character through "a Mark on his left Breast, of a Strawberry, which his Mother had given him by longing for that Fruit." Mother's marks could link a woman to her community, or serve as a resource for the enterprising or desperate, or explain the innocuous.[16]

Circulating stories about the power of the maternal imagination invariably reflected their immediate historical environment. During the English Civil War, which pitted Royalists against Puritan Roundheads, a pamphlet told of a woman who preferred to have a child with no head rather than a round head. The result was entirely predictable. Shakespeare, at least, thought such beliefs had comic value: *The Winter's Tale* stages a ballad about a moneylender's wife giving birth to twenty moneybags.[17]

Amusing or condemnatory, the stories suggest fragile boundaries between bodies, babies, and their surroundings. They presume a vulnerable porousness. Tottering along icy pavements like a misshapen skittle, I can recognize the sense of vulnerability, if not the supposed permeability of sight and soul and infant. The old history of mother's marks does not reach all the way down to us, though we might hear echoes in injunctions against unwholesome desires and inappropriate cravings, or in calls to keep up spirits and avoid depression. What communicates from me to the baby—an orgasm, a cheese sandwich, a wince against the cold? Do the baby's spirits rise and fall with my own?

Exactly when the notion of mother's marks faded, and when these stories stopped circulating, is not clear. The records of London's General Lying-In Hospital suggest that it was not before the 1880s. In the casebooks, there are echoes of the earlier stories. Agnes Reed explained that consuming large quantities of brimstone and treacle, a digestive remedy, caused the red face of her fifth baby. The remarks of one Mrs. Lambert on her ninth child, who was born without one of its hands, recall former concerns about beggars. The hospital's medical officer recorded, without comment, the story that "a beggar in street uncovered his arm without a hand and gave her a fright."

"Would [it] make any difference to a baby," one Connecticut woman wrote in 1916, if a mother "saw a man with a disfigured arm acting on a stage, and it impressed her so much that she became very nervous and had to leave the hall, and has been able to think of nothing else for three days?" Her enquiring letter to the U.S. Children's Bureau, founded in 1912 to improve maternal and infant health, suggests that changes were still being rung to stories of mother's marks in the first half of the twentieth century. The impact of movies, or vaudeville? "My neighbor has a new baby & it is deformed," wrote in another from 1926 Alabama. "People say picture shows did it." In this case, the reply was reassuring: "If you enjoy the movies and can go at times which do not interfere with your eight hours of sleep at night . . . there is no reason why you should not visit an amusing picture show now and then."

Midwestern interviewees of the mid-1970s, in the most recent evidence I find, reported the effects of cravings for strawberries or fish, or marks left by worries. Avoid seeing "freaks" at the circus or the snake house at the zoo, they remarked. Take care! Take care!

I am still working: sitting on the table at the front of the lecture hall, seemliness gone. Work is sliding away from me. There is a last set of student essays to evaluate. I stir myself to deduce final marks even though my mind shrinks away from the narrow lists of numbers and into the expanse of my trunk.

I never want pregnancy to be over. We defy mathematics: one plus one equals one. I am myself and not myself; I am eating for two. The relation I have to this extra life is not unlike that I have to my dreams and thoughts, which I can tell K or a friend, but which cannot be an object for us in the same way. I am happier than usual, though I cry easily.

I cannot wait for pregnancy to be over so I can feel normal again: hug my sweetheart, cross my legs. I bump crankily into older habits only to find the way blocked by my body sticking out before me—hard belly on my thigh as I lean to tie a shoelace, a pull from my side on turning to check that the front door is properly shut.

This is a luxurious tangle of feelings.

At the annual seaside regatta where I grew up, there was a big black boat, a clipper ship perhaps, that served as headquarters for the seaborne activities. The figurehead was buxom and overspilling, with pastel paint peeling off the cleavage. As a child, I always noticed her because she made me uncomfortable, a wooden mockery of my mother's warnings not to behave "common."

Now I am like the prow of an old-time ship, all boobs and frontage, announcing the arrival of cargo. Back when seafaring was still big business and Britain presided over a mercantile empire, a proverb could read "A ship under sail and a big-bellied Woman, are the handsomest two things that can be seen in common." Daily, hourly, my contents are bigger and more separate from me.

At regatta's end, after watching the walking of the slippery pole and the fireworks, we sometimes went back to Mrs. Wass's house for tea. She was old and strict and made fish-paste sandwiches. On a thin windowsill sat a tall sailing ship in a bottle, with three delicate masts on which white sails were suspended. I took it that her long-dead husband—my friend's granddad—had made it, although I never understood how.

The longer we go on, the more I fear I've made a ship within a bottle. All the while a second heartbeat pulses, a sound inside the glass with its own intent.

This Giving Birth

Leaning, squatting, straining, calling out to lovers or mothers or gods, panting, pulling, pushing—birth-givers do not document birth as they labor. This work may be recorded by others—the diary entry by the husband of a long-suffering wife, the notation of payment made in eggs or butter in a midwife's account book, the scoring of a newborn's test in a hospital file—but those laboring leave storytelling to retrospection. They can't take notes. This giving birth, this glistening verb, to borrow a poet's words, gets described after the event.[1]

Because every event has a beginning and an end, here are two moments. First, it is dark outside, and broken waters pool around my feet. The puddle spreading on the wooden floor is clear of blood or stain and smells faintly agricultural, like damp straw. My face reflects in the curtainless glass, a startled glance of fear and a matter-of-fact grin quartered by sash lattice. Several miles away and many hours later, once again it is dark outside a brightened room. Beyond the wide sweep of a hospital window, heavy-coated figures lean into the cold night air. The form of a healthy newborn baby warms my chest. A midwife tidies the foot of the bed.

No two scenes or circumstances of birthing are the same. Some people labor for days, some for hours. Some births are intense and others are ambivalent, some both. People have labored at home, in special huts, in hospitals and clinics and almshouses, or elsewhere, in a more or less intended place: on the steps of a benefactor's house, in a snowdrift, behind a tree, beside a bridge or across the back seat of a taxi, upon a surgical table. They have labored among women friends and neighbors, around doctors, nurses, and midwives, and in the presence of lovers, servants, mistresses, sisters, and mothers. They have blown into bottles to focus breath, and let birthing stools or broad laps take their weight. They have delivered on hands and knees on a rug, over newspapers or moss, or, conscious or unconscious, into hands clad in sterilized gloves.

Yet all births fit somehow into one broad historical change, a single arc of transformation to which every birth refers. That is the shift from birthing among female family members, neighbors, and friends to medical birth in a hospital. Some in the past gave birth alone or among strangers, and some today choose a home birth, but the dominant context for birthing—the set of expectations held by the culture to which we refer, whatever the circumstances—has shifted decisively from a traditional world of female knowledge and companionship to a medical world of technology and expertise. Doctors arrived first in the homes of privileged women, as male midwives and then as obstetricians. Later, laboring women were brought into hospitals and surrounded by beeping equipment, cabinets of pain relief, and white sheets. Most recently, owing especially to late-twentieth-century natural childbirth activists, some of the old concern for human warmth and a birth-giver's experience have been knitted back into labor. Sometimes contemporary birth is a cesarean section that safeguards a life or attends to fear or concern; sometimes labor is a palimpsest of practices old and new.[2]

After the event, birth-givers reach for the analogies they know to make sense of what happened. Early contractions are like small waves at Stinson

Beach (a recent Berkeley woman) or the quick dips and rises of a green contour map (a contemporary poet). The pain is like a red-hot poker (a twentieth-century milliner) or like a fine electric needle outlining one's pelvis (an early-twentieth-century social scientist, following the pains with her mind). Labor is being on the rack, as if each limb were being divided from the other (a seventeenth-century Puritan gentlewoman, identifying with the suffering of religious martyrs). Pushes move like the wind preceding an avalanche (the Berkeley woman again). It was a night that would kill a horse (a Yorkshire woman, when horses were still the main form of transport). Some insights about vaginal birth seem universal: the baby's head crowns in a ring of fire. All these phrases grasp at understanding. Words surely shape experience before and throughout, and they come to hand in retrospect, but birthing itself always exceeds them: elusive, demanding, requiring both presence and loss of self. My words are already receding. As the small pool of broken waters glints at my feet, at first the size of a saucer and then a dinner plate, I inhabit birth's glistening verb.[3]

At first, there is not much to be done except wander around the house, eating toast and faking calm. Where I live, there is a large and lively "childbirth community" committed to natural childbirth. A doula, Molly, who taught our childbirth class, turns up after a few hours to stay and help. Is the smell of coffee okay? she asks to a nod. I put some music tickets that will now go unused in an envelope for a friend. I take an apple from a bowl and put it back again.

In seventeenth-century East Anglia, going from house to house to summon the midwife and other experienced women to the birth was known as nidgeting. Jane Josselin's husband, the minister of Earls Colne, might have gone door-to-door fetching some half dozen or dozen women: her neighbors, friends, sisters, mother. The village of several hundred was set in a countryside of small fields and hedges, alder groves and marshes. Most of the old forest had long since receded, except for a medieval woodland. Accents overheard might show the strains of London, which was linked to the village by road, or of Holland, from where immigrants had come to spin and weave cloth for export all over Europe. Perhaps Jane Josselin could hear voices from the lane, perhaps she noticed the smell of cooking onions or garlic from the kitchen at the back of the house, over-riding the scent of apples or hops in the loft or the oily odor of fresh wool. The chamber that had been turned into a birthing room was kept warm and dark. As the women assembled, thick curtains refused light and air. The keyhole was blocked.

Such birthing scenes could be places of retreat or of suspicion. As a minister's wife in the 1640s, Jane Josselin was the kind of woman deemed an honest matron. Her childbed should have been kindly supported. Rings, laces, knots, fastenings, and buckles might be gently removed to avoid them getting in the way. The hands were familiar and caring. Less fortunate women—the poor, the unmarried—might give birth in fields or in local prisons or under a mistress's glare. Josselin may have seen such a single woman called upon, at the very height of her travails, to name the father. She may even have spoken the words herself, finger-wagging about sin and the Day of Judgment. A poor mother might be standing in the corner of Josselin's own birthing chamber, the menial birth-side tasks of washing and cleaning part of her duties in exchange for receiving charity from the parish.

Perhaps, near the end of her first labor, Jane Josselin heard her husband's cough through the wall. Men were excluded from birth, but timber-frame house walls were thin, with holes and cracks and spaces in them. Ministers like Ralph Josselin viewed birth as something to which women should submit. Labor was God's punishment for Eve's sin, and his rod of correction meted out pains to be patiently borne. Other con-temporary men imagined women in the chamber telling jokes about sex, judging men and belittling their reputations. The attending women were called godsips, or gossips, a term that in the next century came to take on the pejorative meaning of tittle-tattle. Inside the birthing room, though, a midwife saw birth as active, as a woman's hard work. She and the godsips sought to keep Jane's spirits up by talking and sharing a special kind of wine thickened with spice and grain. This caudle was sweet and warm, and mildly softened the pain. Oil of lilies warmed and smoothed the midwife's hands. Candlelight reflected off a pewter plate and the sweat on a woman's brow.[4]

We are staying put, for now, but the house goes silent with each contraction. Each takes all my—what? concentration? absorption? resilience? Panic induces vomit, and I think, I can't do this, and I say so out loud, too, but the resistance leaves as quickly as it arrives. Nothing has ever been as involuntary as these moving pains. I just need to show up, get my mind out of the way, and breathe out. The cramped confines of the bath replace the air of the living room and the old clock on the mantel. The clock has not worked since we brought it here, I notice, and we really should repair it . . . but the thought gets lost. Bathwater contains the scattering pain of each contraction. K pours water over me once, five, thirty, hundreds of times. His presence feels entirely essential but also peripheral to the overwhelming interior rhythm.

Cherokee women of the eighteenth century removed themselves to special cabins for menstruating and for birthing. They called the secluded cabins *osi*, walking to them at some distance from ordinary town dwellings. Within, the usual indoor tasks of producing pottery or cloth, cooking, and taking care of children ceased. The osi's wattle-and-daub walls were well used to rest and to talk. They heard the story of the Corn Mother, the first woman, whose blood had fallen to earth as life-giving corn. They heard other stories of owls and giants, or the White Beaver, who might be called during a river accident. They associated birthing with spiritual power.[5]

A Cherokee woman, with a name like Dawnee or Qualiyuga, might have stood by the hearth at one moment. At another she might have knelt on the ground, holding a chair, at another she sat on a lap and was held around her waist by one of the other women. Her usual garments—of woven buffalo hair or deerskin or hemp and mulberry bark—were tucked up.

Such a woman might hear the medicine man or woman outside, walking around from the eastern to the western corner of the osi. Across the fertile valleys of the Southern Appalachians stretched a landscape of spruce and sugar maple in which women were farmers and men were hunters. Sharpened sticks and stone mattocks served as hoes. Elderly women known as ravens watched over outlying fields of flinty hominy corn, keeping an eye out for crows or raccoons or marauders. Away from the fields, an older mother might be teaching her son to use a bow and arrow, throwing a piece of moss or some other frail object into the air for him to hit. Clay bowls were placed over fires of smoky pitch pine to make the pots smooth, black, and firm. Oil and honey were stored in deerskins. Bread was loaded with chestnuts or beans or pumpkin.

"Little boy, jump down," the shaman might have called at the osi's eastern corner; "little girl, jump down," at the western. Red elm was taken to frighten the child and make it jump down from her body and onto the waiting leaves. Or the warm smell of an infusion of cherry bark was brought close to her nostrils. Women's words aimed to coax the baby out. There were loving promises and hollow threats: "You little man, get up now at once. There comes an old woman . . . Listen! Quick! Get your bed and let us run away!"

We make an odd trio in the hospital parking lot: Molly and K are upright on either side of me, and with wide and unsteady gait I clutch their hands. Cheap men's pajamas, bought at the last minute, poke out beneath a gaping coat. Each pain halts our slow progress, stops us short in strange refusal of the minus temperatures. I do not sense the cold. This is splendid and squalid together: I am reminded of attending a rave during a sadly short period of misspent youth, high on Ecstasy and aware of the warehouse's cold floor and low temperature only because of the bulky jackets of the security guards. Concrete parking lots and gray hospital buildings don't intimidate me today: I am off my head on birth. There's another pause at the foot of the elevator, and another outside a delivery room.

Our midwife is waiting. Eight centimeters' dilation: a nugget of birth-manual talk that seeps into what's happening like the learned fact of a school test. The room is plain and comfortable, and another bath is run. Molly talks me through each pain, which come rapidly now. Perfect. You don't need to do that one again. There are obstetricians on hand if necessary, but we are hoping to do without. My mother's hints about her doctor's belligerence had chimed with birth-class cautions about cascades of medical intervention.

A doctor turning up at the home of a white tenant farmer of the 1930s southeastern United States typically brought chloroform and asked for water to be boiled. He knew the heated professional debate about the failings of hospital obstetrics—the threat of infection, the high maternal mortality—and a laboring woman knew the distance and the cost. There were few hospitals in the flat landscape of crossroads country stores, white chapels, and mud-chinked log barns for curing tobacco. Unpainted one-story weatherboard houses rose out of the red and gray soil. Rural electrification lines ran along highways. Meat was typically served on Sundays with lima beans or cabbage.[6]

For a first birth, such a woman probably chose her parents' four-room home. Usually smoke smudges were left on the walls where kerosene lamps hung. In the kitchen might stand a stove, an oilcloth-covered table for preparing food and eating, and a wooden safe for storage. In the sitting-bedroom there were beds, a sewing machine, and perhaps some chairs around a fireplace. Flour sacks might have been pieced together for curtains, and artificial tulips or calendars or photographs from years past and present adorned a dresser. There were no cupboards or closets, so guns, hatchets, and clothes hung from nails along the walls. Shoes were often suspended by their heels along the top edge of a mirror. Jars of fruit or vegetables lined a kitchen wall or were stacked in a bedroom corner. A pint milk bottle saved tobacco seeds from one year's crop for the next.

An experienced neighbor, often known as a granny, helped out. This was one of those times when a woman needed all the help she could get from anybody. The granny heated the water, gave chloroform to dull the pain, handed the doctor things, and held the woman's hands when she was bearing down. If the birth was hard and involved instruments, the kitchen table would be used. There were a hundred different kinds of forceps. Perhaps the woman's eye was caught by the food dishes, covered separately with overturned plates, or by the brown snuff stains at the corner of the granny's mouth. She might be relieved to have kept a bottle of disinfectant on hand, and to have collected old cloths for pads and navel dressings. Bragging rights came with the extremes of labor's duration—either unusually long or unusually short—and with not yelling. Grannies claimed that if you yell on a pain, you will have to have it over again, or if you yell too loud or too much, you will kill the baby.

The bearing down takes getting used to. This is hard labor: arduous and full of ardor. The hospital midwife is cool-mannered and commonsensi-cal. Curl around your baby. I am surprised the pushing is taking so long. One hour, two hours, three hours. Molly takes down the clock. Between pushes, I disappear into something like sleep before bracing and curling again. There is an air of expectancy. A nurse wheels in a fetal monitor. She monitors and cleans me, monitors and cleans. Maybe there is an air of faint concern, I'm not sure, but I am not worried. I can still feel famil-iar kicks in my belly.

In 1949 New York, Otis Burger wanted to stop each contraction to see what it felt like. It was odd having an entirely new sensation inside. She had been reading the English doctor Grantly Dick-Read—who thought that childbirth should be painless—disliking his determination to reduce women to their biology but appreciating his tenderness. Her fear was the hospital feeling of being naked and at the mercy of strangers, like a spec-imen of some sort. Male doctors were condescending; they seemed to think that the difficulty was all in the mother's mind and that birth was too much of a commonplace for the mother to make such a silly fuss.[7]

The city of this highly educated woman was a world of portable radios and bathing suits, of gelatin desserts and starched clothes, of door-to-door salesmen and typewriters. Jazz was played at the Royal Roost club, and sun worshipping and smoking were deemed safe. A two-bedroom apartment in the Village, with furniture, sold for $750. Otis Burger's mother had a great belief in medicine and in white-coated doctors. What Otis, a recent tomboy, knew about babies she had learned in a college zo-ology class.

Otis Burger drank four Scotches to jump-start birth. She had been shaved by a nurse and given an enema. In the delivery room, the lights were dazzlingly bright. When she pushed, her wrists were strapped down to protect the sterile sheets. Below the waist she was painted with antiseptic. To dull the pain, she was offered, and declined, the analgesics ether and then scopolamine. A nurse told her that redheaded women always have babies quickly. A doctor told her that in the Middle Ages babies were delivered only by midwives, and the first doctor who tried to see an actual delivery by sneaking in disguised as a woman was burned at the stake. (This is not true.) As the baby was halfway out, a medical attendant wearing a mask administered laughing gas, and she was "out" for twenty minutes.

Feel the top of your baby's head, instructs my midwife. I had not planned on this, on exploring my lower body made large and foreign. What's there is sticky and hard behind a tiny slanting slit, forward to back, and offers a daunting, leaping sense of the work still left to be done. K is glowing. The baby kicks again, and I try to etch the sensation in my memory, to lay the feeling down within me. Finally, the baby's head emerges. I think of my sister. Her firstborn also arrived across two separate pushes. In a wide-eyed pause, I wait for the last push. Then there is a flurry of limbs, the edge of a frog kick in the air, and we are parted. The event ends. The doing rushes to a full stop.

This giving birth pummeled time, turning it lumpy and uneven. Now I am once again in this room, in this town, with this man and these women, snapped back into time and place. Molly replaces the hospital clock on the wall, and each minute returns to sixty seconds.

So women birth in and out of normal time. And perhaps their recent past has felt more and less present likewise. In seventeenth-century Earls Colne, the thoughts of a woman like Jane Josselin might have flickered to earlier generations, before the Protestant Reformation. Earlier women in her village labored with the aid of saint's girdles, or relics of the Cross, or the intercession of the Virgin Mary or Saint Margaret. Those habits had disappeared in the Reformation, along with the local Benedictine priory.[8]

As her belly was rubbed with a warm hand to expel the afterbirth, an eighteenth-century Cherokee woman might have thought of former generations and old omens. If a newborn jumped down onto the leaves placed under her and fell on its chest, it would have to be wrapped in a cloth and put in a creek. As the cloth sank, carrying away any ill fortune, the baby would be retrieved. The Christian missionaries moving close to Appalachian Cherokee towns were determined to replace such ancestry and such omens—including stories of the fertility of the Corn Mother—with accounts of original sin and the sufferings of Jesus Christ. From Oostanaula, near the Brainerd mission, a woman called Dawnee married a white man.

White tenant-farm women of the 1930s southeastern United States recalled that *their* mothers had preferred birthing by sitting on slop jars rather than lying flat in bed. These mothers might also have distracted them with tales of their own parents' better days, before the Depression, when tobacco still provided a decent living, or of granny midwives as their sole birth attendants. With luck, such grannies used to say, the afterbirth "falls out like a book." "Granny helps in your misery," observed one such mother; "midwife . . . gives tea etc; and helps with her hands," said another. Granny midwives in these states, both black and white, called the contractions "pains" and reminded that babies "work slowly." Often they matched deep experience with religious conviction: "All I want you to do is be calm and easy," one used to say. "Leave the rest to God. He'll do it."

Otis Burger's mid-twentieth-century hospital experience contrasted with what she knew from nineteenth-century novels, in which there were no anesthetics or adequate medicines. She expected to dislike birth and feel like an invalid, and she did. She also had fond faith in progress and in science. A few days after the birth, Otis pseudonymously penned a first-hand account of childbirth. In so doing, she was ahead of her times by some two decades. Intimate, firsthand childbirth stories emerged in some quantity with natural childbirth activism and second-wave feminism. The retrieval of unmedicalized birth, the arrival of "choice," and the refusal of old silences all made it possible to go public.

The arc of change seems to speed faster as it arrives in our present, an arrow that quickens in its descent to the here and now. In recent generations, fathers were brought into the birthing room from waiting rooms and corridors. Doctors stopped entering laboring cubicles unannounced.

Strange hospital practices, like the slap on a dangling baby's behind to produce the first cry, stopped as abruptly as they had started. Activists campaigning to demedicalize childbirth reimagined labor as an event in a woman's life rather than as an illness, and sought out earlier forms of expertise and experience. At the same time, a succession of analgesics came and went. Cesarean sections became much more common. Hospitals developed policies to support birthing trans men.

In the days and months that follow my labor on this long December day, the birth story will become the child's story. We will come to notice how this baby arrived several weeks early, with determination and intensity and a loud protest at being removed to a set of scales. We will tie the strands of the event into a net of family meaning. For now, the birth story is in uncollected fragments. There is no myth of creation and connection. We are merely gazing at the baby.

8

Hello, You

So an event becomes a thing. A newborn. An offspring.

What we see, and what we have seen, when we look at a brand-new baby depends on who is looking. A modern midwife or doctor focuses on a set of vital signs. A suspicious father might search for signs of his paternity, while an anxious mother might scan in hopes that her transgression does not show. A nurse might see a cranky baby to be dealt with. A hastily arriving minister might see a soul to be saved. A surrogate might see an infant to pass over. Often people already know what they are going to see: a returning ancestor, a beloved addition to a family, a ward of the parish, the boy or girl they have been waiting for, a future king or slave, a bastard, an orphan, an adoptee, an addition to the mother's clan, the spitting image of an aunt.

Otis Burger's baby was seen not by her, but by the hospital nursery staff. The laughing gas had worn off, but the new mother lay awake in a private room until the wee hours, reading novels: "I had seen so little of her, and imagined her so rarely, that I quite forgot my reason for being here." These immediate separations were common hospital practice until recently. In 1967, the young London housewife Ann Oakley watched two medical students in white gowns stand with their backs to her, counting her crying newborn's fingers and toes. Was there something wrong with him?[1]

A Cherokee mother of the eighteenth century might have touched near the newborn's soft fontanel, that sweet spot in a baby's skull where a soul resides that has memories and lives forever. Perhaps she looked hard at limbs and tummy and face. Outside the wattle-and-daub cabin, people might have asked, "Is the baby a bow or a sifter?" "Ballsticks or bread?" (Would this new person hunt and play games or sift flour and make bread—was it a boy or a girl?) Usually, a husband covered and buried the placenta. Inside the cabin, a boy was wrapped in a panther skin or a girl in a deerskin to signal their distinctive future roles.[2]

My own seeing is rosy with hormones: long purple feet, splayed limbs and barrel chest, dark hair matted into fine streaks, some smears of white stuff in an ear, scuffed and shining face, cleft chin. Expansive eyes of dark oil look back at me. Hello, you.

For the gift of an hour or two, the baby is alert. He has an unhurried gaze and a strange air of self-sufficiency, which clings for a few days until he fully realizes he has arrived outside. He seems to know what to do, clamping onto my nipple and then sagging away with his cheek against me. He sleeps behind bruised, wafer-thin eyelids, mouth shaped into an O and fists nudging the edge of a lip. There is a bizarre kind of drained bliss.

Hospital staff come in and out: Here is how to swaddle. The baby should sleep in the see-through plastic crib. That was a good latch. The hearing test department can fit you in at two tomorrow afternoon. Humbling devices and small horrors wait in the bathroom: a vast swing-lid garbage can for dressings, a bloody tiled floor beneath my feet, a pulley for emergencies. I am at extremes of joy and humility, and I'd quite like to go home and get back to normal.

The baby is labeled "Knott baby boy" around his wrist, as if we were not yet certain of his name, and our wrists too are circled with name bracelets. They have bar codes which suggest that the hospital has just manufactured a baby and two parents. The paperwork for a birth certificate appears.

K and I had tussled over possible names. Each sounded more and less right, based on the shape of a surname or the name of a school bully or a character in a film or a stereotype. A girl's name came easily, a boy's name did not. In the car one afternoon, the seat belt pulled as taut as my fraying patience, he had offered a set of four good names plus one I probably would not like. Start with the probably not, I urged—and that was the one. Now the name from the parking lot enters our strange new present and seems to fit.

There's lots of intention in a name. Just occasionally adults have named themselves. Elizabeth Howell, John Powell, and Samuel Stephens did so. These late-eighteenth-century Philadelphians belonged to the first generation of their city's free black community. Under slavery, Elizabeth Howell had been Susanna. John Powell had been Jack. Samuel Stephens had been Jammy, short for Jamaica. Slaveholders did not bother with last names, their business records filled with short forms such as Betty and Ben. Now, freed of slave owners after running away during the American Revolutionary War or through the particular provisions of Pennsylvania's gradual emancipation legislation, former bondpeople gave themselves new last and first names, both. William Trusty, James Jones. Though they left few literary traces, their decisions showed up in the port city's legal records, tax lists, baptismal accounts, and census.[3]

Sturdy, proper. Such new names etched a sharp line between living enslaved and carving out an independent future in a white-dominated world. Freeman and Newman were among chosen last names, making the determination clear. Free black Philadelphians rejected the many kinds of names, most usually bestowed by colonial masters, that they associated with slavery: not Cuffee or Cajoe (after African days of the week), nor Cato or Caesar (from the classical past), nor Glasgow or Bristol or Jamaica (where planters did business), nor Venus, Mistake, or Moody (each a dangerous or derisive name to carry). People like Susanna-turned-Elizabeth-Howell did the same when it came to the more mundane task of assigning a new baby a first name.

We don't know what happened to Dinah, a twenty-year-old woman who tried to free herself by running away from the city "with the last of the British troops" when she was "big with child, and near the time of her lying-in." Was her infant born safely, and how did she name the two of them? The free black people who did make their home in Philadelphia carefully fused their new surnames with baby names associated with autonomy, freedom, and their local church. Charlotte and James Forten, among the more economically secure of free blacks, carefully knitted local benefactors and businesspeople to their family through naming. Robert Bridges (1813), Sarah Louisa (1814), Mary Isabella (1815)—these names also appeared among the family of their white benefactor, Robert Bridges. Thomas Willis Francis Forten (1817) gave a nod to a paternal grandfather and to a local merchant. The baby was baptized with four names, where a Dinah or a Susanna had only one. Naming can be a heady business, can help a child or a family find their way in a rapidly changing world.

Intention flows also in more mundane settings, in places of less distinct flux and lower stakes. In the tiny villages of fisherfolk in late-twentieth-century Scotland's East Sutherland, first names repeated, and just three surnames accounted for most last names. There were many Hugh MacDonalds or John Sutherlands. Fishwives birthed large families in which babies were named after grandparents. Usually the parents swapped turns: the father had the naming of the first child, the mother of the second. Every family had at least one boy and one girl bearing the most popular name. These naming habits made for fine labyrinths of connection among tight-knit communities. Shared names could tie families on dry land to the fishermen plying the herring shoals, the North Sea having no shortage of bad weather. The East Sutherland fishing folk solved the problem of multiple Hugh MacDonalds and John Sutherlands by giving their "fisher bairn" bynames: nicknames used to refer to them, if not to address them in person.[4]

These Scots' contemporaries among the black Seminole on the frontier of Texas also deliberately repeated names. Several habits kept the same names appearing. Namesaking after a relative was one. Esther Factor's son was called Hardy, just like his father. Swapping given names for surnames or vice versa was another, as was reversing male and female names. Clara Dixon's son was given Dixon as a first name. These shared names extended a black Seminole heritage that stretched from Africa to Florida to Texas: a usable past. To differentiate among people with similar names, Texan Seminoles used what they called basket names: entirely alternate names, many of which honored an African heritage. On a Texan frontier, as in an East Sutherland village, being able to tell people apart oils the wheels of a society. Names are filled with communication and social meaning, with personal hopes and historical happenings, with attitudes to life and cultural values.[5]

The baby is wordless and new, and any kind of name seems formal. Hello, you, I find myself repeating each time M opens his eyes, as if to welcome him back into social existence and mark his arrival again. Hello, you.

Events become things, but events are always untidy. Ritual seeks to contain them—the coronation of a king, the confirmation of a judge—but there is rarely a neat before and after, even with birth.

The movement from inside to out, from pregnancy to maternity, is less crisp than I expect. It's barely inches. Immersed in late pregnancy, I thought that the baby's arrival would usher in physical separation and a somewhat welcome autonomy, that the baby would adopt a distance I could more readily perceive. From the outside, birth appears as one body leaving another, extreme unity followed by extreme separation. ("Your baby is seven pounds one ounce.") But in close-up, it is starting to appear otherwise. The frog kick I recognize from inside. When the baby sleeps with arms crisscrossed against his chest, like a priest in pious repose, I am reminded of the awkward position that apparently explains those many hours of pushing. (The pious repose looks pompous and, worse, funereal to me, but I daren't say that aloud.) He is content only next to my skin.

Since the mass entry of laboring women into hospital in the 1920s and 1930s, hospitals have often supplied the rituals for the ending of birth. For two decades in late-twentieth-century Britain, it was customary for a National Health Service midwife to carry the baby to the hospital's front steps and then hand it over to the father. Buchi Emecheta, a Nigerian immigrant, describes the hour just before departure: the big, open maternity ward of the 1960s hospital, full of young mothers comparing nightgowns and cards, and the leave-taking that entailed dressing the baby in his first proper clothes and new shawl, with everyone cooing and remarking on how smart he looks. In Emecheta's autobiographical novel, the young immigrant hides in the corridor, imagining all the women laughing at her poverty and her blackness, while a nurse shows the baby around. Maternity wards could be places of companionship, in which new mothers befriended one another over stays of two weeks (this was, she remarks, when Britain funded a full welfare state). But the wards could also be places of isolation. Even if the women are friendly, she has the wrong color skin and the baby's shawl is much used. To the twenty-year-old, not having a new shawl is the end of the world.[6]

I am transported to the hospital's side door in a wheelchair, with my back to the master of this last ceremony. I see a flash of the orderly's blue clothes, but not his face. As the door swishes open to a gust of cold air, I wonder at the purpose of the wheelchair. Who does the hospital think is greeting us at the other end? Can't I walk? The baby crumples into the outsize car seat, and I voice some first maternal worries to K: Do you think he'll get cold? Should we tuck another blanket around him? Why didn't we think to bring warmer clothes? Gift givers have been more farsighted than we have: thank goodness for the car-seat cover.

It's a slew of maternal worries, and I am not a worrier. Not usually, anyhow.

9

Tears and Anecdotes

The baby is crying. Great, welling cries fill the room. They tear at me. I hold the baby, I pat the baby's back, I pace us back and forth along the corridor by my bedroom, I soothe. The sound ricochets between the narrow walls and soaks into me. After the tactile quiet of pregnancy, there is so much noise.

What exactly does an infant's cry sound like? The Dublin writer Anne Enright, charging herself earlier this century with writing a memoir of early motherhood, takes no less than three pages—THREE PAGES—to articulate the sound of her baby's cry. H-a-N-a-n-g. H-a-N-a-n-g. HaNang. Six hundred "words." Three full pages, until the cry comes to a complete stop.[1]

Enright's challenge was to convert sound into text, into a set of letters on the page, into black and white. Her dilemma was what an insistent cry often, but not always, does: crowds everything else out.

What has an infant's cry sounded like? It's a banal query. Babies cry. Sometimes, such as now, they cry a lot.

But as it turns out, what an infant cry sounds like cannot be separated from the historical environment. For a Californian aunt of 1900, a cry could sound like Scottish bagpipes, with their long, thin snuffle. Or like a penny horn, for a new mother in 1940s Manhattan. Or like the red-headed grebe, for the 1930s Ojibwe living on a reservation in their former hunting grounds. The grebe is a feisty, tough bird, about the size of a duck. A baby's "pitiful hard moan" might sound just like it. How a cry sounds depends on what you are used to hearing.[2]

Or how a cry sounds depends on ideas about babies. In seventeenth-century England, a clear and loud newborn cry was a welcome sign that the baby was expelling the moisture and phlegm of the womb, though intensifying crying caused concern. Vehement crying was thought to tax an infant's delicate bones. Fifty-odd years ago in the town of Nottingham, many mothers thought that small babies cried simply when they needed something. Others saw babies as both willful and cunning, and distinguished between real crying and merely "crafty" crying. As the put-upon wife of a caretaker remarked, "They get very crafty, and if they know that you're going to keep running up and down [the stairs] they do it all the more, and then they stop and they laugh at you."[3]

Or a cry depends on ideas about pain: for much of the eighteenth and early nineteenth centuries, the consensus among Western doctors was that infants were exquisitely sensitive to stimuli. This changed in the 1870s, with many scientists and clinicians claiming that infants were almost totally insensible to pain. That idea was only fully debunked in the 1980s. Did infant caregivers really believe it?[4]

Or a cry is more than just a sound: an "irritating" cry, among eighteenth-century letter writers; a "spine-destroying" cry, in one early-twentieth-century account. So crying can have a bodily quality that leaps over the neat boundary between the carer and the baby, and pushes and pulls at the hard-and-fast division of the senses into five. A cry can be felt as more than just sound. It can touch.[5]

Or a cry depends on local demography. "'Tis better to bear" the sound of noisy, healthy children than "the piercing cries of a sickly child," observed Esther Cox in 1801, when infant mortality was high. The sound of a baby's cry surely seemed different to Lois Larcom, who raised a big, clannish family of ten children in Massachusetts, than to her daughter Emeline. By the spring of 1852, four of Emeline's six babies had died in half-finished cabins on the Western frontier.[6]

Or a cry can be a sound worrisomely out of place. One English-woman was brought before a church court in 1620 Nottingham for bringing "a most unquiet child to the church to the great offence of the whole congregation." The vicar, it was reported, could not be heard for the "offensive noise." An enslaved Southern father "kept a bottle of sweetened water in his shirt to keep warm to give the baby when it cried." Laura Clark recalled that when she was a slave child on an Alabama plantation, enslaved women regularly gave children sweets "to keep us quiet." In a Louisville, Kentucky, jail, before the Civil War, Angie King walked her baby all night to keep a drunk white woman from carrying out the threat of "bashing its brains out against the wall" if it did not stop crying. King produced her "free papers" the next day, to prove to her jailers that her husband had bought her freedom from slavery.[7]

Late-twentieth-century Oglala women following "traditional" ways in Pine Ridge, South Dakota, put a hand over a baby's mouth and nose when it started to cry, gently cutting off its breath and "singing softly at the same time so as not to frighten it." When the baby struggled, they let go. This was training in being quiet, for babies had to be taught not to cry in case the sound spoiled a hunt by scaring off game.[8]

In the former quiet of the corridor by my room, the baby's cry is a refrain, a song without verses, a sermon without words. I listen, I interpret, I comfort, I place the sound in history. Thin bagpipes. A grebe's moan. HaNang, haNang. The crying sounds raw, something innate spilling forth. At the same time, the sound attests that what seems natural is only known through culture. Nature and culture can be different terms for the same thing. No sound can be heard, discerned, or made sense of outside of our historical circumstances, outside the particularities and specificities of time and place and individual. I find the thought comforting, a refusal of false universals.

I also wish the crying would stop. That we knew how to return him, more easily comforted, to his own strength. My godmothers Margaret and Betty, retired London nurses who live together, and are fierce stalwarts of the twentieth-century medical profession, say that it does a baby good to cry. But I don't think that.

The running water of the shower makes its own temporary quiet. My empty midriff is flaccid and unsightly, devoid of interest. Blood circles the drain, along with my fading curiosity about pregnancy. Like hearing a cry, being pregnant had compounded bodies and culture: made by shame and confidence, ignored or celebrated, shaped by clothing and words, a loosened corset, an apron let out or lifted up, a metaphor for touch, a euphemism about sex or size, an expectation of feeling, a technology's arrival, a taboo against seeing or looking, or eating one thing or another.

A baby is always a new beginning of some kind. Now there's my, our, separated state. Almost. Perhaps. My neat autonomy, my firm edges encased in skin, have dissolved. Droplets of milk, like early modern white blood, run off my chest, down the untended, uninhabited tent of my stomach. They join the clots disappearing with the shower water. Lowering the shower heat, the midwife had said, might stop this pale escape.

The baby's crying halts all thought, pulls at my heart. I think of Molly's childbirth classes, how we passed the doll-baby from person to person, faking different forms of comfort, the novice task then foolish and abstract. Now, before I am even dressed: Are you hungry, are you tired? The crying makes everything else discontinuous.

The discontinuity is true not just of today with the baby, but also of what remains to be known about infant care in the past. Be a political historian and search the archives for the records of a Parliament or a Congress, and you'll find a more or less continuous record of political speech. But search the archives for records of living with and caring for a small infant and—if you search hard and have a hunch about where to look— you will find a vast but highly piecemeal and incomplete archive.

The slim shards of evidence about hearing a baby's tears that I found before the birth, for example, came from anthropologists' interviews with Ojibwe or Oglala peoples on reservations, a single remark in a published diary, a stray sentence or two in government-sponsored interviews with formerly enslaved men and women, a handful of letters in manuscript, a seventeenth-century church court record.

Collected up, and thought about, this is an archive from which anecdotes, at best, can be composed. Even the most chatty and literate of past Britons and Americans—the privileged white middle classes and elites who composed hundreds of thousands of letters to one another in the eighteenth through twentieth centuries—rarely wrote about the particulars of daily infant care. "Here evidence is at its most fragmentary," comments the leading historian of Georgian women.[9]

The telling of anecdotes, it is seeming to me, is a peculiarly powerful means of moving between History with a capital H—the institution of slavery, the rise of industrialization, revolutionary ideology—and the mundane stuff of living with an infant. Anecdotes offer the rare opportunity to interpret different kinds of scenes, remarks, or objects that illuminate being with an infant, even where there is no continuous record, and the tiny archival traces that are left usually appear minor or inconsequential. They are the only means to keep asking "What was it like?"

For anecdotes hew close to what is deeply ordinary, mundane, and hidden from wider view. Even today, it is through anecdotes that the experiences of those caring for babies routinely surface—as stories they tell one another. "The postman rang the doorbell just as I was getting the baby off to sleep, and she was grumpy for the rest of the day." Or "He does better with *this* formula." Or "I was so tired I drove straight through a red light." Anecdotes hold the inconsequential and the important together and pronounce them somehow the same. Right here, right now, they are.

The bare anecdotes K and I share grab at explanations for what the tears mean, or what works to stop them: That's a hunger cry. Do you remember yesterday when . . . ? That's tiredness. That's overstimulation. We're not, I realize, with the 1970s Londoner who complacently reckoned she had "a remarkably good baby—what I'd have been like with a crying baby I don't know." Our baby cries a good deal, but I am already an admirer of his determination, his staunch advocate before any critic. In keeping with the times, and with glad relief, we declare to each other that there's no such thing as a bad baby.[10]

Sometimes the tears and crumpled face seem to be our baby's original state. He always wakes with a cry. Speakers of Lakota on the North American plains, I learn, inherit a verb, "to whine, whimper, almost crying, as a child on first waking, and wanting its mother." I reach for vocabularies to describe what I hear, what I perceive, how caring feels. Sometimes knowing about the past expands what can be said.[11]

I walk on eggshells to get things right, and I strain to understand. M's tears are kittenlike, mewlish, before they gather momentum. The tears are mine as well as his. I'm happy-sad and sad-happy, and often I can't hear myself think.

10

Staying the Month

A month. Six weeks. Or maybe just a week, or ten days. Different intervals get allotted for a birth-giver's recovery and a baby's nurture, for the broken and intense early days of keeping a newborn alive. Sometimes relatives, servants, and adoptive parents hover, aid, or replace the birth-giver, counting along.

Staying the month was one designation for the period of recovery. Or lying-in, then upsitting. How did people count and label the time? And what weaves through the counting, gets attached to this new kind of reckoning?

In my dark January house, day and night run wildly together. My past, my usual life, is receding at a great pace; my future is far-off and out of focus. There's just one long, blurry present, counted out in the days of the baby's age. Or maybe my days since the birth. Of the past, there's a series of shards to assemble, the hints of themes to come.

Three days in

"Baby blues" is a modern term. The phrase was once meant as a compliment. Flirtatious eyes, baby blues, reeled in the men. "Your pretty ways, your baby-blues / May give you right to pick and choose" ran a late-nineteenth-century poem. Starting in the 1940s, though, it serves to capture a fleeting change of mood, felt in the days shortly after birth. I recognize that. "By the third day," reckons the feminist collective who wrote *Our Bodies, Ourselves* in 1978, "most women have the by-now familiar 'baby blues.' We may cry; have frightening dreams and fantasies; feel scared or worried by our lack of 'maternal feelings.'" The Irish-born health visitor Ellen George remembers laughing about it beforehand: "If you come to see me on the third day I'll be having my crying day!" Her mum brings her home for three weeks, which feels terrific.[1]

Before the milk comes in, there is colostrum. Early modern doctors thought that a baby should not suck any milk on the first day, and that from the second to the eighth days, the baby should be breastfed by another woman. After a woman gave birth, the logic ran, the milk was watery and thin, "Foul, Turbid and Curdy," and hence inferior. But such views change. In the 1920s you could pick up Truby King's best-selling book about the baby's first month: "For a day or so the baby usually gets scarcely anything—only a few teaspoonfuls of creamy-looking liquid; but every drop of this is precious." This became commonplace. Fifty years later, the ex-barmaid Anne Bloomfield hated breastfeeding, and stopped after four days, but at least her baby "had the colostrum so that's alright, you know, they say that's a good thing." A bottle is her alternative.[2]

Western Georgia, the eighteenth century. If a Cherokee woman dies in childbirth, a white observer records, "any of the woman's relations that gives milk will take the child and give it suck and they will make no distinction between that child and their own children." There is no such category as orphan among them.[3]

In the 1970s, José Bryce, a red-haired and fair-skinned manicurist, feels so dry and salty that she could sell her body to a potato chip manufacturer. Her pregnancy had felt like a "bloody disease." Now there are so many stitches she cannot easily sit down. One is "like a piece of fishing wire, a great knot." The rest of the world has faded: "I look at the news and there could be a third world war and it's really not important at the moment."[4]

I'm on the sofa, facing the fireplace: the baby's four sippy sucks are changing to gulp and swallow, gulp and swallow. The skin on his face, scuffed by birth, is starting to smooth. He has my cleft chin, or K's cleft chin. I'm used to feeling romantic love, so this deep falling in, this toppling, feels unexpected, even promiscuous.

In early-twentieth-century Canada, among the Inuits of the Great Whale River, a new mother remains lying down for about a week, her head toward the tent door. If she is fortunate, a young girl helps her: into the next week, she is to avoid all heavy work. White Canadian mothers in northern Alberta or in Newfoundland are also encouraged to remain supine. They were supposed to eat light food and wear binders made of flannel for abdominal support. Of her midwife care, one later recalls, "You got tea with bread and butter the first day. Then no more for three days, dry toast I lived on for three days . . . You were not allowed to sit up in bed."[5]

Farther south than Alberta, the older women among the Ojibwe, living on a reservation in the 1930s, are bemused at the thought of being confined to bed after birth. In the old days, no: "The mother was lifted up to stand on her feet and given Indian medicine to drink. After that she walked around a little, although she didn't do any work for 2 or 3 days; but she didn't lie down." Newborn babies were wrapped in moss and squirrel or weasel hides. It was said that very few babies died in those days: "They were like little kittens; they lived right on."[6]

Seven days

Our doula, Molly, visits, holding the baby on her lap, legs pulled up on the sofa, baby face near her own. I'd actually rather like her to stay the night and some more days beyond. I'd like her to be my friend for the rest of my life. But I don't say this. Leaky with feeling and uncertain of my ear for tone, I don't say any of this. She knows more about babies than K and I put together. I watch her liking the baby, and love her for it, a new triangulation of feeling.

On the seventh or ninth day, Margaret Charles Smith goes around the house with the baby and a thimble of water as some kind of act of welcome. The baby's spirit is said to be unsettled before then. It is 1926, but such conventions reach back from Alabama to West Africa before slave days. Her mother makes her drink the thimble when she is done. "It was just a swallow. It wasn't a swallow. It was a little thimble." Margaret readily obeys her mother (actually her grandmother, who raised her); she "never explained to me why, but you know she being an old person, I love to obey old people." Then, as she recalls it to an interviewer some decades later, she put the thimble back.[7]

Among the wealthier middle classes of early-nineteenth-century England and North America, it is usual to employ a "monthly nurse" for care of mother and newborn. As the first week is turning into the second, mother and child still reside with her upstairs. In a monthly nurse, a Warwickshire textile manufacturer's wife recommends the qualities of bodily strength and the capacity to do with very little sleep. (The baby sleeps near the nurse in a cot or crib.) Further merits include taking advice well from a doctor; being tender, kind, and gentle but lively; and having experience at encouraging the baby's regularity and cleanliness. By the 1850s, her presence upstairs is becoming an important badge of respectability.[8]

How that may have felt is hard for me to recapture among the nineteenth-century effusions. A nurse known to two generations of women as "Mother Monroe" is described as "full of the magnetism of human love," "as wise as she was good, and as tender as she was strong," having nursed two generations of mothers in Johnstown, New York. An infant "lay as peacefully in her hands," one reckoned, "as if they were lined with eider down." But in *Ruth Hall*, a novelist imagines a young mother silently at war with the monthly nurse. She wondered if she could ask Mrs. Jiff to "take the babe and keep it quiet *part* of the night."

Confederate Texas, at the close of the Civil War, just as Southern slavery is being taken apart. A formerly enslaved woman named Chloe Ann is in her cabin with a week-old baby when "twelve Ku Kluxes done come to the place." Family lore later tells that they came "in by ones, and she whupped them one at a time." Long-standing forms of violence, local resistance to large-scale change, do not stop for a baby.[9]

Nine days, ten days

It is 1914. Vita Sackville-West receives a letter from her husband, Harold, who is caught up at the Foreign Office: "Give a hug from me to that odd little funny which happened the other day." He has left behind a household full of servants and a nanny, along with her and the baby.[10]

The late 1960s. A Korean military bride sings a Korean lullaby to her tiny baby. Her husband shouts, "No Korean!" That's when she realizes that her child is American. The families of such military brides, forming in the United States since 1952, are typically monolingual.[11]

K's immigrant family—Russian and German speakers—were told only to speak to him in English, and that's all we now have to hand on.

A coal-mining district in the north of England, the last decade of the nineteenth century. Her husband is out of work again, so she is intensely preoccupied with their material survival. His being out of work is not unusual: sometimes he works nights; other times since their marriage he has been out of work, and she has returned to her parents' house and he to his. It was the same way during the pregnancy. Her sewing machine was sold to pay for rent. The nurse cost seven shillings and sixpence. "The first night I went out Saturday shopping after baby was born, I had 1s. 7½d. to get meat, grocery, and all else to live on till [my mother] came along . . . her home being near." Her husband tramps from place to place looking for work. There is nothing but "pits for the boys."[12]

The coal miner's wife stayed in bed ten days before that Saturday shopping trip. The women she knows look forward longingly to this time in bed: "to be still and rest was a luxury of luxuries." Many have strong feelings about it. "I was not allowed to get up before the tenth day, and I do not think anyone ought to do so, even if they can." In the months and years to come, there will be four more babies, more help from a mum and a sister, and relieved thanks to a new British prime minister, Lloyd George, for maternity benefit. "Who works harder than us mothers?" she will ask. "I often say we work twenty out of twenty-four hours very often. Some days I don't sit down hardly to snatch a mouthful of food."

Fourteen days

The Vancouver artist Carole Itter, born in 1939, thinks that the exhaustion is like being stuck endlessly on a coach. "Time measured by the emptiness of a tummy to the fullness of these breasts, then reversed. I have never known tiredness like this, as though travelling day coach from Vancouver to Halifax to Vancouver to Halifax to Vancouver, two weeks of it, two weeks old today, not more than three continuous hours of sleep, my dreams rich, strange."[13]

Sometimes the baby sleeps on K's chest, sometimes even as far away as the sofa a few steps from the bedroom door. I am too lumpy and tender to sleep on, but K's generosity feels kind and not quite right, as if my homing devices are alarmed. Usually, the baby seems to disagree likewise, which pleases no one. The baby and I are swimming in a flood of signs, a flux of communication by tears and twitches. He is always hungry, and so am I.

Violet Harris describes, of working-class Lambeth in East London, "you wasn't allowed to get out of bed, not even to have your bed made, for seven days. And then you were got up on the tenth, or eleventh day and then you went out on the twelfth day, you know, to be churched and then on the fourteenth day, like, you had the baby christened, usually, if you was all right." By the twentieth century, churching was either tradition or superstition, depending on whom you talked to.[14]

Nineteen days

On the Maricopa Reservation in Arizona, now the fasting ends. Helen Sekaquaptewa, who was born among the Hopi in 1898, can eat salt and meat again. She's been eating only corn and well-cooked vegetables. It's customary for the mother-in-law to come in every day for a period of twenty days, taking over her chores. Every day, a steam bath helps Helen heal. She stands over a basin of hot rocks, cedar twigs, and water. "It really makes you feel good." She reports all this to Louise Udall, of the Church of Jesus Christ of Latter-Day Saints, who writes down her story. After the account of Hopi customs, Helen adds that, since *her* mother-in-law lived in Oraibi, "she came every fourth day."[15]

The counting in Helen Sekaquaptewa's community, I notice, is marked in corn. "On the first day the mother-in-law draws on each of the four walls of the room, with white corn meal, five horizontal lines, each six inches long, to tell off the twenty days . . . Every fourth day one line is rubbed off each wall."

In the joy and confusion and interruption and fatigue, I cannot yet linger over these historical anecdotes. I can barely see my way into the past contexts that make for such similarities, such contrasts.

My friend Jen, with four-month-old Jack on her lap, talks by the fireplace. She is trying to claw her way back to her former life. Her words are bighearted and witty, her lipstick the usual bright smear of feminist red. I am trying to hold on to history. Each of our projects is just trying to make sense. Our gazes on each other are slightly wild, off-kilter.

Three weeks

Sam is three weeks old. Jo Ingram, a teacher, would really have preferred a girl, but she's just getting on with it. She had wanted pink cotton sheets— she thought they were pretty—but she got some blue as a concession. She had worried about "bringing up a boy, a sexist child." "Now I'm beginning to recognize him as a boy," she thinks. "I just hope it's not going to make too much difference." Maybe she has a sense of herself as out of step: at this moment in 1970s Britain, only about one in five women wants girl children. The popularity of boys is especially strong for first babies. Jo has been cohabiting with Steve, and he deals with the diapers. There are no changing facilities to be found in men's public toilets "because men are not supposed to change babies."[16]

August 22, 1798, Liverpool. Hannah Rathbone, the wife of a cotton merchant, is a diarist of few words. She reports on difficult days with her son Theodore. Then, when he is three weeks old: "The little boy more quiet and easy than he has been any time before." And next: "A stormy night on the 24th, but my dear little boy slept well, as he generally does, which is a great comfort to me." The diary mingles her own state and her child's interchangeably: "Another bad night and day of headache. The child cried a great deal, gave him a little Dalby's" (a soothing medicine).[17]

We are coming to learn that we have a smart, fretful, wakeful kind of baby, a harp of nerves. He will not, quite, let us relax.

Georg'ann—doula, mother of a grown child, childbirth activist, this morning's visitor—is the person who dubs his sensitivity "smart."

At a corn shucking in the 1930s American South, a "smart" baby was, rather, the baby who did not cry for "ninny" very often. A white tenant woman boasted that her baby was so smart that he lay on a bed at the corn shucking for nearly three hours without crying. As recounted to researcher Margaret Hagood, "this feat attracted attention and finally, some of the older women got after her and said, 'You take that baby right up and feed it. You don't have to starve him to death just because he's smart.'"[18]

San Francisco, 1896. Jeong Hing Tong is anticipating her one-month "red eggs and ginger party" after the birth of her first child. She is a Chinese immigrant from the town of Foshan, following a long tradition of immigrants since the 1848 Gold Rush and the first group of American immigrants from Asia. In Chinatown, such women typically lived entirely confined. If they did go out, they were ridiculed for their bound feet. Jeong's plans for eggs and ginger, luck and recovery, will be disrupted by an immense earthquake, however. People will pour out into the streets. Holding her baby in her arms, she will manage to get a ride to the Golden Gate Bridge in a horse-drawn wagon and watch the city in flames.[19]

In rural Mississippi around 1916 or 1918, most black women living on tenant farms tried to follow a tradition that the mother should "stay in her month," in local parlance. "I stayed out of the field my month" is the remark if you are fortunate. Many stay in bed less than a week. The season of the year matters. One woman describes staying in bed only four days with a "summer-time baby," but with a baby born any other time of the year she might stay longer. The busiest farm times are May and June, the hoeing months for cotton and corn, and October and November, the cotton-picking season. The slackest weeks are the middle of June to the middle of September.[20]

There is not much internal life. I live only in the in-between that stretches between the baby and me, and between my former life and whatever mercurial scene is unfolding. I am being for myself and for him. Catching the tail of what is happening is elusive. It's easier to look into his almost lidless eyes, note the white milia on his face disappearing, be absorbed.

I was used to looking out, not down. Early modern Englishwomen were told to "look downward when you are in men's company, and not to stand gazing and gaping as if you were looking babies in their eyes," a remark that tells as much about what *did* seem natural and acceptable in women's behavior as what needed instruction to ensure their subordination to men.[21]

A friend visits while K is at work—his family leave will come next semester—and I pause for a longer thought. Medieval people had an emotion, I remember reading, that was located in the stomach: the sensation of losing one's zeal for praying. Emotions can get lost in time, it seems, left behind in bodies that have crumbled into dust. People have cast their emotions as residing not just in the brain and nerves and heart, the contemporary targets of science and romance, fMRI tests and Hallmark cards, but also in the spleen. The gut. The liver. So it used to mean something entirely bodily when someone was described as being splenetic, or as having gall.[22]

While I nurse, the idea of having feelings in those unfamiliar locations somehow makes more intuitive sense. The milk in my breasts "lets down" (a swelling, tugging sensation) not just at the baby's "latch" but as an empathic response to the sound of his cry, the sound of another baby's cry, a friend's grazed knee, a sappy piece of advertising, the news of a couple's separation. These feeling responses to the world come ahead of what I can say aloud. They are strange and scattershot and oddly exhilarating. They are felt right here in my chest.

Four weeks

In seventeenth-century London, desperate mothers rarely abandon infants under the age of four weeks.[23] The reasons for eventual abandonment are usually illegitimacy, widowhood, or—

I turn the spines of my pile of books on maternal loss or foundling hospitals against the wall. Their subjects make me retch, or panic. I hold, yet more urgently than before, to the guiding topic: the living mothering of a living infant.

The Ojibwe storyteller Louise Erdrich is at her home in New Hampshire. "Writing as a mother shortly after bearing, while nurturing an infant, one's heart is easily pierced," she observes. It is the middle of the 1990s, and she is composing a memoir. Her three youngest daughters are still at home. The last is a baby. "To look full face at evil seems impossible, and it is difficult . . . to write convincingly of the mean, the murderous, the cruelty that shadows mercy and pleasure and ardor."[24]

In 1782 Boston, Sally's newborn is "as knotty a Baby" as her sister-in-law has ever seen. Perhaps the phrase captures the baby's appearance: the spindly, cordlike legs and arms, the limbs entangled in knots. Or perhaps this baby is hard to unravel, difficult to interpret, resistant to explanation or consolation. Or perhaps "knotty," in a usage more familiar to eighteenth-century ears, conveyed a certain kind of character already forming. Hard and tough, rugged even. The baby may have been hungry: the family members that cluster around—her sister-in-law Polly, her husband—are disappointed that she could not nurse. Polly writes that Sally finds "putting out" her baby—hiring a wet nurse from among the many who advertised in the city's newspapers—"worse upon trial . . . than she could imagine before."[25]

In 1785 Philadelphia, Elizabeth Sellers's husband, Nathan, a former scrivener, describes their newborn as a "fine Lump of a Girl." He writes to his mother to request a visit. They need help.[26]

I keep expecting a community midwife or a health visitor to walk through the door: expectations of state support fashioned by growing up under Britain's NHS. But in this small American city, we are left to our own devices. Who watches our upheaval, makes sure we survive and thrive?

Hester Thrale finds a baby's cry distracting. In September 1777 she has four living children from eleven births, and she is trying to compose a book of anecdotes spoken by the lionized literary gent Doctor Johnson. She knows why she's failed so far. She has known why since she first became a mother twelve years earlier . . . that's 1765. Like the irascibility of an elder or like a sudden danger, "the Crying of a young Child . . . will soon drive out of a female Parent's head a Conversation concerning Wit, Science or Sentiment." (It's not just that, she justifies, but "doing" something is more important than "hearing" adult conversation if you are a mother—how else the time for "tutoring, caressing," or "having one's Children about one." Thus her playful and pensive retort to the reproaches of her literary friends. "I . . . feel myself at this moment very miserable that I have at last . . . leisure to write" the *Johnsoniana*.)[27]

So many themes crowd in, all at once. The marking of time and its shifted rhythm, the quality of feeling interrupted. Keeping a baby alive at a breast or with a bottle. Using stuff, like flannel binders or plastic bottles, or squirrel hides or small cotton sheets. Sleeping or, better put, not sleeping. Delegating mothering to and among servants. "Othermothering" by relatives or community members—the term was coined by black American feminists. Mothering as providing new raw materials for experiencing ourselves, others, our worlds. Raw materials being produced between caregivers and babies and historical circumstances.

Eventually all these themes will need sorting out. After this onrush.

March 8, 1980. Londoner Jean Radford becomes an adoptive mother on this day, at the end of a decade of women's liberation. She brings home a baby girl through transracial adoption: "Not much hair, toothless, a fat bald child in a scratchy pink dress. It is love at first sight. The cliché resounds in my head and I can hardly see straight." Radford imagines that for a birth mother, the arrival of a child is a scene of separation, the end of a process, not just a beginning. But for adoptive mothers, "the arrival of the child is a scene of different significance. The desire for the child is 'inside,' but the adoptive child comes from 'outside.' Bringing the two together is more of a union than a separation and for me is accompanied by an almost manic joy."[28]

Five weeks

1861, during the American Civil War. The baby is five weeks old, and Mrs. Slichter feeds it molasses. Her hostess, the Canadian-born Rachel Cormany, a new mother, thinks doing so is outrageous: "She makes a great fuss over it."[29]

After completing her month of lying-in, in 1768, the genteel English Northerner Bessy Ramsden gets to record her relief and to reflect. "Thank God I had a very good Lying in, for had not an hour's illness the whole month and my Little boy as well as myself." Lying-in was also termed being "in the straw." These weeks were the husband's "gander month." The phrase teases, naming the suspension of his usual conjugal rights.[30]

1673. The reader of Hannah Woolley's *The Gentlewomans Companion* is well-off enough to employ servants. About babies: nursery maids should "walk them often up and down" and "take heed they get no falls by your carelessness."[31]

The tube between the baby's mouth and stomach is still so thin, still so close to the skin's surface, that I can hear the milk descending. When we are done, I will walk him up and down the road, looking from darkness into our neighbors' lighted rooms.

A sharecropping farm, 1930s. The seventeen-year-old daughter of the household is unmarried, with a small baby. "The children take turns walking or rocking her if she cries even the tiniest bit at night." The Welfare Department has given the family a mosquito net.[32]

Most evenings, K bathes the baby and I sit very still and write in the quiet. There's a minute, mute semblance of routine.

Six weeks

The six-week checkup is tomorrow, and we will all go.

The ship *Roseboom* arrived in Manhattan from Holland on a misty, still day some six weeks after a lowborn passenger had given birth. The ship's keeper noted that the woman delivered a son on April 21, 1663, but by the time the ship docked, the notation was corrected to "daughter." Members of the Dutch poor like her moved around the Atlantic Ocean as employees of companies, patroons, and wealthy families, a world afloat.[33]

November 2, 1993. San Francisco. The Chicana playwright Cherríe Moraga feels that something has broken within her, yet she is forced to proceed as if everything is normal. She writes: "I am a mother now and I do not yet know how to fully inhabit that place in the world. In the small confines of my home, with Ella"—her partner and lover—"with my familia, there is a sense of rightness, but nowhere else." She is so sleep-deprived that she has started sleeping with her baby on a futon with flannel sheets. They look like odd-size twins. "I worry, what does this mean? The child has moved my woman and me into separate beds."[34]

Then there's a moment of peace: "Getting in the bath with Rafa, I see his body relax in a way I imagine it hasn't since utero. Floating, floating. His fists unclench, his arms fall back to the sides of his head, his chest receives the water." The baby books say that Rafaelito should already be smiling, but he was born prematurely. "His smiles will come."

Throughout Moraga's pregnancy she had kept an almost daily journal, but few moments during Rafa's first year get recorded there. She later summarizes: "It is a series of moments that are the mundane world of sleepless nights, ear infections, and petty arguments. It is hallmarked by the ordinary: baby rolling over, baby sitting up, baby crawling . . ."

For all that being pregnant and mothering an infant are both contained within the word "maternity," they are quite unalike. Carrying and caring are distinct activities. Out goes the single form of the expectant birth-giver. In comes a duo. Or a trio with other caregivers, maybe more. Meanwhile, birth-givers do not invariably become mothers, and adoptive mothers may be no less immersed in mothering even though they have not given birth to the infants they tend.

"Going with child" has shifted beneath my feet. I hold on to thinking in verbs rather than, say, through identities or institutions. To mothering over being "mother" or "mum" or "mom." To caring for the baby over the imperious, scolded, sentimentalized institution of Motherhood.

We have a smart, fretful baby. I want him, I choose him.

Until he smiles, this promiscuous love feels unrequited. Even to write a paragraph requires long preparation.

11

Damp Cloth

Caught stationary, again. I am on the same sofa with the baby, in the same living room. The same pictures are there on the wall when I look up. All morning I have smelled of fresh milk. "Streaked with running milk" reads Li-Young Lee's poem about a nursing mother. The fluid "sweet, iron, . . . astonishingly thin." Thin, yes, at the corners of the baby's mouth. Sweet scent, plus that note of iron. Yes. The damp smell clings faintly in the air, it enters my clothes. The hours on the sofa intensify smell and sight and touch, heightening my senses.[1]

There is a faint line of black under the tips of two of the baby's nails. His fingernails have got a little too long again. It's hard to bring the cool sharp metal of the nail cutter close to their paper edge. A few weeks ago he caught his face with an overlong nail, and now there is a wafer-thin scar just below his left eye. It's the first mark against his perfection, the first visible mistake.

Caught stationary on the sofa, just like yesterday and just like tomorrow, my mind meanders from this room and the baby's face, looking for sustained themes of mothering an infant, starting by imagining other homebound lines of sight, other damp cloth. Other scents.

A middle-class terraced house in Victorian Glasgow. On Carnarvon Street or Claremont Street, most households had five or so rooms. The 1880s. A two-month-old baby meant that the time of "lying-in" was over and the monthly nurse had departed. Sitting still in her parlor, a new mother might have been stitching or mending long white baby clothes, or picking over linens for small holes or stains, or concentrating on the household accounts. A lady's workbasket was placed near her feet.[2]

In the parlor, the gaze of such a woman alighted upon the velvet and damask curtains in red or green. The room was cluttered; there could not be too many objects, provided they were beautiful. Oil paintings included family members past and present, such as a relative whose piety had carried her off to do missionary work in some part of Britain's far-flung empire. There was the piano. A music stand. A Singer hand-sewing machine. The stitched cover on a footstool had been worked in Berlin wool.

A bamboo afternoon tea table might have held a popular Japanese tea tray or the local *Waverley Journal*. With Victorian platitude, the newspaper saw the home as a place for spiritual and moral renewal, presided over by a devoted wife and mother.

The clutter and heavy furnishings generated their own swathed smell. Cut flowers compounded the parlor's scent.

The woman's smell was clean. Eighteen eighties "clean" was distinctive and sharp: the soap used during her morning stand-up wash was made of animal fats and caustic soda. There could be an added floral scent, too, either from the soap or from a lavender perfume.

Other smells had been banished from the house: of the dirty laundry, which was sent out to be washed, or of last night's slops, which had been emptied from the chamber pots by the servant. A single residential servant proved a family's middle-class status. Cooking smells concentrated below the parlor in the basement kitchen.

Follow the sent-out laundry to the house of a local laundress, and there the smell depended on the day of the week. The stale smell of dirty cloth on a Monday was followed by those of soap, bleach, bluing, and starch mixed with steam. Later in the week, the coke or gas stove that heated the irons added its own stench and fumes: the windows would have been closed against urban "smuts." Sometimes there was the smell of the stale beer that helped the laundress get through the day. The verbs ran in order: mangling, starching, ironing, folding, airing. The smoke-laden air of Victorian Glasgow necessitated indoor drying draped over clotheshorses. By week's end, the laundress's home smelled of clean, airing cloth. Washing began on a Monday so that the freshly prepared linen was ready for Sunday. The aim was to return snowy linen, well "got up."[3]

Back in the terraced house, the baby might well have been absent from the parlor. In the nursery, the nanny-cum-servant was responsible for the more mundane parts of physical care. The servant's eyes might have alighted on the nursery wallpaper, perhaps adorned with characters from *Alice's Adventures in Wonderland*. Or they might have taken in the pictures hung on top of the wallpaper (such as a hand-stitched sampler sternly warning "Thou God Seest Me"), or the bars and brass knobs of the crib, or the shape of the horsehair sofa. The servant's clothing occupied a special corner of the room. Nurseries like this were common in British middle-class homes, however small, from the middle of the nineteenth century. Autobiographers of this generation of children, writing in the early to mid-twentieth century, tended to remember their parents as quite distant, not very much around.

The servant took care of the dirty clouts. There was probably a diaper bucket for soaking them. Other smells, such as that of the lard used to prevent rashes, were smothered under the baby's long layers of clothing.

On a sunnier morning, the parlor where a mother sat was as bright as a bit of a Dutch picture. Fresh air blew through. If her husband was considerate, there was not even the lingering smell of tobacco smoke.

Again on the sofa. Fresh milk lightly souring. The shared milky smell is becoming remarkably familiar; it measures a distance from my old body and my former life. At two months, there are fewer daily diapers than in the very earliest weeks. When K is home, he changes them.

The town of Mobile, Alabama, again the 1880s. The thirty-year-old Caroline Bowers was breastfeeding her first (and, as it turns out, only) baby, Willie. She was well used to the smells of damp cloth. Her mother, Lucrecia Perryman—known as Crissy in the family—had worked as a laundress since Civil War emancipation. Doing the laundry for other families had some advantages over other kinds of available work: Lucrecia Perryman could work in her own home; she interacted with local whites only for dropping off and picking up; she kept well away from former slave owners. The family possessed a small piece of land, with an improvised pair of buildings, at the edge of town and opposite the Magnolia Cemetery. This made them better off than many of Mobile's black community. It almost put them among the town's black elite, the owners of grocery shops, restaurants, and hardware stores.[4]

If you worked with laundry, smell was one of your guides. You needed a keen nose. The Perryman women must have known this; their neighbor Emira Hansberry, also a laundress, must also have known this. These women had other knowledge, too: that when laundry was spread under the intense Southern sun, it bleached. That a Little Lord Fauntleroy suit, popular in the 1880s for wealthy boys' formal dress, had a wide-lapeled jacket and broad-collared starched shirt. That children must be kept away from the drying cloth. Caroline Bowers helped raise her younger siblings and step-siblings, spreading the tasks of mothering. In later family stories she was remembered as "Mama Caroline."

Even when a wooden frame house was three times as large as a slave cabin, the smells of laundry and food intermingled readily. There was fried fish from the Gulf of Mexico. There were pungent condiments such as Worcestershire sauce, horseradish, pickles, and mustard. The Worcestershire sauce came from England, for Mobile had strong ties there since the cotton trade. The mustard was a good thickener for fish gravy. If the house had been recently cleaned, the smell of mint from "Dr. Tichenor's antiseptic" lingered in the air. Caroline Bowers, like many of her 1880s contemporaries, knew about the newly spreading germ theory, the notion that contact with germs leads to illness. General recommendations included to ventilate a house well, to let in sunshine, and to pick things up from the floor. These practices further distanced the family from their enslaved days.

Depending on where she sat as she nursed, there might be a couple of cherub vases in the line of Caroline Bowers's stationary gaze. They were arranged as a pair and evoked images of healthy, beautiful children of no particular race. One played the lute, the other playfully held a hand to its ear. Caroline's mother was learning a midwife's trade; perhaps the vases were intended for the gaze of expectant visitors.

A porcelain spittoon was a sign of both the consumption that carried off Lucrecia's husband and of up-to-date hygienic habits. A few teacups had bamboo styles in keeping with the late-nineteenth-century Japanese craze. The "Rebecca at the Well" teapot (either the smaller one or the larger one, for there were two) was reminiscent of the biblical story of Rebecca being chosen as Isaac's wife when she offered to draw enough water from the well to satiate his camels. The lesson was that woman is the spiritual and physical protector of the household.

Perhaps a woman can reach greatness through her children. That was the implication, at least, in the image of a woman feeding an eagle that adorned a redware matchbox. The reference was to the well-known myth in which Zeus took the form of an eagle to seduce Semele. Their son Dionysus made her into a goddess.

Caroline Bowers's stories were repeated down through her family's generations as racial segregation was legalized in 1902 and then overthrown, as electric streetcars and then automobiles replaced Mobile's mule-drawn carts. That during slavery, Lucrecia was a stern mother. That Lucrecia wore her hair in two long plaits because short hair reminded her of the bad old days.

The condiment jars, the vases and teacups and biblical Rebecca teapots, the redware matchbox with the figure of Semele encountering Zeus, these items are known to us because they were discarded in a household pit and later found by an archaeologist. The smells have long since dissipated from the broken ceramics and the teaware.

This late afternoon, the baby is napping on my lap. I cannot move or he will wake, so I reluctantly watch my cup of tea cooling on the table. Do I ever get off the sofa? On the table by the teacup is a spiral notebook in which I write messages for K, who is at work—about "our" day, maybe about something nice or strange that happened. If not, the small things get forgotten, or they have no status next to the real facts of the outside world, or their triviality is overpowered by someone's need to comfort a colicky evening baby.

(How much difference has a baby made to your life? Diana Meade is asked in Edward Heath's Britain. "I used to drink cups of tea all day long; now I don't drink any tea. I can't make it or I can't drink it. [To baby] I can't do anything, can I?" Since tea was popularized in the eighteenth century, how many cups have cooled that way?)[5]

Sitting still with an infant, aware of smells and damp cloth. In rural Alabama, at the center of the Cotton Belt, the heat was so great that the landscape trembled. Odors cooked. Ellie Mae Burroughs belonged to a generation or two later than Caroline Bowers, and to a different race. In the 1930s, she lived far back in the countryside, where the houses were half a mile from their neighbors. Most people were sharecroppers.[6]

The best place for nursing was a hickory chair at the rear of the hall. That was the evening place to sit, before supper or a little while after it, for only in the hall was there likely to be any sort of breeze. The hall was open to front and rear. The walls were six feet apart, and there was no ceiling beneath the pine planks of the roof. From the chair, she could see the hard, bare dirt yard out front, the dogs and hens and, on the porch, the edge of another chair, the rocking chair with its hickory sapling bark. Between some of the wide planks of the hallway floor, earth was visible during daylight. Bare feet had smoothed a path along the bare wooden planks.

The routine smells of the four-room house were pinewood smoke, fried salt pork, fried and boiled pork lard, and cooked corn. At the rear of the hall where Ellie Mae Burroughs sat to nurse, and right by the lean-to kitchen, was a shelf with washbasin and soap. The soap for hands was sometimes strong tan "kitchen" soap, sometimes a cheap white gelatinous lavender face soap from the country store.

Through an open doorway, above a mantel, was a picture in red, brown, and yellow shades. The title of the image was *Just a Prayer at Twilight*: a young mother sitting in a big chair by the fire; a little girl in a long white nightgown kneeling between her knees with her palms together; the mother's look a blend of doting and teaching. One of Ellie Mae Burroughs's neighbors had the same picture. Another neighbor, Elizabeth Tingle, had a welter of images—idealizations of family life and fetching advertisements—pinned up around her fireplace: happy young housewives at resplendent stoves in sun-loved kitchens; mischievous or dog-attended or praying little boys and girls; great rosy blue-eyed babies sucking their thumbs in clouds of pink or blue; close-ups of young women brandishing Lysol.

In a wardrobe near the mantel, a heap of overalls, dresses, shirts, and bedding, ready for laundering, added its own smell.

On Ellie Mae Burroughs's lap the baby was wearing a plain dress of white cotton or a homemade dress she had sewn from a top of gray denim and a shirt of yellow and white checks. Her own clothes she made from cheap unbleached cotton, cut and stitched to be tall-skirted and short-waisted. It was the decade of the Depression: her neighbor was reduced to making sleeveless dresses from fertilizer sacks. One company deliberately printed its sacks with a calico pattern.

A visiting journalist spent many pages describing cotton growing in great detail, but he did not depict Mrs. Burroughs laundering. But a woman visitor to some other white tenant families, in the same Depression decade, recorded, of diapers: "If the baby only wets them, they are often simply dried without being washed. When hung before the fire from the mantel or on chairs, the odor is suffused throughout the room."

The journalist who stayed with the Burroughses did describe Ellie Mae's slantwise gaze while she nursed. She looked quietly down past her child's head into the junctures of the earth, the floor, the wall, the sunlight, and the shade. For him, the dominant smell of the house was that of the pine boards heated in the closed and darkened air, the fetid corn, and the fresh and stale human sweat. These made up "the nostalgic odor of poor white southern country houses."

Smell is a fleeting sense, said to leave no traces. Smells dissipate into thin air. At the same time, though, smell is a language of airborne shouts and whispers that travels across rooms. Smell is suggestive.

Although odors often dissipate moments after they have been encountered, the smell of cloth gathers up several mainstream histories of mothering. Two of the histories are remarkably continuous: infants swathed in cloth were changed regularly and washed frequently, and laundering was invariably women's work. The first continuity is what babies need, the second is a particular domestic arrangement. That female labor was not always maternal: the soaking and washing of the clouts was the lowest of lowly domestic work, and the employing classes got out of it when they could. An eighteenth-century servant might agree, on being hired, to clean the baby's dirty clouts for an extra two shillings a year and a new gown.[7]

The smell of damp cloth gathers change as well as these continuities. In the seventeenth century, an English or colonial mother was defined in part by the amount of cloth she produced for her family. Clothes were changed frequently, as the friction of cloth against skin was understood to keep a body clean. Then, with cloth's mechanical production, and with a new ethos of domestic refinement and germ theory, what came to matter was less the production and the amount of cloth than its cleanliness. This was measured in the odorless, dry whiteness of the linens. Sixty-year-old New Englander Ruth Henshaw Bascom was on the cusp of these changes. She spent many of her life's daylight hours weaving cloth. In 1840 she voiced little patience for younger women who spent more time on washing and cleaning than on making. "'More nice than wise' ladies," she called them in her diary. Invoking the well-known proverb "More nice than wise" was brisk shorthand for fastidiousness and fuss.

In these seventeenth-, eighteenth-, and nineteenth-century pasts, those mothering knew so, so much about cloth. If you lived well above the ranks of the poor, clothes and linen were washed seasonally or quarterly (the seventeenth century); once a month (beginning with seventeenth-century townswomen); or weekly, with Monday as washing day (from around the early nineteenth century).

The workaday household labor of weaving large amounts or washing fastidiously made for a whole language of cloth—a textured, fine-grained language—that captured exactly what was material about it. In a kitchen of the 1830s might be found knife cloths, dusters, tea cloths, and glass cloths. Knife cloths had a harsh feel, dusters could pick up dust and were made of cotton or flax, while tea cloths and glass cloths were made from old bed sheeting and had a lint-free nap. It all depended on what kind of filth they should address.

Thus "linen napkins" came to lend their name to nappies. "Diaper-weave linen" lent its name to diapers. This inferior linen was woven with a small, simple pattern formed by the different directions of the thread, causing the light to reflect at different angles. Cloth talk could get very specialized. Early-twentieth-century mothers of the Lancaster textile mills knew that the "wiper"—a fluffy, flannelette-type material issued to workers for cleaning the machinery—could be used to make baby clothes, and "proper rags" substituted for wiping down.

There was not always enough soft cloth, or any cloth at all. The poorest Victorian mothers laid babies down on straw with oilcloth underneath. Commentators on working-class London in the early twentieth century remembered babies as always wet and smelly. Diapers were made from the tails of worn-out men's shirts, with loops and ties sewn on, and were insufficient to their task. In some times and places, cloth was not the thing at all. Dried swamp moss served as an alternative for Native mothers on the Vermilion Lake Reservation. Moss was gathered in the spring and summer, dried on bushes, and then shaken and pulled apart to rid it of insects and dry weeds. Those tending babies kept a supply of it on hand, in the kind of birch-bark *makuk* or sack also used for storing maple syrup or wild rice. In the 1930s, one woman recalled, "The baby seldom became chafed, and when it was unwrapped you could smell only sweet moss."

In recent times, people have deodorized and deep-cleaned and spring-cleaned and vanquished smell. They have put the washing on and noticed how much more often they do so when a baby is in the house. Electric washing machines became common after the Second World War. In our house, the washing machine is tucked away in a back room, its whirr a distant hum. The washing powder K uses carries a different smell from my mother's Persil Automatic. I know from her to choose clothes that are 100 percent cotton, but I've not spent much time thinking about cloth before.

A middle-class home in 1880s Victorian Glasgow; a wooden structure in Mobile, Alabama, in the same decade; a sharecropper's cabin in rural Alabama, in the heart of the 1930s Cotton Belt. Sitting stationary with the baby once more, I'm struck that the white middle-class Victorian mother had been the first figure who came to mind. Perhaps that's because we know more about her than almost any other maternal figure from centuries past. This Victorian Mother was domestic, devoted, moral, and selfless. She was richly content in her economic dependence. She took shape in hundreds of pages of Victorian ideology: newspapers such as Glasgow's *Waverley Journal* or advice books or household guides. "The perfect Victorian lady," Martha Vicinus titled the essay about her that she published in 1972, in the first wave of women's history.[8]

Or perhaps the Victorian Mother came first to mind because this selfless, idealized figure still holds many contemporary imaginations in thrall. She does so together with the figure that seems to repeat her: the homemaking 1950s housewife, with her gleaming refrigerator, clean-faced husband and children, and uncomplicated smile. This pair of images is often behind the question that is asked of "stay-at-home" mothers—namely, how do they do it? Or else they stand for what is traditional or usual, stable or "good." Say "mother," meaning noun, and these historical figures routinely come to mind. They seem excessively visible in contemporary culture, sticks to beat people with.

The figure of the Victorian woman certainly haunted the liberationist writers of the 1970s who were trying to make sense of maternity. Writing in 1976, the lesbian feminist and poet Adrienne Rich reported what she had not realized before becoming a mother—what educated and middle-class women like her had simply not appreciated in the late 1950s. "I did not . . . understand," she reflected, that we "were expected to fill the part of both the Victorian Lady of Leisure, the Angel in the House, and also the Victorian cook, scullery maid, laundress, governess, and nurse." Rich wanted neither to be the domesticated, moral mother nor the poorly paid drudge. "I *knew* I had to remake my own life," she wrote, and to find some distance from "the repetitive cycles of laundry," the exclusive devotion to "children's welfare" and "husband's careers." Victorian womanhood needed to be named in order to be roundly dispatched.[9]

There have always been idealized figures of Mother and child—in the *Waverley Journal* close at hand to a Glaswegian Victorian stitching white baby clothes, or pinned up around a rural sharecropper's mantel in the 1930s. "Babydom," Frances Murray called it, visiting a friend in Victorian London's suburbs, and commenting on the "conventional dullness" of her hostess's domestic life. In fact, she put it more tartly than that: the "apotheosis of babydom." Sometimes ideals were and are relentlessly constraining. Worse, ideals have been, or can be, pernicious or impossible to attain. Where a "good" mother exists, swaths of real-life "bad" mothers surely follow, whether in their own eyes or in the gaze of institutions—the state, the law, the doctor, the social worker.[10]

The scene of Caroline Bowers in 1880s Mobile, Alabama, suggests, alternately, that one set of ideals can be used to push against another. The cherub vases on her mantel made the claim that black women, too, were good mothers. This was despite the racist conventions of late-nineteenth-century white Alabamans. In the Magnolia Cemetery opposite her home, a tall Civil War memorial commemorated the many Mobile men who had died in the Southern states' violent fight to preserve slavery.[11]

So some ideals, some idealizations, are more usable than others. Writing in the same liberationist years as Adrienne Rich, the poet Lucille Clifton explored a sturdy history of black maternal resilience. Clifton was the child of a steelworker and a launderer-turned-homemaker, people who had come north during the Great Migration. Her 1976 book *Generations* evoked a history leading back to another Caroline, a woman who was "born in Afrika in 1823" and died free in Virginia in 1910. Caroline Sale Donald was a mother, a midwife, a life-giver. "Don't you worry," read one of Lucille Clifton's lines, quoting an ancestral remark. The maternal hauntings, Clifton's own series of historical idealizations, ran back from Buffalo, New York, through the slave-plantation South to nineteenth-century Dahomey, in what is now southern Benin. Her figure of "Mother" was dark and tall and skinny. She walked "straight as a soldier": a heritage of unflinching black maternity to be pondered and sat with.[12]

12

Time, Interrupted

Think of the day in four parts, my friend Myfanwy advises during a phone call. Morning, afternoon, evening, night. That sounds familiar enough, except that it's not: the point is that each part can be wildly different. The baby can be content one moment and miserable the next. The good bits are lived in swinging buoyancy, the bad bits are staccato chaos. There's rhythm and interruption.

Around three months, the doctor advises, crying peaks. There's crying and holding, crying and pacing, crying and singing, crying and walking in circles, crying and pressing on the creak in the floorboards. We've learned why we are always holding M upright: he is not just a colicky baby; he has reflux. The condition means that our baby is frequently in pain, pulling up his knees, arching his back, and vomiting acid. Hold the baby vertically, confirms the doctor, and there should be less throwing up. The baby will be less uncomfortable.

You scream as if you are trying to climb out of your own skin. I am halted and taken apart by the wails, halted and taken apart, too, by your blistering radiance and my relief when the sound stops. Hold the baby upright. Walk on eggshells.

Out in the world, I obsessively notice the babies that lie flat. Is there Velcro in their strollers? On that outdoor rug here in the park, as parents look away and talk so unconcernedly? My impulse—wrong, of course— is to pick the babies up. This baby, my baby, is always picked up and swung up to my shoulder, picked up and tipped into a sling. For me that's what babies are, that's what a baby needs. That's what mothering is.

Morning, afternoon, evening, night. These are the rhythms of the daily round. The halting, the interruption, constitutes the everyday. I am mid-thought, mid-sentence, mid-task, and then I am stopped.

MORNING, AFTERNOON, EVENING, NIGHT.

Interruption comes into view wherever the archive gets closest to mothering. Shimmy near. Pause softly if you can. In the present, the essayist Lisa Baraitser reckons the interruptions to be so relentless and so formative that she proposes them as the main condition of maternity. Place her before a baby and a mother and she sees a scene of interruption.[1]

There's one such history of interruption to be found among the reams of late-eighteenth- and nineteenth-century letters. Broken-off letters, short letters, impoverished letters, unwritten letters: when educated women took to letter-writing in the eighteenth century, mothers' attempts to keep up with their correspondents often told about interruption. Jane Scrimshire was stopped by "a thousand Petits riens that happens in Familys." She had already warned a friend that "when you become a Mother & a Housekeeper you'll be as bad as some other people"—the thousand little nothings fragmented time.[2]

That mothers of infants, or indeed children under five, were terrible correspondents quickly became a platitude, even an occasional scapegoat, in such letter-writing circles. In 1787 Halifax, Nova Scotia, Rebecca Allmon apologized to her aunts for the interruption in her usual attentive letter-writing: her "constant attendance on a dear lovely infant" had incapacitated her.[3]

Bessy Ramsden started a letter that was finished by her husband, William: "Mrs. R was called up to the nursery," he added in his own hand, "or she would not have left off so abruptly." This kind of interruption is being summoned by the present, being called away from a task. It is being pulled into what is immediate, the here and now, with the past left behind and the future postponed. In later years, Bessy kept reaching ahead to the chance of concentrating or being absorbed in a singular task:

"If I do take a pen I always meet some interruption";

"As I have Lay'd by my cradle"—her infants have grown—"I shall have more time."

But: "My little folks are now pestering me [for] their Tea, so shall conclude."[4]

Or there's Anne Livingston in Philadelphia in 1783: "My Child calls for my assistance. Therefore I must defer writing what I intended till Evening." Or Ellen Parker in the early nineteenth century: "[Elizabeth] is crying to Mama to nurse her, *therefore* you will excuse a short, hasty, & uninteresting letter." Or Frances Smith at Fort Pickens in 1846, to her career officer husband: "Fanny will stay in my lap and interrupt me so much that I must stop." Or Louisa Wylie Boisen of 1878 Indiana: "As I have to be continually running after Baby I will use a lead pencil"—considered inappropriate for a letter—"as it is more convenient." Or Boisen's relative, three years earlier, in the same redbrick house: "Baby is stirring so I must stop."[5]

To write a letter at all, or to start to write a letter, already means such a woman is literate, already means there is most likely some fragment of time called her own. Probably it means there is a servant on hand, if not a peer. These women were all members of the eighteenth-century and nineteenth-century employing classes. Rarely do they write about what happened at the cradle, or when they went upstairs—that was apparently too mundane, too much of a given to share with their correspondents—but in the interruptions themselves they hint at a feature of mothering. At first I notice only what these writers omitted, the silences that frustrate my curiosity. Now I notice the stutter step of the downing of the quill and the drying out of the ink in its stand, the misuse of a pencil, the halt to whatever task was at hand or thought was in composition.

AFTERNOON, EVENING, NIGHT, MORNING.

Sometimes a mother with her hands full is visited by an interviewer. In the early 1970s, first mothers with babies of a few months in age spoke to a research officer from Bedford College, University of London. The academic was sympathetic—a feminist, a former housewife, a mother herself—and the women opened up.[6]

Sandy Wright was a secretary, and now, "all the time I'm thinking, I'm going about doing bits of housework and thinking am I going to have time to do this before she wakes up? . . . You know because if she *does* cry, there isn't anyone else who can go and see to her, you've got to stop what you're doing."

Or there was the former civil servant Lily Mitchell: "I don't do half of what I'd like to do at all . . . people say that you're at home all day, but I don't *start* the things—if it is something I really want to get stuck into I don't start it. And then after I find I would have got it done I think I should have started it."

Interruption, 1970s-style, was described in relation to housework and a baby's naps. These women were home alone, housework was a woman's task, and a baby in a crib was laid down and picked up. Lily Mitchell reckoned "it's the way it's been going on for years."

The confiding, commonplace tone of the reporting suggests that there were more remarks like this—that this experience of interruption was entirely usual. That's the implication, too, of Lily's weary sense of timelessness—

Ah. The baby just woke up.

EVENING, NIGHT, MORNING, AFTERNOON.

As the day's fatigue accumulates, what evidence I find seems merely to echo my own sense of things. Sharp-edged specificity gets lost in my sluggishness. Historical particularity disappears from sight. As the baby lies fitfully asleep in the next room, I read:

"You who are a mother can understand what it is to commence a letter and then have one child cough and another child wake and cry for water."[7]

This is Mollie MacEwan in Alabama in the late 1860s, writing to her sister-in-law in Glasgow. Mollie explains that she never tries to write during the day, as the distractions are "greater then." She can no longer afford a "house-girl." Absorption is her wish, an expectation deferred to the promise of evening's stillness.

I rush on in my reading, fearful of the comeuppance of the baby waking. I do know that there was less labor in reprising a letter in Mollie MacEwan's 1860s than for the correspondents of a century before: just the picking up of a steel-tipped pen, not the making up of more ink and the scratch of a fragile quill.

NIGHT, MORNING, AFTERNOON, EVENING.

I dread the night.

Some days, still, I am unprepared for the joy of his presence, the prone content of our intimacy.

He is finding his hands. It's as if cognition is traveling down his body. First arrived the smile. Now hands can be pressed into his mouth, my mouth. They slide, and pull at the interior of my lip.

This morning, the tighter I hold on to the notion of interruption, the more the idea slips away from me, fails to fall into shape. It can't be readily generalized about. Or perhaps, being interrupted can't be specified historically without noticing its opposite or outside. And what is that? What exactly is being interrupted? Concentration, absorption? The rhythm of the daily round? Other familiar rhythms?

Interruption could be declared as, actually, the usual condition of most ordinary people's experience. Interruption is the condition of caretaking. Being interrupted is the workaday experience of anyone who is mostly beholden, at some kind of first hand, to someone else, time not being their own. Wives to husbands, in patriarchal times and places. Early modern apprentices to masters. House slaves to slaveholders. Domestic servants to employers. Nurses to doctors and to patients. Secretaries to bosses.

I am most alert in the morning, and so, in between naps of forty minutes, forty-five minutes, is the baby.

Can the rhythms of earlier daily rounds be uncovered, the ways in which people experienced the shape of their day? For Margery Spring Rice, surveying the health and conditions of more than a thousand "working-class wives" in 1930s England, this was a question worth a chapter in itself. For Rice, as for her informants, "wife" compounded the roles of housewife and mother. "It's the old idea that we should be at home," observed one woman, describing a life "penned in a kitchen 9 feet square, every fourteen months a baby." The average age of first marriage was twenty-four.[8]

The daily round for most of Rice's informants opened with waking around six-thirty, unless their husbands were miners or bakers, or had a night shift, in which case the wife might get up at four to make breakfast. The baby, who slept in the same room, would in any case not give his mother much peace after 6:00 a.m. The morning was spent working and caring in the kitchen, at the end of which her husband came home from work for "dinner." Very often, she did not sit down herself; Rice remarked that "she finds it easier to take meals standing. If she is nursing a baby, she will sit down after that, and in this way 'gets more rest.'" Then, in the afternoon, the husband having returned to work, she might have the chance to tidy herself up, rest, go out, or sit down. Perhaps once a week or once a month she went to the Welfare Centre with the baby, or to the local recreation ground, or to see her sister or a friend in the next street. But mostly there was no opportunity for this sort of leisure, for there was sewing and mending and knitting to be done, plus the shopping. When her husband returned home from work, there would be tea. Thus the morning and afternoon for a typical 1930s working-class mother.

Come evening, after having been twelve or fourteen hours on her feet, she sat down and perhaps had "a 'quiet talk with hubby,'" or listened to the wireless, their "'one luxury.'" Perhaps her husband read the paper to her. She had a lot of sewing to do, so she didn't read much herself. She might or might not have a bite of supper with her husband, cocoa and bread and butter, or possibly a bit of fried fish. And so to bed, mostly at about ten-thirty or eleven. Margery Spring Rice noted that the woman with a first baby, or just a couple of children, generally got out more and lived in better financial circumstances. Largely, the rhythms and the interruptions lived by these women appear cut off from the outside world. Their interruptions were made in and marked by their solitude at home; made in and interrupted by the needs of husbands and children.

Or there was the daily rhythm of a middle-class housewife of the early 1950s, as recounted to Mass Observation, the British social research organization. A typical report read: "7:30 a.m. Got up, washed and did hair." She got breakfast, bathed, fed and dressed the baby and then herself, and headed out to the shops. "Bought meat, vegetables, fruit, sweets. Bought myself a pair of stockings and rubber pants for baby. Brought laundry back." That's an hour, from ten to eleven. Then she took off the baby's outdoor clothes, changed the diaper, made herself a cup of tea, washed up the breakfast things and made the beds, cooked dinner at noon, and sat down to eat it at twelve forty-five. She made up the baby's feed, gave it to him, put him in his crib at one, and had another cup of tea. She did some of the baby's washing. "Took it easy—didn't rush over it, it being Saturday." She took the baby out for a walk at 3:00 p.m., her husband heading out elsewhere on his own. This was the report's first mention of the husband.[9]

The baby must have slept in the pram, because after she got in, "4:30 Baby woke . . . Busy with baby from 4:30 to 6:00." The baby was put back in the crib, and she headed out to the library to change books—presumably taking advantage of the husband being at home, it being a weekend day—then did the ironing and mending, got supper ready, listened to the news and read the paper, had supper at 9:00 p.m. She fed and changed the baby again at 9:45 p.m. and returned him to his crib. She cleaned up and headed to bed, like her 1930s working-class counterpart, between ten-thirty and eleven.

There's a clear rhythm here, determined by the tasks of cooking and diaper changing and clearing up and putting a baby down to nap. And there's interruption, documented almost in passing: "Baby woke." Public commentators noticed it, too. Marjorie Lloyd argued in the pages of the 1955 *Manchester Evening News* that such women needed "uninterrupted time," that is, the leisure already afforded to their working husbands who clocked off at regular hours.[10] Too often, a thirty-six-year-old shorthand typist observed, "a man regards his day's work as done when he 'downs tools' at 5:30 p.m." But the mother could always be interrupted. She inhabited unending broken time.[11]

Before the baby, my daily round had been coordinated with the rhythms of working life—teaching, meeting, writing deadline, weekday, weekend, term. K's disappearances and reappearances repeat that coordination, but for now I am living within morning, afternoon, evening, and night. There's no mother or sister on the next road; that's an immigrant's situation. But there is a group of new parents I encounter at a community center most Tuesday and Thursday mornings. Margery Spring Rice would have called our meetings "leisure" and noted our standard of living as well as our ability to get out of the house.

The talk at the center is of three- or four-hour schedules or of breastfeeding on demand. Some are fretting about the return to work, U.S. law allowing for only six weeks of leave, and some are planning to remain at home. The tone veers from mutual comfort to stark shock. We vent, exaggeratedly, about not being able to finish a meal, to hold a thought in mind, to speak to the end of a sentence. It's a long way from Thursday afternoon to Tuesday morning. Each Thursday I throw the ship's anchor ahead, trying to pull the baby and me into next week.

Friday afternoon. K is cycling down the road, and any moment now he will arrive. My diary on this day reads: "K came with me so I could get my hair cut. He walked M about—showing him the cars and clouds passing—for three-quarters of an hour before M called for me again." The entry's final comment documents this as the longest time the baby and I have been apart since he arrived more than three months earlier.

As I walk with the baby up the road, I think of where the archives don't get so close to mothering—but where they offer an alternate account to the constancy of maternal interruption, an apparent alternative to the rhythm of being absorbed and interrupted. Contemporary Native storytelling suggests, indirectly, a study in contrast.

"Like many women of my generation," Maria Campbell observed, "I grew up with stories, lots of them, and all kinds." Sacred stories, family histories, riddles. But "it was the stories about the women I loved best." The storyteller from Gabriel's Crossing, Saskatchewan, described Monday washdays in her mid-twentieth-century Métis community. Laundering was collective: "Maybe eight or ten wagons of us would go to this big pit about half a mile up the road." Huge cast-iron pots of water were heated on fires. Children swam in their underwear in the clean water. The lunch was Sunday supper warmed over. When a woman had a baby, she did not take part in the heavy scrubbing, but handed over her laundry and tended the cooking instead. She was surrounded by people.[12]

These communal habits ended with the arrival of gas washing machines. But in the decades immediately before, as Campbell told it, Métis women most often labored communally, not in solitude. For these women, mothering's interruptions had none of the isolation, the nine-foot-square autonomy, that so marked the broken daily round of their contemporary English counterparts in nuclear households. Margery Spring Rice's informant's casual reference, in the 1930s, to "the old idea that we should be at home" or Lily Mitchell's sense in the 1970s that "it's the way it's been going on for years" reflected a belief that mothering had always been isolating and isolated, that this was the natural and age-old state of affairs. In fact, their domestic solitude and solo responsibility was distinctive and far from inevitable, other historical possibilities being far more various, far more specific.[13]

The sense that things could be otherwise informed the Bedford College researcher's conclusions about housewives in 1979. "The effect of having constantly to interrupt other tasks," she summarized, "may be experienced as incredibly frustrating." These were conditions that made a mother's solitary labor as alienating as any factory worker's, she thought—even if they ran alongside addictive pleasures such as the smile from the crib, the classic noises of post-feed contentment, or the clear healthy skin in the clean clothes that became almost daily too small.

On a good day, on one of those days when the baby and I are in sync, setting interruption and rhythm apart seems like sophistry. Interruption slides into absorption with the baby, unruffled by irritation or discontent. Rhythm is the mode he and I inhabit together; I get what's needed done. On bad days, like yesterday, when K went back to work after a weekend here and when the baby is grumpy, there is only chaotic interruption. The absence of flow. Lisa Baraitser, that contemporary theorist, does not take sides. For her, maternal interruption is neither edifying nor to be overcome, just the tiny staccato place, the split moment, that answers the question, What does maternity feel like?

Night approaches again. In the 1940s, the anthropologist Margaret Mead, back in the United States after her most recent field research, wrote about the unkind expectations that medical opinion had for new babies. They should be ready to sleep through the night, "already," as she tartly put it, "resigned to a world whose imposed rhythms are strange and uncongenial."[14] What seems historically certain is that mothers' rhythms, babies' rhythms, and the rhythms of society are never wholly identical to one another. Maybe maternal interruption resides in the misfit.

And maybe maternal interruption shows itself—is at its most staccato, most abrupt—most powerfully wherever those mothering have social expectations of being absorbed in other tasks, and where they largely spend their days alone.

Night approaches. Contrast these interruptions to being a secretary, Deidre James remarked in 1979. "You're on the go from seven in the morning and you're on call more or less all night, every night, whereas you're not when you're working. Your boss isn't going to ring you up at eleven o'clock at night and say come and take a letter. Whereas if the baby cries, you can't say I've finished for the day, tough luck."[15]

13

The Middle of the Night

The darkish stillness has made room for three of us. This dark, this still, once was a covering blanket. Sleep felt simple and unchanging, even natural and timeless.

My old body expected eight hours of solid sleep, maybe eight and a half. The eighteenth-century writer James Boswell called such deep sleep, such dead sleep, "absolute, unconscious, and unfeeling." I find these delicious, heavy words. They are words of removal and restoration.[1]

Now, with an infant on hand: "Your sleep," wrote poet Alicia Ostriker in the late twentieth century, "is like a dirty torn cloth." English speakers of Boswell's time had other phrases for broken sleep, words that conjured the light sleep of small and vulnerable animals: dog sleep, cat sleep, hare sleep.

At night we might seem to retreat to our more bodily selves, our minds absenting themselves. Yet the sensations of night, its feel, are as particular as those of the day. In bed so many hours of each twenty-four, and awake for so many of those hours, I suspect that the middle of the night is maternity's most concealed past. Hard to fathom, yet perhaps most important to a person mothering.

On a spring night, our bedroom is dark by nine-thirty. The baby's four-month-old body is turned toward mine, his face an inch from my chest. Lying stock-still, I am stiff as on the first night of a camping trip, before my sides and back get used to the lumpy ground. Any movement will wake him. The bedroom has the faintest uncolored glow from the factory lights down the road—so slight I cannot see his features or even the top of his silhouette above the bedclothes. There's the clack of K's keyboard in the next room, an occasional ambulance siren. How to know the pasts of the maternal night?

Sounds loom differently as sight recedes, I think in the dark. When sight fades, and touch is bound by stillness, sound amplifies and disrupts. In past nighttimes, people have heard mosquitoes, mice, snores, barks, bellows, drays, curfew bells, church bells, fire bells, plantation bells, hackney coaches, garbage trucks, factory whistles, milk floats, shrieking trains, leaking roofs, creaking boards, the cries of the night watch, the calls of newsboys, the voices of next-door neighbors, birdcalls, alarm clocks. Their daytime sight has receded because of the particular dark cast by a place's sunsets and seasons, or with the putting out of candles or street lighting or electric lamps. People have had a particular sense of their surroundings: a bed's scale and surface; any bed hangings; the ceilings, walls, and proximity to floor; a habitation's size; the presence of other sleeping partners. They have had former habits of sleep before a first child, usual expectations about what a night should bring—and then, with an infant, how *this* baby has been sleeping, and in what proximity.

Start with a bed, perhaps, for most societies designate a special space for sleep. Early modern English peasants slept on straw pallets, covered only with a sheet, under coarse, shaggy covers made of "dagswain" or "hap-harlots." Or they slept in closed beds capacious enough for an entire household of family and servants. New immigrants to the Chesapeake region commonly used a mattress on the ground. According to a Jesuit observer, their Algonquian counterparts in Maryland longhouses spent the night on "mats spread on a low scaffold half a yard from the ground." Enslaved Igbo people on eighteenth-century Virginian plantations placed skins, and parts of a spongy tree known as plantain, upon platforms raised three or four feet above the ground. In the Shenandoah Valley, a French traveler in the same century saw, within a slave house, a bed constructed from "a box-like frame made of boards hardly roughed down, upheld by stakes [and] some wheat straw and cornstalks, on which was spread a very short-napped woolen blanket that was burned in several places."[2]

Into more modern times, there have been flock beds, which were stuffed with wool; boarded bed steddles made of hewn timber; settle beds; standing beds; rope-strung beds in which it was hard to lie flat; folding beds; and four-posters hung with curtains, their frame replacing wooden or metal poles attached to a ceiling. There have been canopied half testers, iron bedsteads, twin beds, the "black and brass," the "white enameled kind," divan beds, and futons. There have been truckle or trundle beds, which were low on the ground and rolled on castors, to be easily tidied away by day beneath a higher, main bedstead.[3]

Beds are usually just taken for granted, felt as normal. Sometimes they are the occasion of nostalgia or of determined innovation, and get commented about in more detail. "Do you remember those big beds in which everyone slept together without difficulty?" a member of the nobility recalled of the closed peasant bed of the Middle Ages.[4] When the big, square Victorian half tester replaced the four-poster bed of the well-off in the second half of the nineteenth century, the novel "hygienic" circulation of air substituted for older sensations of enclosure. Hanging curtains gave way to airiness. Twin beds, which seem so prissy to us, started to become popular in the 1890s as a deliberate rejection of Victorian ideals. The old availability and deference of wife to husband looked old-fashioned as the nineteenth century turned into the twentieth. In the new aesthetic, identical twin beds stood for a husband and wife's mutual satisfaction.

As nighttime furniture, felt beneath a person in the dark, beds speak several stories. One is about material resources: what is, or can be, afforded. An eighteenth-century Polish visitor to George Washington's Mount Vernon plantation read the "mean mats" of the slave quarters as a sign of enslaved people's deprivation.[5] In eighteenth-century Europe, a bed might cost—be worth as much as—a quarter of the value of a laborer's property. Together with the chimney, the bed was the most important feature of a place to live. Substantial beds of any kind were important goods to display and to bequeath: they turn up in wills, to be itemized and passed carefully on to a favored descendant.

Another story tells of increasing privacy and rising expectations of comfort: from closed beds for a whole household and servants, say, or from the low-platformed mats in a substantial Algonquian longhouse, to separate beds designed for one or two. From a bed's surroundings in any part of an interior, to spaces set out expressly as bedrooms, just for the purpose of sleeping. (In England, the separate bedchamber was usual from the eighteenth century, just as straw and thatch roofs were giving way to tiles and slates.) From the utility of trundle or truckle beds, fitting under a main bedstead by day and pulled out for the use of servants or large children, to their unheralded disappearance from use. And from coarse dagswain covers and shaggy hap-harlots, or wool or canvas next to the skin, to smooth sheets with thread counts. The standard-issue modern bed stands in a room as furniture for sleeping solo, or with a sexual partner, in consumer comfort.

Maternal nights, in particular? Those mothering infants?

Late September 1937, in the mountains of Caney, Kentucky. Verna Mae Slone spent the night with her four-month-old baby in an iron bedstead. Verna Mae's new husband, Willie, was away from Sunday to Friday night. He boarded at his grandfather's house by night and earned money logging for him by day. Verna Mae's nighttime was pitch-black, for there were no neighbors close by and no roads to speak of. Her habit, as she recalled in a plain-speaking memoir, was to go to bed "with the chickens," that is, at the same time the chickens went to roost.[6]

The ceiling above Verna Mae's head was tall for those parts: some ten feet from the floor. She lived where there had once been "a log house, one larger room with a very large chimney" plus another room added from "sawed lumber." The log house had been torn down, leaving the remaining plank room. Aside from the iron bedstead, the room held a walnut crib, a smooth-topped table made from split boards, her sewing machine and Willie's "talking machine" (a record player), a trunk that once belonged to her mother, and a wood-burning stove. There was a wall shelf for the dishes. The floor below her bed was usually smooth: a "puncheon" floor in which split logs were laid side by side, the split side up, and hewed flat with a broad axe. Such a floor was scrubbed with a broom and with sand made from pounded rocks from the creek. Chickens clucked beneath the floor by night if a skunk got among them. There were no other farm animal sounds: getting a cow would wait on more household earnings. She was twenty-two, Willie a little older.

Verna Mae was well used to sharing a bed. She was the twelfth of twelve children in a poor Baptist rural community in which siblings routinely slept with their parents and one another. It's "what you grow up with," as another Kentuckian observed of sleeping alongside his mother as a boy. "If you ever take off from home, you'll just crave it." In 1930s Caney, ask a growing child how old they are and the answer might come, "old enough to sleep by myself." The routine habit of bed sharing extended to familiar visitors. There was a children's rhyme for when you sleep three in a bed, which often happened "when folks stayed overnight."

By day, the baby was kept in the crib, or on a quilt under the shade of the tree, while Verna Mae worked outside. But at night she let him sleep and nurse with her. She made no immediate report of these nights, but their memory only gained in retrospect. Four more boys and forty years later, she described "the pleasure of sleeping with your child, and letting it nurse" as "two of the greatest blessings that God gave mothers." These tactile pleasures, she remembered, made for "a closeness that cannot be understood unless you have experienced it." Her recollection of the middle of the night, that distinctive intimacy, was fond, prescriptive, and defiant. "I don't care what doctors say, I believe it is best for mother and child to be together."

The memoir's phrasing was defensive against medical advice, but not strongly so: in 1937 and at the time of writing the memoir forty years later, bed sharing was typical among the rural, laboring Kentuckians of the Appalachian Mountains, even if it went against educated trends. A schoolteacher who did otherwise in the 1930s remembered being scolded by a censorious "country woman" who thought that mothers who did not share their beds with their babies were neglectful. Appalachian mothers continued to bed share as the Depression passed, and as they moved from log cabins and frame houses into homes with central heating. Bed sharing was a social habit, a value, not just a practicality compelled by cold winters and one-room cabins.

When the winter nights of Verna Mae's 1937 drew in, the step stove came into nighttime use. Its name was thanks to the two back caps or lids that sat higher than the two at the front. The stove had lost all its legs and most of the doors. An iron teakettle replaced a missing lid. When Willie was there, before coming to bed at night, he poured water on the wooden replacement legs he had made, so that they didn't catch fire. Rain spattered on the board roof. Perhaps there were words: "Move over, you are scrouging me"—Kentuckian for you are sleeping too close. The baby nursed. Morning began with what Verna Mae thought of as "the challenging crow of a rooster." One crowed to be answered by another on a far-off farm, and then another and another. Perhaps the crow sounded like the challenge of a new day's arrival after what Germans have called *Ammenschlaf*: the light sleep of the wet nurse or new mother.[7]

Bed sharing? That distinctively light sleep of those mothering infants? The lightness of sleep makes any thought hard to follow through. At the community center, someone asks, to shared laughter, what is "sleeping like a baby" again? Some bed share, some have their babies in cribs at the side of the bed, others put their babies in their own room. It's a charged topic; you can hear the straining generosity when the subject of where comes up.

My sister bed shared with her first baby—"It's easiest if you are breastfeeding, in the early months"—and I am following suit. M's reflux is so severe that there's not much choice in the matter. Whatever offers most comfort, whatever keeps him stably propped up surely makes sense. In the first ten days, he slept sometimes in a Moses basket. I know, because I still have the photos. But since the reflux began, I sleep right next to him. That's breathtakingly intimate for a person who has only ever slept with lovers. I hear the small intakes. The downshifts in exhalation as sleep descends. Our breath shares a space. I like knowing he is right there. If the oak tree fell against the house, we would live or perish together. I also recall the ordinary pleasure of eight solid hours, my wistfulness as hard as an acorn.

The yearning for solid sleep is not historically peculiar. There are terms for sound sleep in almost every language. But the notion of a solid eight hours *is* idiosyncratic. Historians know that the very idea of an ordinary and undivided eight hours is particular to modern times. There's nothing natural or timeless about it. Before industrialization, before artificial lighting and electrification, men and women in Western Europe and North America thought of sleep in two parts, sometimes named "first sleep" and "second sleep." The first part of the night began as light faded. First night, or forenight, was when sleep was deepest. Then came an interval of wakefulness often described as watch or watching. Then there was second night, a phase of lighter, often dream-filled sleep.[8]

These habits suited a world of agrarian rhythms, of absence of light and seasonal need for warmth. Rarely were they the object of direct comment. We know about them only through so many chance references as to constitute a convincing preindustrial pattern. Call it segmented sleep, or sleep in two phases. First night, then second night.

On initial reflection, those long nights, and the ordinariness of being wakeful during their middle, appear not unlike the way I am sleeping now. Segmented sleep sounds almost convivial. Others were up in the middle of the night, too! How much easier to be mothering an infant among such scenes. The intermission of wakefulness, I read, had a pleasant, unanxious quality. People prayed, chatted, had sex. They got up and did a spot of work about the house. Sleep was interrupted, wakefulness was sociable.

Perhaps those longer, more interrupted, and sociable nights encapsulate the sleep habits of preindustrial mothering. But more likely that neat pattern of segmented sleep barely begins to account for mothering's middle of the night. Such a possibility has hardly been researched. I'd like to know, was preindustrial maternal sleep, too, a dirty, torn cloth?

The few chance references I find suggest a pattern of disruption, a tearing of the usual fabric, which thoroughly disturbed two-part sleep. First night, second night seems not to have been the maternal mode. Seventeenth-century anti-wet-nursing moralists presumed that to be entirely self-evident. Mothers "put out" infants, they huffed, in part "for ease and quiet, because they cannot endure to have their sleep broken, or to have their children wrangle and cry." Easeful quiet contrasted with noise and soothing. An infant cry broke the night, and summoned due attention. "Wrangling" sounded vehement, insistent.[9]

"Tossing and tumbling" with a baby in the night was another brief mention. Or "sudden cryings out in the forepart of the night." Or there was the washerwoman Mary Collier, in 1739, penning a rare poem about the lives of laboring women, her target the lamentations of a male peer, the working-class poet Stephen Duck. Who had it harder? The nights of laboring women were distinguished by "little Sleep" because of "froward Children" who "cry and rave," she reported. "We have hardly ever *Time to dream*," she elaborated, as if a mother had too little forenight sleep to arrive at second night at all. Early modern adults may have slept in two phases, but then as now, people agreed that babies sleep in many. Our contemporary scientific term, distancing and polite, is polyphasic. Collier's "froward" is more fraught, more close at hand: nighttime crying, she wanted to convey, can be unreasonable, difficult to deal with.[10]

And then there are the individual exceptions that make me tremble in envy even centuries later. The baby "sleeps all night without nursing more than once sometimes not at all," noted Narcissa Whitman on March 30, 1837. They were, some might say, sleeping like a baby. Narcissa Whitman's days were marked by the physical demands of pioneer life in Oregon, but, unruffled, she *was* getting enough sleep.[11]

In some preindustrial communities, religious beliefs and habits rang their own changes on first night and second night. I trace the example of the Puritan goodwives of seventeenth-century Andover, Massachusetts. For them, the call of God and the cries of a living child together made of the middle of the night a cycle of sin, confession, and absolution. Sleep was believed to be sinful at origin—proof of man's degenerate and lowly state—and watching or wakefulness was an opportunity for prayer.[12]

Some Andover rituals of the night had little to do with Puritanism in particular. Preparing for bed by hunting for fleas or bedbugs was an early modern habit, as was combing out lice, banking the hearth to keep the embers at a safe distance, donning a chemise or smock, and snuffing out candles. The baby was fiercely swaddled, the many bands and layers rendering its body rigid to the touch. The dark shrouded such objects as the family Bible, whose flyleaf recorded the minute, hour, day, and month of a child's birth, or the wicker or wooden cradle, with its deep hood to keep out drafts and its firm mattress of cloth packed with straw, feathers, or oak leaves. At four months of age, by night a baby was still likely to be in bed with the goodwife.

For the devout, Puritan spirituality infused night as much as day. Settling Massachusetts villages and towns like Andover, Ipswich, and Boston had offered these supercharged Protestants the prospect of leaving behind a less pious English society. A feature of their holiness was constant awareness of God's presence. The ambition was to fall asleep with your mind focused on godly matters, and to ensure that your first thought on waking was of God. Night's rhythms and requirements were marked out by prayer. Before sleeping, the goodwife might utter, "Let the bed, O Lord, strike into our hearts that the grave is almost ready for us. Which of us can tell, whether these eyes of ours once closed up shall ever open any more again or no?" Midnight wakefulness was for drawing a soul especially close to God through prayer, meditation, or self-questioning. Waking and rising early—in contrast to the less devout, sleeping out their second night—should mark the shift from night to day.

The goodwife with a first living child was encouraged to sing her baby to sleep with the "Cradle Hymn." The infant was at home with her—not put out with a wet nurse—because she read the Puritan moralists, or attended to a minister's sermons or followed the vigilant, spiritual ways of the women around her, and because nursing was going sufficiently well. Andover Puritans knew the verse of Anne Bradstreet, whose poem *The Four Ages of Man* placed in an infant's mouth a description of the night's disturbances: "With wayward cries, I did disturb her rest, / Who sought still to appease me with the breast; / With weary arms she danced and *By By* sung . . ." The mother's rest was disrupted by sound; her limbs moved wearily; she sang. Ministers in this fiercely patriarchal society liked to use an infant's contentedness at the breast as a metaphor for eternal joy, but Bradstreet's infant was not so easily "appeased."

An infant's nighttime needs could interrupt prayer or provide its occasion, allow the night to end at dawn or weaken a mother's vigilance at early rising. For well-regulated nights and early risings were believed to allow the faithful to perform better service. Sensations of weakness or drowsiness might reflect or provoke lack of spiritual fortitude. (Falling asleep in church was an especial evil.) So providential punishments and deliverances, both, hovered over nighttime mothering. Anne Bradstreet's poetry was shot through with tensions between the requirements and pleasures of godly religion and those of earthly family. These tensions, and the cycles of sin and absolution, marked the middle of the night as much as the daytime hours. Even in the dark, they set the vigilantly pious of Andover apart from their merely observant contemporaries.

First night, second night, torn apart. Or first night, cry pray nurse, cry nurse pray . . .

On my Tuesdays and Thursdays, the sleeplessness forges a defiant and secular camaraderie. I'll think about you, too, feeding at 1:00 a.m., run the promises. Or maybe at 3:00 a.m. I learn much later that those who are sleeping better or longer just kept mum about it.

Preindustrial habits of two-part, segmented sleep slid away first in the cities and towns of the later nineteenth century, and then in rural areas. It seems that first sleep started and ended later, second sleep was shortened, and the period of wakefulness was decreased. Eventually both the memory and the terminology of first and second sleep faded into oblivion. Intervals of non-sleep were fretfully recast as insomnia. Segmented sleep was supplanted by one compressed cycle of sleep optimistically named "eight hours."[13]

Exactly among whom, and why and how, this started to happen is not entirely clear. Certainly the privileged and modish of the eighteenth century led the way. In 1710 London, *The Tatler* captured what the fashionable periodical saw as disappearing English ways and emerging new ones. Once, the periodical explained, night used to last longer. Nature threw the world into darkness, and mankind followed that simple cue, dedicating nighttime hours to rest and quiet. The evening curfew bell of eight o'clock signaled the time to snuff candles and go to bed. Now, in 1710, fashionable urban types stayed up late, playing cards or talking politics and then sleeping well into the morning. There was "scarcely a Lady of Quality in Great Britain," *The Tatler* reckoned, "that ever saw the sun rise."

Such habits of staying up late were encouraged by the spread of public street lighting in cities, which made late-night leisure safer, easier, and more visible. In the nineteenth century, the core of economic life moved from agriculture to industry. With factories and with industrial life, there arose an ethos of productivity, efficiency, and consumption. Labor was increasingly clock-oriented rather than task-oriented. These demands bled into the clock regimentation of daily routines. By the twentieth century, compressed sleep suited a society that was work-dominated and efficiency-driven. Electrification—whether in London or in Massachusetts or in Kentucky—made staying up late cheap and easy.

In my hankering for a solid eight hours, in having the distinct impression that this need is written into every cell of my body, I am a creature of modern times.

At a certain point in this fourth month of reflux and sleep deprivation, just as I am wondering about my own sanity, I start to document the nighttime wakings. Tiny columns of cramped writing crowd out the other brief notations in my diary—the doctor's appointments, K's work schedule.

The columns form a testament to sleeplessness. They offer cold comfort in the form of evidence for why I feel mildly insane. Later, when I go back to the diaries, I find that M did not sleep more than an hour and a half or three hours at a time until he was fifteen months old. Doctors say that this is not uncommon for infants with reflux. Some people lament their former autonomy. Sleep-stricken, I was grieving for rest, and for the ability to put this sensation or any thought adequately into words.

By day, I lose nouns. I drive through red lights. In the mirror, my face is fainted away almost beyond distinguishing, as if by the continual brush of waking activity, the features had softly withered.

In contemporary San Francisco, the poet Brenda Shaughnessy reaches for a thought, and composes, elegantly, "I'm trying to explain it. / I repeat myself, or haven't I already?"[14]

I scrawl my fear that M might be "disformed," staring stupidly at the page, unsure whether the sentiment or the spelling is wrong.

If one could raise the entire skein of sleeplessness from the historical archives, like a conjuror, I suspect it would be made up of such slurred words, phrases that trail off, half-vacant sentences that fail to land. Some venom, some acquiescence.

Sometimes the tiny, more recent reports I find come warmly alive: Olive Morgan, a Welsh tin miner's daughter who was born in Llanelli in 1914, reported that if "the baby cried all night, the mother nursed the baby all night." In the daytime, she said, "I would sit on the settee with the baby on my lap, and the bottle would often drop from my hand to the floor. I was so whacked."[15]

Or a former secretary, born in Preston, England, in 1931, reports, "He never slept for the first few months, it was awful with him. I was like a zombie."[16]

9:03 p.m. 11:30. 1:00. 1:45. 3:30. 5:00, read the notations in my diary. 8:30. 10:45. 12:00. 2:10. 4:50. 5:45.

So once, babies sometimes, or usually, disrupted first night and second night. And then, sometimes, or often, they disrupted the usual modern eight hours. "So whacked" spoke Olive Morgan in 1914. "Like a zombie" reported the mid-twentieth-century secretary. The vehemence of their words suggests that torn sleep feels more pronounced, more fine-edged, when sleeping all night is the usual expectation. Or perhaps not. What roads have been traveled since Mary Collier's "froward" infants or seventeenth-century tossing and tumbling? *Ammenschlaf*, the light sleep of the baby's caregiver, may deserve global translation: a kind of constant possibility, weaving through shifting expectations, to be understood among the details of individual circumstances. 8:55. 11:15. 1:00. 3:05.

And bed sharing, or solitary sleep, among these shifting expectations, among these individual circumstances of the night?

Washington, D.C., the summer of 1880, among the direct descendants of Massachusetts Puritans. The regular notations Mabel Loomis Todd made in her diary in the summer of 1880 recorded the winding of the bedroom clock, the baby's weight (sixteen pounds at four months, seventeen pounds at five), and her nighttime sex life. #21, #22, #23. Each number marked an occasion of marital sex, counting forward from January.[17]

This baby, Millicent, had been born in a boardinghouse, where Mabel and her blond, bearded husband rented rooms. Many financially unstable middle-class families did the same. David had slept "downstairs" for the first six days after the birth. Now the trio, plus Mabel's parents and grandmother and her mother's live-in servant, Molly Peyton, had moved into 1413 College Hill Terrace. It was tight quarters but an improvement on boardinghouse life. "No more boarding, with indifferent outside people in the same home," sniffed Mabel. Just below the hill, she noted happily, the "city lights" of Washington, D.C., "gradually sparkle out" until it seemed "a sea of brightness." Electrification had arrived, and the sunrises and sunsets calendared in the diary's front matter bore no relation to the beginning and ending of Mabel's nights. Time was becoming standardized in glass reflection of a clock-oriented world. When it was twelve noon in New York City, it was 11:47 a.m. and 53 seconds in Washington.

David Todd claimed to have descended from a famous New England Puritan divine, a heritage of which Mabel was proud. Theirs was a claim on American lineage more than the reflection of ongoing and shared culture. Little in her diary's loving self-documentation echoed the world of Puritans or their early modern times. Mabel refused notions of the wickedness of human nature or a punishing God. She liked to read Dickens, Emerson, and *Harper's Magazine*. Unlike in seventeenth-century Andover, the couple's sleeping space was entirely private, initially by dint of the lock to the boarding room's door. Their bedstead—part of a comfortable black walnut chamber set purchased for the new house—was purely marital. The term "bedfellow" had long since dropped out of common use, its meaning as bed sharer having outlasted its meaning as lover.[18]

A Puritan forebear would have been surprised not by the marital sex—poet Anne Bradstreet was in tune with her times in having eight children—but by the regulated coitus interruptus that made Millicent an only child, as well as by Mabel Todd's sensual and unflagging self-documentation. "#44 for me" recorded one notation. After retiring to bed, regular sexy evenings were "radiant": "a very happy few minutes of love in our room," "an hour's joy together."

Bed sharing with a baby was out, but co-sleeping in the same room was in. The baby was "put to sleep" and then laid on a mattress in the crib beside the walnut bedstead, "a permanent bed for the little one's own," as David put it. An early night was 8:30 p.m., maybe 9:00. There's no documentation of first or second nights; the diary marked time by the hours of the clock.

June 3, 1880: "Millicent awakens sometimes as early as five o'clock, and I then have David bring her from her crib to me, where I play a little with her, though three quarters asleep the while . . . About six o'clock Amelia"—a black maidservant—"comes for her, & she is wrapped up & taken out while I sleep an hour or so."

The summer of 1880 was hot and muggy, like most Washington summers. Mabel had been used to traveling north to New England with her mother and grandmother in the hottest months. They had shared a rented room while her father moved into single lodgings. Her only record of fatigue now concerned the heat. "Quite exhausted with the strain of so many hot days." "Very tired at night. The day has been hot—exceedingly." Perhaps Mabel Todd owed her usually adequate sleep to Millicent's praised good nature, or to her own robust constitution. Certainly it relied on the maidservant's labor, on her arriving for the day by 6:00 a.m. Amelia—the diary does not offer her last name—replaced the monthly nurse who cared for mother and baby after Millicent's birth. The "wages by the week" printed by the publishers in the diaries Mabel purchased suggested a "usual calculation of ten hours a day."

There's a hint, too, of sleep training. After Amelia left her post, grandmother and mother attempted to teach the baby to go to sleep by herself. One night, she did it "to perfection," lying awake for half an hour and then sucking her thumb and "finally falling asleep deeply." Better: "She did not awaken for twelve hours—until six the next morning." Mabel believed that "we shall triumph in this respect, very soon." But the family's habits when Millicent turned a year old belied that optimism: she was not falling asleep alone in the crib, but still being "nestled" or rocked.

Sometime in the mid-nineteenth or twentieth century, depending on where you lived and who you were, the middle of the night became subject to sustained and routine recommendations for babies and mothers to sleep well apart. Because doctors were often ignored in Verna Mae Slone's 1930s Kentucky, social workers advising urban immigrants, women's magazines at the local newsagents, and ubiquitous how-to guides all issued variations on the theme of solitary sleep. A mother and a baby (the gaze only ever fell on mother and baby) ought to sleep properly apart, with the baby in a crib in the next room. "American babies sleep alone; my babies too," remarked a Polish immigrant in 1939 Chicago. In co-sleeping with Millicent in 1880s Washington, D.C., her baby in a crib nearby, Mabel Todd was halfway there.[19]

Sometimes the prescriptions about solitary sleep, and what babies should do, were greatly at odds with existing habits or what seems humanly possible. In the 1920s small babies were supposed to spend most of every twenty-four hours sleeping alone. At other times, the prescriptions came closer to a working set of norms. "The baby goes to bed a little after seven and sleeps in her own bed until seven in the morning," reads a 1918 letter from rural Pennsylvania. In the 1970s, the feminist Adrienne Rich wondered what happened to the "unconscious" of the new mother,

her dream life having disappeared. She got up to go to her infant, and then returned alone to her own bed. In that decade, solitary sleep was typical throughout Britain and North America.[20]

The sensations of the night in these modern decades were distanced from former ways, but new arrivals brought their own range of nighttime habits. Japanese immigrants to the twentieth-century United States knew all about bed sharing: in Matsumoto or Kyoto, mothers lay with babies until they went to sleep and shared a futon with them all night. First-generation Bangladeshi mothers in 1980s Cardiff, unlike their Welsh-born counterparts, also slept in bed with their babies. Medical expertise was not always followed. National recommendations voiced by GPs and pediatricians were often honored only in the breach.[21]

Maternal sleep is a dirty, torn cloth. The exceptions reside among those centuries' worth of mothers who "put out" their babies to wet nurses: royal mistresses, genteel ladies, plantation mistresses, and better-off working-women unwilling to risk less rest. Or they reside among those with servants who lived in or, most recently, perhaps, the mothers for whom sleep training had a successful outcome. Otis Burger, the Manhattanite who published her 1949 birth story, complained that at six weeks, the baby still didn't "sleep through the night" with any regularity. One night, the baby slept eight hours; the next night, she was up every three. But "she is learning that when the lights go out and the parents become resolutely quiet in their beds that it means Time to Sleep."[22]

Many more sensations of night are lost to the archives and to my research: of the early modern wet nurses, for example, sleeping with another person's child at hand; of the eighteenth-century "female husbands," close by their wives, who are yet more elusive; of those woken by the sound of the antebellum plantation bell; of an Amelia arriving at her Washington employers' home on College Hill Terrace before 6:00 a.m.

8:20. 10:00. 11:45. 2:00. 5:00. 5:40. And then we are up.

14

Pent Milk

Novice nursing was all humiliation and excess. Too much milk, too many cushions to be arranged just so, too much distress. Rings of milk marked shirts, muslins, and sheets, one circle overlapping the next like an infantile Venn diagram. Some milk went into the baby's tummy, only to return, quickly, expelled by the force of the reflux. Love was unrequited.

Now the baby and I know what we're doing, more or less. We can be merely mutually absorbed, reciprocally endeared. "Sat we two, one another's best," as the poet John Donne wrote of another kind of pairing, in another time and place.[1]

Distress receding, love steadying, the subject of milk can come more readily into focus. Nursing, breastfeeding, giving the breast, milk nursing, giving suck, suckling, letting down, finger feeding, hand-feeding, bringing up by hand, bottle-feeding. Or, more colloquially, giving the baby the tittie. These are verbs of holding and feeding, with roots in care or agriculture or commerce. Such verbs—the actions, the sheer labor of it— are easier to identify than the attending sensations. Scientists experimenting on people today offer a clinical, hormonal description. Oxytocin, the "love hormone," is produced in nursing mothers, they suggest, and also more generally in giving care to an infant. Holding *is* attachment. But you can't take any one body out of its historical circumstances, so a scientific account of oxytocin is only a faint guide to the past.

Holding and feeding can be labor, then: experienced as work, as something a person can get better at, as entailing practice, as taking a lot out of you, as depletion, as bound up with matters of immediate resources or competing interests, as potentially taken on or handed off to someone else.

Holding and feeding can also entail sensations and feelings, dimensions of being that are to me in this moment entirely paramount, but are harder to locate in the past or to put readily into words: as tactile, sensual, bonding, even erotic. Nursing, Adrienne Rich reckoned in 1976, was like a sexual act. The least embarrassed version of this insight dispenses with the analogy: this *is* a love affair. The attachment, the love, can run the gamut from the prescriptive to the subversive. Victorian woman, you *will* find in breastfeeding the highest pleasure. Or, to paraphrase writer Maggie Nelson more recently: eros without an end point.

I found the Donne poem this morning. The relation described is that between two lovers reclining wordless on a bank (a "pregnant" bank, no less). That nursing pulled John Donne's phrases to mind, from the dim memory of a school classroom, makes sense. The baby's gaze fixes on me with an unwaveringly loyal and mature look, a steady contemplation. Donne describes how "Our eye-beams twisted, and did thread / Our eyes upon one double string." The sexy chastity of the poem stirred my mid-adolescent self, but this line was entirely too material and too weird. I like to blink. Yet in the long, slow exchange of M's gaze, I'm newly amenable to Donne's conceit of connected eye-beams.

Today, my conspiratorial lover gives a crooked smile out of the top corner of his lip, milk edging below. As *like* an erotic act, Rich wrote in the

1970s, suckling a child can be a "physically delicious, elementally soothing experience, filled with a tender sensuality." Or likewise, "tense, physically painful, charged with cultural feelings of inadequacy and guilt."
What of earlier acts of holding and feeding, the entwined labors and feelings to do with milk?

Two Margarets, who lived in the very middle of the eighteenth century,
turn up among the books I read as I walk up and down the garden path,
the baby asleep in the sling. If he naps upright like this, away from traffic
and noise, the milk is more likely to stay down. We go in and out of the
sunlight filtering through the oak tree, back and forth alongside the frayed
stretch of the washing line. Fifteen pounds of weight settle down my
shoulder blades and across the back of my waist.

The two Margarets lived at the end of what I am coming to think of
as the first regime of milk, a way of doing things that lasted from before
the start of the seventeenth century to these women's mid-eighteenth-
century decades. The regime's key feature—its underlying question, if
you like—was *whose breast?* Answer: always the breast of a recently enough
delivered mother, usually the infant's own, but sometimes a wet nurse who
lived elsewhere, a woman paid to share her breast milk, her caregiving,
and her home with another person's child.[2]

Margaret Collier lived in the parish of Chertsey, Surrey, a large market town just down the river from London, in which the smell of malting
barley often filled the air. In the winter of 1756–57 she had one infant of
her own. For poor English families, money was especially tight when infants were small. So Margaret Collier added the labor of wet-nursing and
took in another infant that January. Nursing an extra child—in this case,
a foundling from a London hospital named Ann Stafford—could make
the difference between remaining independent and being forced onto
the parish's poor relief. Taking in two foundlings, for Margaret added a
second girl from the hospital in March, made for an even better balance
of income and cost. The hospital records kept track of the infants' comings and goings. For Margaret Collier, her employment made for three
infants: one household. An intimidating ratio.[3]

In 1761 Philadelphia, the second Margaret nursed her daughter Deborah. Margaret Morris—"Peggy"—was the daughter and wife of Quaker merchants whose business dealings crisscrossed the Atlantic Ocean. A letter from her father in Madeira nagged that nursing Deborah might be "prejudicial" to her health. She should put out the baby "to Betty Shute's youngest daughter" or "some other wholesome body," or even "bring her up by hand." Stop soon, he directed, before "it"—nursing, or the baby?—"takes too much hold." Use a wet nurse.[4]

Coming from a merchant born in 1698, the direction to use a wet nurse was not unusual. Employing a wet nurse was an entirely typical routine among women of status of the seventeenth century, and remained routine, if declining, in the families of aristocrats, the gentry, the clergy, lawyers, slaveholders, merchants, and physicians. These women were required to run households or businesses or to reproduce again, and they had the resources to employ someone else. Among the better-off, convention held that lactating prohibited sex, increasing the impatience of husbands already chafing at their gander month. Lactating was also thought to make a new conception less likely. (This last was in fact the case, demographically speaking, if not individually reliable.) Margaret did not take up her father's recommendation with Deborah, though she would do so with the twin sons who came along later.

Seventeenth- and eighteenth-century infants such as Ann Stafford or Deborah Morris were nursed sometimes for a year (typical foundlings), or for nineteen months (demographers' average calculation), or to a second summer (a frequent seventeenth-century recommendation), or up to a year (the eighteenth-century learned view). That's hundreds of hours apiece. The labor was mainly measured in infants' growing bodies and health. Nursing and infancy were assumed to define each other. The baby was a baby—"a suckling" or "a suckling child"—as long as it was "hanging on the Mothers Breasts."[5]

Among Englishwomen and North American settlers during this first regime of milk, that work began with lying-in. A new mother's breast was sucked by a midwife or another lying-in attendant to bring in her milk. A 1682 satirist of the pleasures of matrimony remarked on an inadequate lying-in nurse with such a squeamish stomach that she "cannot suck her Mistress." Someone else had to be found "to suck the young woman's breasts for twelve pence a time; or else her breasts will grow hard with lumps and fester" for lack of "being drawn." The usual attendant *did* suck to draw the milk.[6]

Perhaps breastfeeding was learned in the same way that such women acquired other familiar adult gestures—more by proximity and observation than by technical description. Unfolding clothing modestly, positioning a child at the breast, these may have been movements as early and as easily learned as holding hands clasped in front of the body, in that usual seventeenth-century posture of secure, enclosed chastity. Certainly breastfeeding was ordinary and unsequestered, the kind of everyday activity witnessed across a room. In seventeenth-century Maryland, Rose Ashbrooke was "Suckling her own Child upon the left breast" when a visiting neighbor, a man sitting at the table, remarked that she had "good Store." I nurse in public, but I don't expect a man to comment on it.[7]

However easily learned or hard won, the physical effort needed to be managed. Handwritten recipe books and women's letters to one another recognized the scale of the labor and repeated advice about what to do when breasts hardened or inflamed or milk dried up. Avoid getting cold in case lumps gather, Esther Cox warned her daughter in 1800. The delicate English rampion plant, whose roots oozed white juice when broken, was recommended to improve supply. Likewise lady's mantle. "Everyone knows how many breast troubles nurses suffer from, such as superabundance of milk and its excessive flow when it is too thin," wrote the much-translated commentator Bernardino Ramazzini. ("Nurses" here meant both women who suckled their own children and those hired to suckle the infants of others.) Ramazzini cast the infant as benefiting at the nurse's expense. "As the infant grows bigger and sucks a great deal of milk," he reckoned, the nurse's body is "robbed of nutritive juice . . . and so from exhaustion they become thin and reedy."[8]

Peggy Morris's father's worried reproach of 1761, that nursing is physically consuming, was more or less routine. Perhaps the equivalent remark in modern times is caloric: breastfeeding an infant, I read, takes the same energy as walking seven miles a day.

The at-home wet-nursing undertaken by Margaret Collier or recommended to Margaret Morris peaked in the eighteenth century. In the mid-century parish of Chertsey, there were hundreds of women like Collier who took in local or London nurslings. Call it a cottage industry. One way it was done was through word of mouth, perhaps via a wealthier neighbor or a former employer. Another way was to advertise in the London press, for Chertsey could recommend itself as a healthy, countryside environment for urban babies. A hopeful wet nurse placed an ad reading, "A woman of good Character with a fine Breast of Milk, would be willing to take a Child to Nurse; she lives in a healthy part of the country." Such advertisements used the same rote language, and they are as close as we can get to the actual words of wet nurses like Collier. This is the only literature, the singular poetry, of the wet nurse: "An healthy Woman, with a good Breast of Milk, in an healthy Air, would be glad of a Child to suck."[9]

Wet-nursing in the employ of the London Foundling Hospital, as performed by Collier and many of her Chertsey neighbors, saved the expense of a newspaper ad and made for certain and regular payments. Every month, Chertsey women streamed over the town's wooden bridge, passing the Thames barges headed into the metropolis, to collect their earnings of two shillings and sixpence per week per nursling. Male farm laborers in the vicinity might earn nine or twelve shillings a week for six days' work. Women farm laborers might earn between three and five shillings, depending on the season, so taking in two nurslings served to replace lost wages.

For Margaret Collier to nurse a foundling like Ann Stafford was to hold a baby in the hospital's standard first-year uniform: caps, clouts and pilches, shirts and linen sleeves, shoes and stockings. A blanket served as an outer wrap in winter. These clothes may have been peculiarly lightweight to Margaret's touch. The baby on her lap may have seemed strangely supple and loose of body. The hospital physicians were on a campaign against stiff rollers and swaddling bands, the more usual attire of the times, which they deemed to cause overheating and fits. The institution deliberately did not provide either kind of clothing.

Or perhaps Margaret went her own way. Swaddling can keep a baby quiet and more content. Perhaps she wrapped Ann tight in the way she knew from her own child. Perhaps she did the same with Maud Saunders, the second foundling, that March. When the hospital inspectors visited town, they complained in their reports that wet nurses from their first calls sent word ahead to other wet nurses that they were coming. Put Ann, put Maud in the right clothes, went the whispers. Make sure your own children are not wearing borrowed hospital attire.

There were other places like eighteenth-century Chertsey, spots close to English and American cities and large towns that had parallel cottage industries. Near Philadelphia, for example, where Peggy Morris could have looked in 1761 if she wanted to follow her father's advice and if Betty Shute's daughter turned her down. The coastal towns outside Boston. More places in the orbit of London: Dorking, Epsom, Reading, Woking-ham, Hornchurch, smaller spots along the capital's access roads. They were only the most visible manifestation of a wide and long-standing communal use of wet-nursing. Breastfeeding was the only reliable way to keep a baby alive. Raising by hand, which Peggy Morris's father was ready to recommend, was recognizably risky.

How to choose a wet nurse if you were well-to-do? Families like the Morrises were recommended to look for women who were "healthy, sober, good-tempered, cleanly, careful" as well as having "plenty of good milk"—"wholesome" in Peggy's father's parlance of 1761. Living nearby helped, so that the child could be easily visited. A common fret was that the distance "estranged" the parents from supervising the baby's care. There are glimpses of visits back and forth; in 1750s Pontefract the genteel Jane Scrimshire put out her first son, Tom, and recorded two visits. Her daughter was put out and then weaned much earlier—at five months rather than fifteen, even though, as the Yorkshire woman worried, "the learned" reckon a baby should "never suck Less than half a year." The occasion was a visit from wet nurse and baby: Jane did not want to send her back.[10]

Thus the labor of nursing. What about the attendant feelings? Such scenes of labor were always shot through with feeling. But the sensations of nursing are hard to discern retrospectively. What feelings accompanied

Margaret Collier's labors, the strong clasp on her nipple, the weight of one or more babies across her lap, the relative stiffness of clothing and the winter blanket? What ambivalence accompanied nursing her own baby and the January foundling in tandem, or weaning her child? What pleasure or irritation or rage attended the offering of comfort? Absent the words of the wet nurses, the possibilities can only be guessed at from outcomes or later behaviors. Foundling babies, arriving in new households in a fragile state, were more likely to perish than other infants. But older foundlings might call their nurse "Mammy," and many poor families eventually asked to keep their hospital charges.

Or the feelings of the entirely better-resourced Peggy Morris, nursing her own child against the scolding of a merchant paterfamilias? The evidence of bonding in general—and of a range of feelings, more particularly—is elusive, even among the most well-to-do. An elite 1636 gravestone suggests that a child nursed on "unborrowed" milk—its mother's own—might be singled out and preferred over others. Some wills of the same century left such children more money, making a similar kind of point.[11]

In what I find, there's no exact seventeenth- or early-eighteenth-century equivalent to recent notions that nursing is like a love affair, that it *is* a love affair. There's no anticipation of the literary analogy of erotic romance, or of the best hormonal description being a substance—"elixirs of contentment"—also made when we kiss. It's not that sensations—whatever exactly they were—were absent, it's that they left little or no written trace to be discovered now.[12]

Or perhaps there is a seventeenth-century equivalent, only in metaphorical reverse. In 1692, Londoner Anne Bathurst, member of a mystical religious society, was searching for a metaphor to illuminate her rapturous union with God. She reached for what was apparently familiar and intense: lactating. "The word divine multiplies in me & fills me," she began writing one night, "taking my heart's life into it." And then: "O, a fountain sealed, breasts full of consolation. I am as pent milk in the breast, ready to be poured forth & dilated into Thee, from whom my fullness flows with such fullness and plenitude & pleased when eased." Pent milk, a fountain unsealed, fullness eased, pleasure released, nurturer and nurtured as one. I am hard put to find a description of hotter emotional temperature. This is Adrienne Rich—"like a sexual act"—in divine register. It is desecularized Maggie Nelson, "eros without an endpoint": religious erotics with an ecstatic finale.[13]

"Succeed pretty well in nursing" wrote the missionary Mary Richardson Walker in 1840 Oregon country. "Am greatly rejoiced that I succeed so well in nursing . . . spent much of the day in fruitless attempts . . . Felt much better. Feed the babe for the most part, mostly with breast milk." Nineteenth-century women's diaries recorded the kinds of short phrases we might imagine being shared aloud from a century or two centuries before, reporting ordinary rhythms of establishing and maintaining lactation.[14]

From the middle of the eighteenth century to the close of the nineteenth—the second regime of milk—*whose breast?* remained the central concern about holding and feeding. What most distinctively changed was the arrival of sentimentalism—a new way of venerating motherhood in popular culture and a way in which the labor of nursing combined and recombined with emotion in specific and distinctive ways. The change was consequential for those nursing their own children, as well as for those nursing another's.

There had always been sentiments, but an "ism" is different. Isms dictate and describe and shape and redescribe how things are and should be. They take what's various and try to press it into a single discernible shape. In this case, the ism was focused on feeling: the natural and intimate proximity of mother and child. The sentimental bonds nurtured by breastfeeding should be mothering's fundamental feature. Suckling your own child, if you could, was necessary, sacred, and delightful.

From the late eighteenth century on, the pleasurable sensations of breastfeeding were newly and distinctively prescribed, moralized, voiced, felt, recalled, and written down—sentimentalized. Moralized with effusion: cheerfully fulfilling the obligation to nurse allows the "sweetest pleasures of which the heart is susceptible" (the bestselling William Buchan's *Advice to Mothers*); breastfeeding is "a very high source of pleasure, of the most tender and endearing kind" (U.S. midwife Mary Watkins in her 1809 *Maternal Solicitude, or, Lady's Manual*). Cautiously felt: "a pleasing, although a painful sensation" (Cincinnati author Ann Allen in 1858). Fashionably voiced, upon weaning a one-year-old: I miss "her dear little eager mouth at my breast" (the Duchess of Devonshire in a letter of 1784).[15]

"So sweet an office . . . giving nourishment to my darling," recorded an Arkansas lawyer's wife of 1857, in remarks shaped and dictated by sentimentalism. "Are these foolish tears that dim my eyes when I think of the times, when he will no longer nestle in my bosom through the silent watches of the night?" Deeply invested in sentimental mothering, Rebecca Turner kept a diary for her "Little Jesse" that described breastfeeding as a treasured task. Sweet sensations were felt and told and felt, or perhaps told and felt and told again, in a reinforcing circuitry of nature and culture, physiology and reporting.[16]

Among the well-to-do, breastfeeding now appeared as a matter of feeling—rather than, say, of bodily health or of Puritan godly duty—and could lend a saccharine judgmentalism. "She has a good sweet babe," remarked the high-society Southerner Eleanor Lewis in a letter to an old friend in 1827, "but she is a helpless Mother, she cannot suckle it, and knows very little about the care of children." The clincher was in the comparison: "I hope you will see *my* little treasure next autumn, and his *devoted* mother." The devotion! announced the italics. The refinement of maternal feeling![17]

In these altered times, weaning was still seen as a generosity to husbands, but they were first encouraged to enjoy gazing, in a way that now seems mawkish and slightly creepy, upon blissful baby and mother. The wife "with a little one at her breast" was, or should be, "to her husband the most exquisitely enchanting object upon earth."[18]

As isms do in any unequal society, sentimentalism played unfair. Catering to this literate and sentimentalizing audience, the advertisements of the wet nurse had to change their opening phrase: "*Wants a wet nurse's place*, A Young Woman, aged twenty-one, of a sweet temperament with a fine breast of milk three months old." "*Wanted a wet nurse's place*, for a healthy young Woman, with a good Breast of Milk, *just come out of the country*." No longer, that is, did the wet nurse take her charges away to her own house. Taking a "place," now as a live-in servant, she kept employer and child together under the same roof. She highlighted the merits of her person and character rather than the health and cleanliness of her home and its rural location. I am healthy, I am sweet.[19]

No longer a supplementary form of household labor, wet-nursing became a temporary form of domestic service that separated nurses from their own children. Imagine, for we can only imagine, the labor and sensations of an Irish-born woman, Mary, in 1880s Worcester, Massachusetts. Her record-keeping employer, Fanny Workman, was the kind of upper-class Victorian who could climb mountains—glaciers, no less—and contribute articles to magazines. (*Babyhood* was a favorite.) She was well read and well versed in "educated" beliefs of the superiority of white upper-class society, of Anglo-American "civilization" over the worlds of those of different hue or origin.[20]

That the Irish immigrant Mary had a baby of her own meant that wet-nursing was a possible income and occupation for her. Mary came to live in the Workman household, she was outfitted in new clothes, she profited (so Workman complained) from tea, ice water, and pickles handed out surreptitiously by the cook. But laboring away from her own child in domestic service proved unsustainable. Her child became ill, perhaps in the hands of a relative or of a wet nurse lower down a chain of care, and Mary sought to resign after six weeks. Workman, frantic about her own baby's health, arranged for Mary's child to be brought and then organized what proved to be an unreliable place for the baby's care. The worries cost Mary both her milk supply and her job: her milk dried up through stress, and she left both her post and our retrospective view.

This nursing was partly a monetary transaction. The exchanges of feeling between Mary and her own baby, Mary and Workman's infant, or Mary's feelings about her employer are hidden to us. What's certain is that Fanny Workman ignored Mary's feelings, perhaps agreeing with the doctors of her class who thought that such women did not truly care for their children. Sentiments, they conveniently believed, were only for the privileged. Those of Irish women, or black women, or foreigners were deemed lesser, even absent.

As a way of describing mothering as mainly a matter of feeling, sentimentalism has taken multiple forms since the nineteenth century. Theories of maternal attachment are one example. The twentieth-century idealization of the softhearted working-class mum is another. So, too, is the emotional texture of recent maternal memoirs, or the question driving my initial curiosity: What did mothering feel like?

As for the particular sensations that went with wet-nursing, already almost always lost, they have faded even further from view with the disappearance of that waged work. There is no evidence of wet-nursing in Britain or North America after the 1930s. No single explanation accounts for why. Perhaps wet-nursing ended because more appealing factory jobs were increasingly available to newly delivered working mothers; perhaps because employers so manifestly disliked their dependence on these short-term servants; perhaps because of new foods for infant feeding; perhaps because medical experts of the 1920s and 1930s betrayed so little interest in its merits; or perhaps because of the hospital milk banks that flourished in some places from the early twentieth century into the 1960s and 1970s.

Among the last of wet-nursing sensations were those of the women employed at the Sarah Morris Children's Hospital in early-twentieth-century Chicago. A special wing of the five-story brick hospital housed wet nurses who were employed for nine or ten months to express milk for hospitalized babies. In this last soft-palated gasp, wet-nursing kept the wet nurse together with her own infant once again. Both mother and baby lived "in." The "natural stimulation" to the working breast, doctors noticed, ensured an ample supply of milk.[21]

The attachments forged by wet-nursing have since lingered mainly as family stories, small histories belonging to the distant past or to immigrants' homelands. A long generation ago, the American historian Gerda Lerner recalled her wealthy Viennese mother relying on "wetnurse's strings." The West Coast immigrant and poet Marilyn Chin, born in the mid-1950s, pictured the wet nurse left behind in her Chinese homeland. The recollected voice of the wet nurse appears in the poetry of her American charge, full of advice and admonition. A 1986 poem bids farewell to the ancestors, farewell to the wet nurse.[22]

Reflux milk spatters on the garden path. Breastfeeding Jackson Pollock. I'm told it's only a few tablespoons, but it looks like a small pool of white paint. It is less than the broken waters that pooled at my feet five months before, and larger than the saucer we put down for the neighbor's cat.

A few tablespoons of milk traveling across four or five feet—baby vomiting, me standing—usually hits the ground with exactly the same sharp, conclusive sound. Sometimes M looks surprised. Often I cry, especially in late afternoons when his emptier stomach predicts shorter segments of sleep.

What does breast milk look like? I pause there. Often the stuff passes unremarked and unseen between mother and baby. What it looks like, or what it's imagined to be, usually depends on other perceptions. Seventeenth-century people thought of the stuff as blood turned into milk. Into the eighteenth century, this white blood might be expressed for medicinal use. "Women's milk" was commonly used as an ingredient in homemade remedies for hysteria, or faintness, or blindness, or ear and eye problems. Take a spoonful of woman's milk, read one 1716 recipe for eye-water, and add larger quantities of rose water, fennel juice, sugar, and "White Vitriol."[23]

Or, the expressed milk of a wet nurse might be examined by a nineteenth-century physician, once medical men muscled in on the domestic transaction between mothers and lactating live-in staff. The milk on his fingernail: Is the hue blackish, bluish, gray, or reddish? Does the drop taste sour, sharp, salty, or brackish? Mrs. Beeton's household guide made such queries about the mother's health well known to many later-nineteenth-century households.[24]

In the twentieth century, the question of *whose breast?* would shift with the third regime of milk: *breast or bottle?* Breast milk came to serve as the standard for commercial foods, and vice versa. "Milk" of all kinds appeared increasingly frequently inside glass or plastic, measured against black lines marked out in fluid ounces or milliliters. By the twenty-first century, breastfeeding advocates had coined new phrases to recapture breast milk's particularity: not white blood, but white gold, liquid gold.

Tucked in the back of our pantry, behind the cereal boxes, is a single carton of formula. It's an item from the early days of nursing, when I was unsure of milk and of baby alike. A receptacle of reassurance and anxiety together. Perhaps my milk might fail. The baby won't starve, but no one in this household knows how to give him a first bottle in the middle of the night. How much formula does a five-month-old need at one sitting?

The sudden and remarkable change to a third regime of milk—to *breast or bottle?*—occurred when nonhuman foods met with pasteurization, clean water supplies, refrigerated transport, and domestic iceboxes or refrigerators. In the 1920s, conditions newly pertained that enabled artificial foods to pose little active danger to infants. *Breast or bottle?* became the meaningful question, the general point of reference for holding and feeding.

Certainly there had been earlier and occasional Plan Bs, alternatives to breastfeeding forced by milk failure or maternal isolation, by death or diverted resources. Plan Bs depended on local ecology. The "traditional" Cherokee alternative (the term belonged to 1930s anthropologists) was corn hominy. Among the Algonquian-speaking people of James Bay, the alternative was fish liquor. If a mother cannot nurse, take an animal bladder, pierce a few holes in it, and fill it with fish liquor, on which the infant can suck. Fish roe can be cooked and added while the liquor is cooking. But try rubbing goose fat on the breasts first to help the mother's milk come in. Sadie Neakok, an Inupiaq woman living in Alaska in the early 1940s, "ran out of breastmilk and that fall had to feed Billy fish roe and broth."[25]

"Pap" was the alternative wherever the English, or English speakers, dominated. The term derived from the word for breast, nipple, or teat and endured from medieval times through to the nineteenth century. Ramazzini, the popular early modern commentator, identified pap as made of cow's milk, egg yolks, and sugar. The base ingredients of cow's milk and something sweet were strikingly durable. Consult the 1881 cookbook of one Mrs. Abby Fisher and you find "a Southern plantation preparation" called "Pap for Infant Diet" made of boiled milk and sugar with boiled flour, to be given "whenever you are ready to nurse or feed the child." Abby Fisher had likely lived as an enslaved woman in or around Mobile, Alabama. Was the recipe in her San Francisco publication, now that she was free, a serious set of instructions to be used, a historical curiosity, or an 1881 jab at a nasty pre–Civil War past? "I have given birth to eleven children and raised them all," Fisher remarked alongside the recipe, "and nursed them with this diet." Throughout slavery, enslaved mothers had routinely served as wet nurses for others.[26]

The full routinization of commercial foods began with ads for American infant food in 1869, half a century before such products became routinely safe. "No More Wet Nurses!" promised Liebig's in the pages of *Hearth and Home*. More products were swiftly marketed throughout Britain and North America, their capitalized names typically proclaiming similarity to human milk and scientific approval. Depending on when and where a person lived, what she picked off the shelf might be Allenbury's Food, Arnott's Milk Arrowroot Biscuits, Carnrick's Soluble Food, Cow and Gate Baby Milk Plus, Fairchild's Peptogenic Powder, Farex, Horlicks, Just's Food, Liebig's, National Dried Milk, Nestlé Condensed Milk, Nestlé's Milk Food, Ovaltine, Revalenta Arabica, or Robinson's Groats. My favorite title is "Lacto-Preparata," which placed on either side of the hyphen the old history of lactation and the new need for formal preparation, glossing the whole with Latinate authority.[27]

Formula—"a detailed statement of ingredients"—seems a fair way to capture such products from their commercial beginning. Mellin's Food, for example, was named after the chemist Gustav Mellin and composed of "soluble, dry extract of wheat, malted barley and bicarbonate of potassium . . . converted into soluble carbohydrates, maltose and dextrins, and by evaporation reduced to a dry powder consisting of maltose, dextrins, proteins and salts." This powder was to be mixed with a specified amount of cow's milk. Many products became household names. The baby's face on the Gerber carton on my shelf has been familiar to shoppers since the 1930s. But away from the laboratories or the shops, what new combinations of work and feeling characterized this historical change? What was the ordinary experience of breast or bottle?

In the Piedmont region of the United States in the 1930s, a seventeen-year-old girl, the unmarried daughter of tenant farmers, was breastfeeding, but the baby was losing weight. She was advised to change to a bottle. I don't know about her feelings, but the labor of this was immensely tricky.

Without a cow, or ice, or money for buying milk or training in preparing it, a visitor reported, she found this very difficult. For one week's supply, the "Welfare" gave her a can of powdered milk. But she fixed too much at once and it soured and made the baby sick. She hoped her aunt's cow would "freshen" soon, and she could send her little sister the two miles every day to get milk.[28]

Impoverished Englishwomen emigrating to Depression-era Won-thaggi, a coal town southeast of Melbourne, Australia, either breastfed on demand like their mothers or used artificial foods. Take Milk Arrow-root Biscuits, soften them in boiling water, and add condensed milk. Condensed milk was cheap. The tin was neat. Local medical experts reckoned that "everyone likes" the taste and texture. But better-off mothers in the town would not hear of condensed milk and biscuits.[29]

In 1940s Philadelphia, where Margaret Morris had breastfed or "put out" her infants more than two hundred years earlier, a Jewish woman named Selma Cohen used bottle-feeding. The twenty-something was the daughter of Russian immigrants and the wife of a man in the scrap metal business. For her, holding and feeding was a labor of frustration. Being a modern, assimilated mother in South Philadelphia meant doing things the right way—that is, according to American books and doctors. But her son was a "horrible eater" of artificial foods, she told an interviewer; she "couldn't hold him" properly because she "had to use two hands" to ma-nipulate both bottle and supplementing spoon. The anxiety and sense of inadequacy meant that as her baby gained weight, she lost it. Instruction sheets from the neighborhood doctor explained the formulas for bottle-feeding and infant cereal.[30]

In the post–Second World War English Midlands, breastfeeding was on the decline. In the 1960s a pair of sociologists learned that perhaps 60 percent of Nottingham mothers bottle-fed at four months, 90 percent at six months. Bottle-feeding shared the "labor-saving" association of other processed foods. Starting bottle-feeding, if you birthed the infant yourself, entailed taking tablets to "get rid" of your milk. Stilbestrol and hexestrol, freely available on the National Health Service, might "swill" away what's no longer needed. The baby bottles were lightweight and un-breakable. Find the right size or shape of teat, find the right match of artificial food for the individual baby. Some propped the feed up on a pillow; bottle props were available in the United States in the 1960s, but not in Britain.[31]

"With a bottle you know exactly what you're giving them," remarked a Midlander departmental manager's wife to the sociologists, adding, "at least they can cry it out afterwards and you know they've had enough." A bricklayer's wife was glad to be able to head to the park on warm days: "You could just take a napkin and bottle with you." In places like King Edward Park, benches sat alongside children's playgrounds.[32]

Yet among these 1960s Midlanders, the labor of the bottle was not always as easy as expected. A cycle-packer's wife found that "with a bottle I feel like a woman with two left arms. I don't seem to get *near* enough." Others worried about how often to schedule feeding, as preparation of a bottle takes time and effort and you don't want to waste any. Nor were the attendant feelings straightforward: the mother who resorted early to the bottle might feel guilty for denying her child what the magazines declared was its "birthright." "Idle," "shirking," failed duty—all these were emotive charges laid by some women at the feet of others or themselves.[33]

Those Nottingham women who breastfed for a sustained time often did enjoy nursing. The long-timers were in a minority; the 1960s may have been breastfeeding's nadir, before increasing rates up to our own day. The Scots-born wife of a Polish steelworker, whose baby was born prematurely, remarked, "I don't think there's anything nicer!" A miner's wife reckoned, "You like to feel her lips to you, kind of thing." A shop manager's wife thought breastfeeding made for "an extra something between you; you feel more . . . as one, say . . . there's nothing quite so nice—when they just lay there and you feel that closeness to you." A clerk's wife noticed a difference between the child she breastfed and the child she did not. But this warm bonding did not hold for all; the wife of a university lecturer, for whom it was "just another job," found no special pleasure in it.[34]

Those who stopped or never started nursing highlighted the challenges: you are tied down to the house; your "clothes never seem clean at all, like—always wet through"; your milk was too watery, too sour, too rich, too thin, too insufficient. National Health Service hospitals prescribed breastfeeding, often with great heavy-handedness, but their simultaneous insistence on strict scheduling meant that determination and/or luck were preconditions for success.[35]

Most strikingly, compared with earlier times, embarrassment clung to the whole business. Gone were the days when a woman could casually nurse in the company of her male neighbor. You feel "a bit conscious" or "a sort of disgust for it," observed interviewees; "children . . . ask things"; they "notice more, and they think more, and they say more." If not your own unease or children's words, the problem was husbands: a machine operator was "a bit funny about breast feeding—he says it's dirty, *he* does." Public breastfeeding was a relic from a bygone era.[36]

The choice between breast and bottle meant that each version was compared and understood in light of the other. Who wants to experience "let-down" if you can avoid it? ran Hilary Jackson's logic in 1970s London, where about six in ten mothers were breastfeeding at five weeks, and about four in ten at five months. "I've been out with people for a meal and it's all leaked and you know friends have been really distressed over it. They've walked down the road and seen a kiddie, and it's started, this is the type of thing." The catering manager remembered bottle-feeding in hospital. She had said to the others: "When can you lot open the curtains?" The ward looked to her "like cowsheds, the girls in their cubicles."[37]

Or breastfeeding was "stupid" because "you can't see what the baby's having, you don't know whether it's being fed properly." Vera Abbatt preferred clearly calibrated measurement: "If you're feeding it out of a bottle you can tell exactly what he's having." The 1970s canteen worker made up her baby's bottles in the cramped quarters of two furnished rooms.[38]

Wherever the traces of the past are richest, the sensations and feelings show the greatest complexity. In the 1970s London of Hilary Jackson and Vera Abbatt, bottle-feeding might alternately feel satisfyingly convenient, guilt-inducing, and reassuringly measurable. You might be "happier . . . because . . . more relaxed." Breastfeeding might alternately feel satisfyingly convenient, pride-inducing, painful, and then enjoyable, not "physical" or "sexual," but "nice." Or there might be pure pragmatism: "I felt absolutely nothing."[39]

On this afternoon, with this refluxy baby, I am relieved that the spilled milk fell on the garden path rather than indoors and that there's no one to judge his rage. The sunshine suggests cheerful resilience. Sluice the milk off the path, turn your face into the sunlight, wipe his face, kiss him again. That's my specificity of the day.

Holding and feeding a baby can seem elemental, as fundamental a human activity as there is. But perhaps it's exactly the most elemental activities that are the most various.

In 1998 the Glaswegian poet Jackie Kay published a short story entitled "Big Milk." The opening pages are part vent, part rant, part meditation about the storyteller's breastfeeding lover and baby. "I love my lover and I love her baby," but . . .

The closing pages are part vent, part rant, part meditation on the storyteller's own birth and adoptive mothers. The birth mother had spoonfed her for two weeks and then left. The adoptive mother had "fed me milk from the dairy and Scots porridge oats and plumped my pillows at night." There are seven or eight pages narrated across a single night, and all about milk. Holding is attachment and—but—it's complicated.[40]

Kay's 1998 story marks out continuity and change, a blend of the past and late-twentieth-century novelty. Her opening line echoes the tight earlier association between nursing and infancy itself. The suckling child— who is two years old—"wasn't really a baby any more except in the mind of the mother, my lover." Meanwhile, lesbian mothers were visible, readily "out" in late-twentieth-century Scotland as elsewhere, undoing once-given associations of maternity, birth-giving, and heterosexual reproduction.

The storyteller's lover labors even in her sleep: "The baby is still suckling ferociously . . . It is beyond belief . . . No wonder the lover is drained. The baby is taking everything. Nutrients. Vitamins. The lot. She buys herself bottles and bottles of vitamins but she doesn't realize that it is all pointless; the baby has got her. The baby has moved in to occupy her, awake or asleep, night or day. My lover is a saint, pale, exhausted. She is drained dry. The hair is dry. The hair used to gleam."

Nutritive juices drained, "prejudicial" nursing updated. Echoes of sentimental, saintly devotion. Nursing, or the baby, taking "hold," perhaps too much: the "baby has got her." Now replacement vitamins. Now a detail of once-gleaming hair. Jackie Kay lends the baby's possession of his mother a wry feminist critique: "A woman is not free till her breasts are her own again. Of this I am certain. I am more certain of this than a woman's right to vote or to choose." Kay's other feminist commitments are unstated but evident. There's no embarrassment or shame about women's bodies. Sex is mentionable. Rights to choose encompass "breast or bottle" as well as reproduction.

Breastfeeding's labor appears through the storyteller's jealousy and love, through the prism of feeling. "You are worse than a man," observes Kay's lover, firm and exasperated. The lover reaches for a metaphor that makes sense only with postindustrial agriculture or with the arrival of the electric breast pump at Boots or at Sears; her "breasts are milk machines only for the baby."

In this 1998 story, the recent past casts a shadow as family history, as a maternal generation. "Skin a different colour from my mother's" explains a sidelong remark about the storyteller's infancy, imagining herself as a dark-skinned baby with a white-skinned birth-giver. Kay's own biography features a Scottish birth mother, a Nigerian father, and adoptive parents, left-wing types who worked for the Communist Party and the Campaign for Nuclear Disarmament. There was neither a foundling hospital nor wet nurses in 1950s Glasgow. An adoptive baby could be kept alive with safe purchased milk, could be beloved. The story asks if that's enough.

After so many shards from the archives, so many small and unsustained anecdotes from the first, second, and third regimes of milk, I am grateful for the humor and the immediacy of detail: "I never noticed my lover's breasts were lopsided until the baby started naming them separately . . . The left breast was enormous. The right one small and slightly cowed in the presence of a great twin. Big Milk." Or the consequences of "a two-hour-and-twenty-minute anniversary meal" out on the town. The lover's breasts were heavy and hurting. "When we got home my lover teemed up the stairs and hung over the bathroom sink. The milk spilled and spilled. She could have shot me with it there was so much." Not just pent milk: "Big gun milk."

15

Uncertainty, or a Thought Experiment

The problem is, I didn't read the small print. The short, winsome sentence that spells out that maybe this baby guide, maybe any infant manual, might not be effective for a child who is always refluxy, more or less but never dangerously unwell.

Instead, I am still shuttling between days when we muddle through and days when I walk the garden path with a how-to guide. Do this, do that. Try this, try that. These twenty-first-century guides take various positions. Do whatever works for you and your baby, and cuddle her a lot. Or don't be a "facilitator mother" who encourages bad habits; put him down. Often enough, nothing is working. And who wants to be called names? The most generous tip I get is from someone at the community center: befriend the dark-haired woman over there, called Sarah; she already has two children so she knows that you won't sleep much and that every baby is different.

Contemporary how-to guides like to assure the reader that a state of uncertainty is both common and temporary. Perhaps feeling uncertain, not knowing what to do, is akin to being interrupted or to night waking: an elusive dimension of mothering with echoes in the past. What is the history of knowing or not knowing what to do? What is the history of how-to guides?[1]

Here's a miniature thought experiment. Walk into a magnificent archive, a repository of all published books. Ask the archivist for every how-to guide or infant manual published in Britain and North America since the seventeenth century. Arrange them in order by century of publication, then alphabetize by author. Browse.

On the seventeenth-century shelves, the first will be Allestree, Richard, *The Ladies Calling* (1676). The copy is bound in brown calf leather, with the corners of the front cover and spine lightly tooled. The Oxford printer and the binder did an elegant job. Much about the book feels pretty familiar. There is a title page with the author's name. The ninety-five pages are numbered. Less familiar is the quirky range of fonts; the long "s" that looks like an italic "f." "Sucking" looks like "*fucking*." Handwriting in this particular copy inscribes "Sarah Buckridge her Book 1688." Then, as if Buckridge is young and enthused about the book, or young and enthused about her penmanship, "SB" appears in elaborate curlicue script above her full name, written again in the tiniest of inked letters.[2]

The shelf of seventeenth-century books is slim pickings, a mere armful of volumes. The archivist has had to interpret her remit generously: none of the volumes are how-to guides as such. Allestree's *The Ladies Calling* is a guide to female conduct in general—to good morals and behavior—that identifies motherhood as one stage in being a wife. Caring for a baby is a simple question of physical attention: "The very first part of their infancy is a season only for those cares which concern their bodies." There are other female conduct guides, plus medical treatises that include treatments for infant illness, and a few midwifery manuals focused mainly on pregnancy and birth. Among the four-hundred-plus pages of Jane Sharp's 1671 *The Midwives Book* are five postnatal pages "on the child" itself: loosen the arms from the swaddle around four months; crying a bit is fine because it opens and discharges the humors and helps the brain and lungs; crying a lot is dangerous—an infant will get "broken bellied by its over-straining."

The eighteenth-century section runs to many shelves. An anonymous book by an "Eminent Physician" may lay claim to being among the first how-to guides proper. Of twenty-five brisk chapters in *The Nurse's Guide: Or, the Right Method of Bringing Up Young Children* (1729), sixteen concern feeding: the "Nurse" of the book's title is a nursing woman, whether a "Mother" or a "Country-Nurse" in her employ. Teething, sleep, and exercise gain individual chapters. The shelves display that the how-to genre, composed exclusively by male physicians, takes off impressively in the second part of the century. Some of these how-to authors proclaim experience in foundling hospitals on their title pages: this is not knowledge won at home. These authors are the same kinds of medical men who left aside swaddling clothes when they sent Ann Stafford and her gear to wet nurse Margaret Collier in 1750s Chertsey. Others among them are male midwives or apothecaries or obstetrical surgeons. Most are motivated, they explain, to reduce infant mortality.[3]

These shelves pull the eye to the books that run to the most editions. That's a ready-made hint of popularity. There are ten English and four North American book spines announcing Michael Underwood's *A Treatise on the Diseases of Children*, one substantial part of which concerns the general management of infants. The first edition is 1784, in the decade that U.S. independence was recognized; the last, over on the nineteenth-century shelves, is 1848, when mainland Europe erupted again in revolution. "Intelligent parents" (Underwood's back-patting phrase) between these revolutions would do best to consult the detailed table of contents: "Meconium, what?" Turn to page 15. The late-eighteenth-century reader can treat the contents page as some kind of index. "Retention of" meconium, "an occasion for disease," 15. "Proper remedies to expel it," 18. And later: "Watching"—staying up all night—"or want of Sleep"? "On MOTION and REST" (exercise)?[4]

These officious medical manuals are interspersed with publications of lighter and more literary bent. *The Ladies Library* (first printed 1714, eight editions) suggests that a human is born as a blank slate. Education is all. The engraving opposite the title page depicts a well-dressed woman in a tall-ceilinged home library. She peruses an immense tome. Winged cherubs play, apparently without distracting, at her feet.[5]

Thus far in this browsing, the books on the shelves are printed on paper made from linen and cotton—the paper's surface is sturdy and slightly uneven. The page size is fairly uniform and typically "octavo": made by folding larger sheets of paper three ways to produce eight leaves apiece. These octavo books line up along the shelves fairly evenly. They sit similarly in the hand. Turn to the nineteenth-century books, and by the 1870s, the paper is made of wood pulp. Their innards become brittle easily and turn yellow. The typefaces are more regular, with fewer different fonts or random capitalizations. The long "*f*" for "s" has disappeared.

The nineteenth-century books fill an entire wall of shelves. Multiple editions by respectable wife-and-mother writers newly appear alongside those by doctors: Mrs. Child, Mrs. William Parkes, Mrs. L. H. Sigourney, Mrs. Warren. Their tone is sentimental, matronly, confident, and confiding. *Letters to Mothers* by Lydia Sigourney opens with a cloying, chatty scene: "You are sitting with your child in your arms. So am I. And I have never been as happy before. Have you?" *Domestic Duties* appears as a series of conversations between the experienced Mrs. B and the novice Mrs. L, staged to bring the new mother up to speed. Infancy, Mrs. B tells, requires both physical and moral education. (The nurse should never leave the infant alone, so a housemaid should bring coal, water, and meals to the nursery.) "A child of four months old should begin to spring in its nurse's arms; to crow at the objects which attract its attention, and to grasp, though with imperfect vision, at the things beyond its reach." One small late-nineteenth-century cohort of books, with such titles as *The Biography of a Baby*, is written by self-proclaimed devotees of the Child Study movement. Another is composed for the residents of city slums and printed in tiny pocket-size volumes. Also new are whole runs of specialist magazines: *The Mother's Magazine and Daughter's Friend, The Mother at Home, Babyhood.*[6]

Browsing suggests that by the late nineteenth century, sentimental advice cedes to scientism. L. Emmett Holt's *Care and Feeding of Children* is a white-coated catechism of Q&As. *At what age may a child be given a full tub bath? How should the bath be given? At what temperature . . .* The tone is brisk and precise. There are several blank pages at the back for a reader's "Memoranda." The sixth edition trumpets "constant use" as a "manual for nursery maids" and a means for mothers to know the needs of the well child. (For ill babies, a physician must always be consulted.) So: bathing, genital organs, eyes, mouth, skin, clothing, napkins, nursery, airing, weight, growth and development, dentition; thirty-odd chapters on infant feeding; and then miscellaneous topics largely concerning when a baby is unwell but not seriously ill—disturbed sleep, for example, or nervousness or colic. The symptoms of this last are a strong, hard cry, drawn-up feet, "contraction of the muscles of the face," and "signs of pain." If this continues, Holt instructs, inject the bowels with ten drops of turpentine and rub the abdomen to get rid of the wind.[7]

Finally, the twentieth-century shelves slouch with mass-market paperbacks. An interwar softcover looks to have cost little more than the price of ten cigarettes. Truby King, Benjamin Spock, Penelope Leach, and the also-rans were household names. The *Mothercraft Manual* of 1948 has diagrams crammed with little clocks and weight markers and exact directives. For a six-month-old baby like mine, Truby King's diagram assesses: "sleeps 18 hrs," weighs 16.5 pounds, "put on floor, can have cool sponge," and "first grows aware of self, plays with fingers, toes and toys, teeth may appear." In the pages of Benjamin Spock's baby books are situations that are new to the manuals. In the first edition of 1946 he casts adoption as a "special problem," alongside separated parents and working mothers. In 1998, the last edition, he adds gay and lesbian parenting.[8]

I recount choice pointers from all this bookish advice-giving to the dark-haired woman, Sarah, liking her offhand calm and trading my historian's know-how for her present-day insights. Maybe the babies are just old enough to be trusted not to wake in the early portion of their night, she suggests. Maybe we can slip out and meet halfway between our houses, take her dog out for a three-quarters-of-an-hour walk, taste a sliver of conversation, of our adult selves?

So much advice dispelled across the centuries. From slim seventeenth-century pickings to mass-market modern books, from paper made of linen and cotton to wood pulp, from medics and then from matrons, the volume of books and commentary is overwhelming. Dwell a little longer among the century-by-century shelves, and further historical patterns appear.

Whatever the century, the preeminent concern about infant care is nursing, feeding, weaning: about milk. Other routine topics are sleep and evacuations. All babies eat, sleep, and shit.

Other themes come and go. Themes that disappear: the dangers of colostrum, the merits of the cold bath, and innate infant depravity (still lingering in the 1930s). Themes that arrive: scheduling (especially from the late nineteenth century), tackling bacteria (with the valuable bacteriological insights of that same moment), and burping and winding (an apparent side effect of modern recommendations for solitary sleep, a baby being laid down flat and left alone). The merit of exposure to fresh air comes and goes and comes back.

Formal medicine has a constant voice across the centuries. Other fine-grained bodies of knowledge and disciplinary subfields—some directly related to medicine and some not—impose on the guides across time. The list across the shelves runs: midwifery, philosophy, phrenology, anatomy and physiology, psychology, pediatrics, eugenics, dietetics, behaviorism, psychoanalysis, anthropology, neuroscience. For a hundred years, phrenology studied the human mind from the assumption that different parts of the brain were correlated with different mental powers. Pediatrics emerged as a distinctive and steadfast branch of medicine in the mid-nineteenth century. Eugenics in the late nineteenth and early twentieth centuries studied how to produce fine offspring and men of supposed "high type" and later disappeared on being discredited as a racist pseudoscience. Behaviorism interpreted infant psychology from babies' observable responses to their environment. Psychoanalysis offered new models of infant development and such concepts as neurosis or oral gratification.

Each of these disciplines asked different questions and tried out different answers. Eighteenth-century philosophy: If the mind is a blank slate, how should an infant be raised and educated? Nineteenth-century eugenics: What tendencies exist in the stock from which the baby comes, and how can the white master race be protected? Twentieth-century anthropology: What are the different infant-care practices of people like the !Kung of the Kalahari Desert or the Yequana of the Amazon, and how do they compare with Western modes of care? Often, both the discipline and the underlying questions exist between the lines. Only the answers— the telling a person "how to"—appear innocently in the text.

Metaphors for babies lapped up the times. In the late eighteenth century, when Britain had a maritime empire, a baby's underside could be reminiscent of "the keel of a ship." Just as the keel is a ship's stable foundation, so a baby should be laid down to rest on his back. Sentimental nineteenth-century matrons, meanwhile, imagined babies as tender sprouts, sending out feelings and thoughts like "timid tendrils." When Edison's telephone was invented in the 1870s, the baby's nervous system was reimagined as a freshly installed telephone system. With evolutionary genetics, babies could be like monkeys—they sit "with their little feet facing each other"—and an infant's individual development taken to mimic man's Darwinian evolution from the apes. With behaviorism, babies were, rather, just like dogs, as trainable as house pets.[9]

The occasional seventeenth-century midwife and the matronly nineteenth-century voices aside, the dominant impression is what we now call mansplaining. In 1695, Henry Newcome saw himself as addressing the "inhumane and degenerate Slothfulness" of mothers. The usual eighteenth-century medical manual was "purposely adapted" to a presumptively poorer "Female comprehension." John D. West devoted two and a half pages of *Maidenhood and Motherhood* (1888) to explaining, if in a more friendly tone, exactly how to bathe an infant in tepid water. Some authorities recommend soap, some do not, he itemized: my recommendations are to steer a middle path. In the 1970s, publications of the British Medical Association intoned "never worry your head" about medical examinations of you and your baby. And: "Every woman enjoys shopping for the pram." Really?[10]

Include the matronly voices of the nineteenth century, and an equally strong impression is added of bossy delegation. Instruct the wet nurse, the monthly nurse, the lady's nurse, or the nursemaid, and when your infant starts to talk, don't let him converse with lower servants. These figures of delegated mothering disappeared, to be replaced by a mother-baby dyad, only in the late nineteenth century.

A final pattern—the one that seems most familiar from the contemporary guides—is the oscillation between stringency and spoiling, austerity and cuddling. Pushing on one side of the pendulum is: "Most Children's Constitutions are either spoiled, or at least harmed, by Cockering"—gentle rocking—"and Tenderness" (1693).[11] Or, a child cannot have too little affection (the entire behaviorist school of the early twentieth century); put your baby down and leave it alone. Pulling on the other side is Lydia Sigourney's 1848 opening scene of sitting with a child in arms or Benjamin Spock's warm 1946 recommendation to be companionable.

One afternoon a woman with a stroller glances my way, defensively interpreting the sling I wear to keep M upright as a statement on attachment parenting. "I couldn't try on clothes in town if she wasn't in the pushie."

The thought experiment is not pure fancy or fantasy. For Britain and North America, walk into the British Library in London, then add the Library of Congress in Washington, D.C., plus the Library of Canada in Ottawa, and you more or less have it in real life.

Entering the Library of Congress in Washington, the thought experiment might feel peculiarly private and small next to the shelves of formal records of politics, diplomacy, and warfare. But then not: the stakes claimed by the manuals are often remarkably imperial or nation-size, deliberately blown up and large-scale. During the mid-eighteenth century, when the Seven Years' War pitted the British Empire against the French, foundling hospital doctors, with foot soldiers and mobilization in mind, sought to improve infant mortality. Or there's Lydia Child's archetypal dedication of *The Mother's Book* to "American mothers, on whose intelligence and discretion the safety and prosperity of our republic so much depend." Once the United States became a republic whose future depended on citizens, a continuous stream of manuals reckoned that motherhood was a national bedrock. Then, in the mid-twentieth century, Benjamin Spock promised a more peaceful future. Children properly raised would "grow up to help others, strengthen human relations, and bring about world security."[12]

Or conduct the experiment on a smaller scale: head into the Library Company of Philadelphia to consult the two-hundred-strong collection of mother's manuals donated by the historian Charles Rosenberg. The archivist, James Green, might tell you how his mother's ideas about babies changed in the twinkling of an eye with the publication of Benjamin Spock's *Common Sense Book of Baby and Child Care*. His brother was born under the more austere, pre-Spock regime of 1944. Jim's babyhood was very different. ("Trust yourself," reads the library's 1946 edition of Spock. "Enjoy your baby.")[13]

Or take the discreet lift to the archives of the Kinsey Institute for Research in Sex, Gender, and Reproduction, as I try out one day. The archives are tucked away on a third floor because not everyone supports sexuality research. Entering the Kinsey, where the beige corridors are hung with erotic artwork, research on recommendations about infant care might feel starchy and prudish. Mumsy. Conventional. Heteronormative. Women are making progress, insists the Kinsey Library's copy of Mary Melendy's 1903 *Perfect Womanhood for Maidens-Wives-Mothers*, but, "we must not lose sight of her most divine and sublime mission in life—womanhood and motherhood." But another stream of commentary, such as *Concerning Children* (1900) by the progressive feminist Charlotte Perkins Gilman, takes feisty positions against convention and mainstream gender expectations. The Kinsey's late-twentieth-century lesbian materials—mainly underground publications—presume that baby-making entails not just retooling reproduction but remaking the family. The subtitle to Gillian Hanscombe's 1981 *Rocking the Cradle* reads *A Challenge in Family Living*.[14]

Of course, you can't usually take a baby into an archive, but since old books are being digitized, you can read them on a laptop at home or from a scan. You can contact an archivist and hear a story about his mom.

Every time I pick up a contemporary guide, reading makes me miserable or angry. Reading puts a "should" or "must" in front of what M is doing, raises the stakes, shows we are failing at one matter even if we are doing okay elsewhere. I lose sight of him, and of us.

Why does he never nap more than forty-five minutes? Is it mistaken to nurse him upright and then slide him dozy into the sling? While reading old infant manuals, I take absurd, extravagant delight at learning that one school of thought held that the best babies do not nap. They prefer stimulation. The delight is fleeting—M is as tired and grumpy as I am, he needs more sleep goddammit—but I like the two fingers I can raise to other schools of thought, to all the dubious certainties and grandiose stakes. Sucking, napping, and *fuck* you.

The defiant feminism I inherit from my former life is only of limited help. That particular version of feminism—that gender and sex are socially made, that declarations about femininity are only declarations, that gender and sexuality intersect with race and class—helps me perform ideology critique on the manuals. Left, right, left, right, progressive, conservative. But such critique holds neither the fatigue nor the uncertainty at bay. In the blur of the here and now, and to my dismay, I mostly want to know what to do next.

History tells that feminists have fought many battles—over the vote, or sex discrimination, or reproductive rights, or universal childcare, or whose lives matter. They have won some and lost others and forged new coalitions. In the 1970s, the most decisive victory was to blast open cultural decrees about gender and desire and to separate out femininity from maternity. A woman no longer needed to be a mother to be a "real" woman. Meanwhile, even if motherhood was an oppressive institution, mothering could be recuperated. Thank goodness. But feminists didn't tend to tell others what to do. Mentoring, yes; modeling, yes; prescription about motherhood, not so much.

M is asleep in the sling as I enter the park, walking away from the mechanical grind of a lawn mower toward a quiet stand of fir trees. The silhouetted edges of the trees shimmer in my fatigue. The trip to the archives is a thought experiment because I don't really believe in it, don't really think there's much correlation between a history of books and a history of how we know what to do, or how uncertainty gets dispelled.

For starters, there is the question of who was reading these books before the mass markets of the late twentieth century. Think of Britain in 1688, when Sarah Buckridge carefully penned her name in Allestree's *The Ladies Calling*, and the Glorious Revolution bloodlessly overthrew King James II for King William III. Less than a quarter of women were literate. Most could not afford a leather-bound book even if they did read. Most did not see themselves as "ladies," but counted themselves among the laboring classes. There were more illiterate delegated mothers—more wet nurses, more domestic servants—than literate mother-employers. On the other side of the Atlantic, meanwhile, the Native nations that dominated the North American continent had primarily oral and face-to-face means of making and handing on knowledge. Some among the encroaching white settlers may have cared about a lady's calling, but most never came across a bookstore. The slaveholders among them tried hard to deny literacy to enslaved peoples, even enshrining those attempts in law.

Two centuries later, as the sentimental guides of the nineteenth century were ceding to scientific manuals, a fifth of the United States population remained illiterate—more than 10 percent of whites and nearly 80 percent of everyone else. (This is how they got counted in surveys—white, or "Negro and other.") In the twentieth century, and even where literacy was widespread, how-to guides frequently went unread. In 1916, Mrs. Carlin, the winner of a Milwaukee baby contest, remarked, "I raised this baby to suit myself. I didn't . . . read any books." She rejected the world of printed advice. "I raised him myself and I guess I haven't made a failure of it." Even in 1956 and 1968, when Benjamin Spock was revising his bestselling guide, working-class women in Lancashire reported rarely reading a childcare guide by him or anyone else.[15]

Another issue—the arguing in my head blows through some of the fatigue—is that the guides are typically not descriptive, showing what people know and do, but overtly reformist instead. This is what people *ought* to know and do, not what they *are* doing, and what a new mother should know to do, too. The seventeenth-century midwife Jane Sharp was an early and rare exception. Her scant five pages on infant care end, rather defensively, with the admission that she is just documenting what her readers already know: "Some things may seem to be needless to tell to those that knew them before." But "they that know some things may be ignorant of other things: what one knew before, it may be another knew not: and what she knew not, another might know." Otherwise, contention and novelty are the genre's hallmark, especially among the mansplainers. Reform is the how-to guide's very first rule. Michael Underwood's 1784 *Treatise* reads "Dry-nursing, Arguments for it usually futile" or "Errors in regard to the first clothing of Infants" or "Caution against the use of Opiates" by caregivers looking for an easy ride. "The myth that children have no sexual feelings" reads one chapter title in a psychoanalytic guidebook of 1949.[16]

Finally, there is the question of the unlikely babies and improbable mother figures who waft so easily through most of the guides. *Should* glides easily into *are* or *will*. Nineteenth-century sentimental mothers were effortlessly self-denying and patient in the face of infant need. At most, cultivating infant tendrils might necessitate a little extra prayer. An early-twentieth-century "Truby King baby" was not too fat, the "happiest thing alive," and chillingly compliant. He would sleep twenty-one hours a day at one month, and eighteen hours a day at six months. The baby's voice in one Truby King manual ventriloquizes a 1944 timetable: "6am I wake. Mother changes me and feeds me; then I go back to bed and sleep." At 9:30 or 10:00 p.m. (a rare ambiguity): "Mother feeds me again, in a darkened room so as not to wake me up too much. Good night, everyone! You won't hear anything more from me till the morning." Poor blighter.[17]

So the basic question—What is the history of knowing what to do, what is the history of uncertainties felt or dispelled?—remains somewhat unanswered. It's one of the few moments in which the research fails me. It remains a thought experiment because the thinking failed. Even the arguing in my head stops.

In the woods, the massive undulating sound of frogs mating can almost be heard twice. Once, out there, hovering and swirling over the greenish marsh, and once inside your eardrum, bouncing and ricocheting, as if you've held a shell up too close. M is stunned into silence, flattened back against me. He points an arm out, vainly, toward the sound, not finding a visible origin. If you turn your head too fast, the sound ricochets harder, like slurred speech finding a sharp edge. If sleeplessness were a sound, I think, this is how it would be.

One afternoon, in pure serendipity, I encounter a reader's voice within a 1942 baby guide. It's Anderson Aldrich and Mary Aldrich's *Babies Are Human Beings*, a text on the warm and fuzzy end of the spectrum. On page 60 of a university library copy, a reader has taken out a pencil and marked a section of text with the words "Oh my how true." The person kept reading and kept adding notes. A little later, another penciled piece of marginalia adds "I got a kick out of this." Then there's another, apparently with a particular growing child in mind: "I wondered about Susan's appetite."[18]

In 1942, when *Babies Are Human Beings* became part of that university library, American college women wore short-sleeved dresses that skimmed the knee, and campuses swelled with army and navy trainees headed to war. Perhaps the book was checked out and scribbled in right away. People have been getting "a kick out of" things since before the 1940s. "Oh my" has a decidedly old-fashioned ring.

"Oh my how true," page 60. What rang startlingly true to the reader with the pencil was the "cloud of conflicting ideas" that the Aldriches reckoned a mother—an "average, young" college-educated mother in the book's terminology—might hear on having her own child. I separate out their many different sources: "The doctor's careful and scientific instructions; what both grandmothers advise; stories the nurse relates about her other baby cases; suggestions brought in to her by friends as she receives visitors from her hospital bed; and most of all, perhaps, vague memories of her own bringing up."

The Aldriches reckoned that all this created "a fog of anxious uncertainty" in a new mother's mind. The reader's exclamation is: yes!

I stare at the page. The jolt of serendipity comes less from the confirmation of one mother's uncertainty than from the spontaneous affirmation of a whole range of sources of information.

A person's own childhood, knowledgeable senior women, medical professionals, friends and peers; memory, instructions, stories, advice, suggestions: the reader's enthusiasm for this 1942 list suggests some categories for a more face-to-face history of knowing. This is the kind of knowing what to do that includes, in my present, a becoming-friend like Sarah.

Even better, the list suggests that, after all, how-to manuals are a small part of the history of knowing, if approached differently, if read as a set of proposals or attempts, many of which failed or went stale, rather than as a representation of the knowledge people actually held. Some people did read how-to books. Indeed, it is safe to say that by the late twentieth century a majority of infant caregivers probably read books. But book know-how invariably intersects and contends with many other kinds of gaining knowledge, more of which occur in person. That includes the constraints and vagaries posed by a particular baby.

Mothering is tangible, sensory, and material, I am reckoning, and it unfolds at first hand. Babies are never pure thought experiments.

16

Queer Ideas at the Clinic

Sometimes, when Sarah is not around, or when it's too late to call a friend, I read contemporary memoirs and essays, the twenty-first-century voices of those knowing and doing. Lisa Baraitser in London, Rachel Cusk in Cambridge, Anne Enright in Dublin, Lonnae O'Neal Parker in Washington, D.C., Rachel Zucker in New York, and Maggie Nelson and Sarah Manguso in Los Angeles, who think in anecdotes, too. There's a preponderance of what one reviewer calls straight-white-lady motherhood—like me, I suppose, with an immigrant twist. But not only so. (The pile will keep growing: the Chicago writer Eula Biss, the Maryland essayist Lia Purpura, the Winnipeg trans man Trevor MacDonald, the Brooklynite Rivka Galchen.) As I get absorbed, the "should" or the "must" I feel on reading contemporary guides disappears. M comes back into focus.[1]

A past memoirist comes back to mind, a contemporary of the marginalia writer on *Babies Are Human Beings*: Otis Burger, the redheaded, upper-class Manhattanite whose pseudonymously published 1949 *Diary* had so intimately and unusually described her hospital birth. The diary kept going into her child's infancy, when Otis switched from reading Grantly Dick-Read on birth to Dr. Spock on babies, when she came home from the private hospital room to her five-room apartment in the Village. It's worth returning to.

At a different pole of the 1940s there are the forthright, vibrant recollections of the black Alabaman midwife Onnie Lee Logan. Voices like hers are remarkably unusual in the archives. But in 1989 she recounted an oral autobiography that was ushered into print under the title *Motherwit* by a well-connected Harvard graduate. ("I know you don't understand two-thirds of it," Onnie Lee remarked to Katherine Clark about pre–civil rights Mobile, amplifying and adapting her story for the younger, white interviewer.) "Motherwit" connoted "common sense" about babies as much as about birth, as well as—for a churchwoman like her—"wisdom come from on high."[2]

So here's a method for the history of knowing, then. Take the Aldriches' list of sources of knowing what to do—memories? grandmothers? doctors and nurses? friends?—and, starting with the 1940s worlds of Otis and Onnie Lee, radiate out. Find a richer history of knowing and doing about babies, lifted off the page and into the wider living world of relationships, in which know-how is most usually made.

"Vague memories of her own bringing up"? My own infancy entailed 2:00 a.m. bottle-feeding, a stay-at-home mother, and a salesman father. "Vague memories" is about right. What fills a pause of recollection is the white scratch of a summer blanket, the backlit still of evening curtains, high words between my parents, great emotional warmth. I do know I was well loved. But I'm unsure where my own memories end and tabletop stories of infancy and childhood with my parents begin.

What I'm most struck by in retrospect is the utter absence of babies. Our family was unhitched from relatives. Infants were only elsewhere: up and away in a pram across the pavement, in a far-off vista of the library or recreation ground. There's no residual baby know-how, just the distant reverberation of a single little sister kicking my seat on the pram.

Memories of her own upbringing for a 1940s woman like Otis Burger? According to the Aldriches' *Babies Are Human Beings*, the residual impression of infancy and childhood among the college-educated classes was a loose sense "that it is wrong for babies to be mothered, loved or rocked." Babies of their generation had been raised strictly, regularly, and with minimal cuddling—"'untouched by human hands,' so to speak, and wrapped in cellophane like the boxes of crackers we buy." That characterization of the decades during and soon after the First World War is familiar from the how-to manuals. Untouched babies, packaged and unwrinkled in cribs, and left alone, are a characterization or a caricature of the guide-reading middle and upper classes of the Truby King era. "Too much emphasis cannot be placed on the necessity of establishing regular habits for the child," noted one mother.[3]

If Otis Burger had memories of her own privileged infancy and childhood in the 1920s, they did not explicitly surface as she wrote in her New York apartment. But an aunt did make her newly aware of the strict scheduling of the early twentieth century. Her first baby, the aunt recounted, adapted easily to the schedules, but the second spent most of his first year screaming in hunger. Perhaps this was the explanation, Otis wondered, for why her cousin was now so restless, so reluctant to be contained? Otis the child had been a "tomboy." Not only were there no babies to be cared for, she did not play with dolls either. What filled the apparent vacuum of knowing about babies, before her own arrived, was the odd magazine photo or a cartoon of a weary parent pacing the floor with a screaming baby.

The 1940s world of Onnie Lee Logan, and her memories, by contrast? New York, with the arrival of the United Nations and massive corporations, felt—to the well-off—like the prosperous capital of the world, but in Alabama the lingering effects of the Depression compounded a longer history of slavery and racial segregation. Black maids like Onnie Lee entered white homes only by a back or side door. Onnie Lee's childhood memories had been formed in Sweet Water, Marengo County, where she

was taught to help collect plants as remedies. A salve made from turpentine and the dripping of "fat hog meat" might be rubbed into the gums of
a teething baby. Bitterweed, a plant with a little yellow flower, was good
for summer fevers. These remedies were said initially to come "from Indian people," and they were preserved and handed on by midwives like
her mother.[4]

Poor black families of these decades were typically large compared
with the families of the white upper classes. Onnie Lee was the fourteenth
child of sixteen, so she may not have lugged many siblings around. But
there were plenty of extended family members who had small babies, and
lines between generations and households were blurry. Older folk were
strict. Childhood was a time of following or going by the rules and of becoming competent at helping out. Margaret Charles Smith, another Alabaman living a little way north in Eutaw, recalled, "I was raised to learn
a little of everything I could learn possible, because you don't know when
it's going to come around that you may have to do some of these things."
Her learning about remedies came down from local Choctaws.

Radiate out from the particular memories of Otis Burger and Onnie
Lee Logan? What memories of upbringing have later surfaced among
adult ideas? Occasional anecdotes, surfacing retrospectively in a memoir
or an interview, illuminate memories that seem to matter—particular
conditions of childhood, familiarity with babies. Such anecdotes are the
memories of memories, piecemeal fragments of the piecemeal.

"Mother carried me on her back. I was restless and she had taken me
off the cradleboard. I remember being there on mother's back." The first
recollection of a Winnebago woman, born in 1884, was of swirling water
and a woman carrying an empty cradleboard. Mountain Wolf Woman
told her adopted niece, a University of Wisconsin anthropologist, that she
and her mother and older sister were heading back from town. Together
they crossed a rapid creek. As her sister carried the unoccupied cradleboard ahead, she held up her skirt just high enough to wade through the
water. Most early memories are vague, but a single shard can be remarkably crisp-edged and precise. Mountain Wolf Woman's mother thought
she remembered Levis Creek and the empty cradleboard because of feeling scared. The anthropologist-niece thought that she remembered this

because recalling an event as early as your second year is considered by Winnebago people to be a sign of great intelligence. How that memory later shaped the grown woman's use of a cradleboard, we do not know.[5]

"I had grown up among babies and cared for them when only a child myself," recollected the white settler Maria Brown of an Ohio childhood in the 1820s and 1830s. Her mother used to leave the Amesville settlement's church and hurry home to the baby when she felt her milk "come." Relatives with children also lived in three of the house's rooms. Maria's father's early death at thirty-three prompted her mother to remarry, and the first half sister was born when she was eight: "I took entire care of her just the way I'd seen my mother take care . . . She said she had nothing to do but take the baby to nurse." Watching had led to doing. The effects on Maria's own mothering, when her son was born in 1846, were minimally useful, however: "I was hardly prepared." What may have mattered more after her son's arrival were family expectations. The growing half sister became helper in turn—usual habits in extended families on the nineteenth-century frontier.[6]

That one particular daughter should help tend her siblings, making baby care a feature of upbringing, was formalized in certain times and places. The role of deputy mother was assigned to the eldest daughter in large, comfortably well-off Victorian families. Margaret Mcewan was left to look after her five younger siblings when her parents left for their summer holidays on the Clyde coast. A paternal letter instructed her to enjoy herself, to govern her temper, and to show an example in getting up on time in the morning.[7]

Twentieth-century working-class girls in a whole variety of ethnic communities routinely recalled looking after their younger siblings: Anne Megna Dunst, born in 1905 and later a playwright, was the oldest daughter in a Sicilian American family in which she looked after the babies. "Hold your little sister while I finish my work," said her mother. Anne's memories of herself at six included being given high-button shoes and making a muslin cap for a new baby brother. The smallest sister shared her bed. Some of the babies Anne delighted in, some she did not. "Of course everybody played with babies," recalled one Mrs. Phillips, an English shopkeeper from Preston, Lancashire: "You didn't play with dolls, you played with real babies. There were so many knocking about and you were glad to get somebody to nurse for a bit." She was one of seven. In the Lancashire of her youth, gender roles were strictly demarcated. Girls acted as apprentices to their mothers, while boys were more often sent out to help on an allotment or run a shopping errand. The interviewer pressed for a label for this role: "So you were really a kind of mother's stand-in?" The reply: "I was like a little old woman."[8]

Sometimes looking after a baby felt like child's play, sometimes caring was hard work. Across the centuries of slavery, enslaved girls tended to have early experience with babies, black or white. On a North Carolina plantation of 1828, Elizabeth Keckley cared for her slaveholder's newborn when she was only four years old herself: a black child called Elizabeth tending a white baby of the same name. Her job was to rock the cradle and keep flies away from its face. The memory is tinged with violence: a fierce lashing upon letting the baby tumble to the ground.[9]

Anecdotes of caregiving seep through the memories of former slaves that were retold, and sanitized, to white interviewers in the 1930s: Mary Smith, who was seven years old when slavery ended, was left in charge of her younger siblings. She knew that a piece of fatty meat could help keep a baby quiet; her mother used to "pin a piece of fat back [meat] on my dress before she went to the fields and when the baby cried I took him up and let him suck it." A once-enslaved woman like Sylvia Witherspoon recognized the exact weight and feel of an infant: her mother would "tie the smallest baby on my back so I could play with no inconvenience." Daytime slave quarters on large antebellum plantations were filled with young black children watching over black babies.

Some valued memories of growing up around babies. In the 1970s, Cathy Cade relished knitting childhood pleasures into a lesbian adult identity: "Whole parts of me that helped and enjoyed my sister and brother are alive again. Motherhood satisfies a lot of the butch in me, or is that the dominant femme?" That in 1942 the Aldriches included childhood memory in their list of sources of knowledge surely reflected their own psychologically inflected notions of how we are formed: memories are a gateway to the psyche; the psyche shapes how we experience and act. But memories of upbringing also turn up as apprenticeship, or child's play, or trauma. Memories carry different charges and consequences. Of infancy and babies, my own memories feel thin and distant, too insubstantial even to surface as the topic of a phone conversation with my sis.[10]

"What both grandmothers advise"? The knowledge of seniors, or elders, appears in the Aldriches' phrase as the words of a relative in a nuclear family. Paternal and maternal grandmothers each offer their own advice. Pressed on to a wider canvas, the phrase invokes powerful intergenerational bonds. Senior women of all kinds—granny midwives, "the older people," "old heads"—have been repositories of know-how that got passed down.

The baby's grandmothers are largely absent from my week-to-week. M has three: One tends my frail dad far away. Another, on K's side, is a stepmother without children of her own. Another, K's mother, drives hundreds of miles for a visit and tells kind anecdotes, but is careful not to tell a daughter-in-law what to do. "He is really having a hard time, isn't he?" The empathy stirs, even transforms, my intimacy with her. Judiciously, she asks, not tells. "Is his tummy doing any better?"

One set of Otis Burger's relatives lived out in the New York suburbs, and her mother lived just a few blocks away. Knowing little of babies, Otis reported to her diary that she felt herself at a loss. Having an infant in her Manhattan apartment was a "major crisis" that she was facing without anyone really to consult. What she needed was "experienced advice, or someone I knew." Otis related to "Mother" as "Authority and the Ways of the World," but she appears in the *Diary* as more a figure of generational contrast than of valued experience. The new mother rejected rigid scheduling as hailing from a different era and found her own mother's deference to medical advice infuriating. "If I ever find I am more engrossed with the routine of caring for the baby than the baby itself, I will know I've failed," the diary remarked. Otis adopted psychoanalytic approaches—maybe the baby hated the bath because of the damp trauma of birth?—but her mother did "not believe in psychology."[11]

The occasional comment from the baby's other grandmother was not that well received, either. Otis's demand-feeding, child-centered approach meant "you must pay great attention to interpreting and observing." But this grandmother did not think the sounds a baby made were a means of communication.

These intergenerational disconnections may have been sharpened by other family dynamics, additional and unspoken cultural changes. When Otis's mother first became a parent, maternity was a dominant ideal for women, an all-encompassing identity based on mother love, self-sacrifice, and scientific advice. She had remained in an unhappy marriage, privileging duty over spontaneity in a way her daughter could not condone. Now new to the 1940s cultural mix was a toxic anti-mother mood. Philip Wylie's quickly bestselling *A Generation of Vipers* coined "momism" to capture an apparent problem with domineering, moralistic mothers. Many young white women found in the attack an acerbic and welcome critique of Victorian-style sentimentalism and prudery. Some feminists called out Wylie's flamboyant misogyny. Others discerned that inequality had forced mothers to seek inappropriate power, their lives being so narrow, so domestic.

Otis's casting and uncasting of her mother as "Authority and the Ways of the World" belonged to these changing times. In the college-educated 1940s, what a grandmother advised could easily be heard not just as outdated but as domineering, edging quickly toward excess authority about how things should work. Her mother seems to have known this. The diary reports: "Mother says, resignedly, 'Well, I could tell you about feeding schedules and give you some little knitted suits, but I understand that's all *passé* now, and the modern baby wouldn't be seen dead in a knitted suit.'"

Mainly by watching, mainly by doing, was how black Southerners of the 1940s learned mothering from their mothers. Shirley Elliott, whose first child was born in 1943 North Carolina, said to an interviewer, "Oh, I don't know much about learning, but you know, just seeing how, you know, how [Mother] fed them and changing them, you know. Just watching. 'Cause you know, mothers . . . they didn't, you know, take time to tell you." Ruth Cooper described it as, "My mother laid out the pattern for you to grow by. That was knowing how to take care of your children . . . she would tell you what to do and what not to do . . . when she had children,

I used to do a lot of taking care of them." In place of the generational contrasts of Otis Burger's world, there was continuity and kin. Observation
and action overwrote and extended memories of upbringing.[12]

In this black Southern world, being around your own mother was
complemented by the mother wit of granny midwives such as Onnie Lee.
These communally respected women knew babies as well as they knew
birth. Onnie Lee traced midwifery back through her own mother, who
had died young, and the grandmother on her father's side, who had lived
under slavery. Her Alabaman contemporary Margaret Smith traced her
know-how to the African-born grandmother who raised her: "My grandmother, who was brought to this country and sold, taught me everything
I know. She knew these things because she was a big old girl, the way she
talked, when they brought her to this country." Standard medicine, local
Native remedies, and African practices blended together in what Onnie
Lee and Margaret knew and showed. For cutting teeth, the know-how
might be to string "tread sash" around a baby's neck or to put moles' feet
upside down in a little bag around their neck. For nursing problems, "take
a comb and comb that breast down. A hair comb breaks it like you do a
cow bag." Familiar rural experience shaped understanding between midwives and breastfeeding mothers: the comb breaks the "clots, like holding the calf when you milk her, first time you milk her, feel it come down
in the titties."[13]

By the 1940s, such lay midwives' know-how had been somewhat re-
shaped by state-required training and licensing. The medical rule book
was there to be followed. As Onnie Lee later recalled to her Harvard-
trained interviewer, she knitted standard medicine into her existing
practice, "progressing out of her mind," as she put it. Onnie Lee explained
how she improvised in order to stop babies from sleeping with their parents. The training required having a baby in a bed to itself, even "if we
had to get a dresser drawer and put a pillow in it." Onnie Lee mostly got
a little pillow and mattress and put a baby in a pasteboard box, or she put
two cane-bound straight chairs together, fastened a sheet around them,
and put down a pillow as a mattress. In Eutaw, Margaret Smith more usually bucked the medical training. She knew cane-seated straight chairs;
they were good for birthing mothers to lean upon. She had been clearly

instructed that a baby should sleep "in a cardboard box with cotton around." But, she said, "I usually put the baby in the bed with the mother." Perhaps Onnie Lee was more of a rule follower, or perhaps she was guarded in talking with a young white woman: Margaret Smith's words were documented in collaboration with a black, Jamaican-born researcher.

When seniors and elders give advice, the way in which their words are heard and their actions get read by new parents depends heavily on context. Some societies presume continuity and tradition. Others expect progress or a generation gap, or they treat maternal care with skepticism. An early modern proverb held that an ounce of mother wit is worth a pound of clergy, favorably pitching maternal common sense against ministerial sermons. But "mothersome" in the 1840s meant anxious like a mother, and the verb "to mother" can mean "to look after in an *excessively* kindly way." There has been more than one way to dismiss maternal advice.[14]

"I don't know how you learn," remarked sheepherder Helen Claschee, "except by observation and listening you begin to know that some things are good and some things are bad." Helen was born in the Navajo Nation in the 1880s. As a young woman, she occupied a world in which sheepherding, hoeing, harvesting, and lambing were shared between women and men. Men also planted and cultivated, women also cooked and wove and nursed. Of mothering, Helen recalled, "The lecture simply was 'Be a good mother. Be a good provider. Think right.'" Navajo examples and words were strongest on a mother's side, as residence patterns were matrilocal: mothers and children stayed close by the *masani*, the maternal grandmother. Interdependence and reciprocity were fostered between generations, and grandmothers often provided childcare. But Helen's grandmother, Big Gap Woman, was so abusive that Helen stayed out of her way, a negative example to learn from.[15]

Grandmothers' advice carried great authority in 1950s Bethnal Green, in working-class East London. Joan Wilkins lived in Tabernacle Buildings, just around the corner from her mum's. If anything went wrong with the baby, she remarked, "I usually go round to my Mum and have a little chat." It was usual to spend the morning shopping together and maybe pop in later for tea or dinner. But that proximity and easy sharing of daily problems was changing. When young families moved out of the East End and into new housing estates such as Greenleigh, young mothers missed their mums.[16]

Grandmotherly knowledge could cross distances, shared by letter where travel or migration impeded presence. Frances Tuttle, an American missionary to China in 1903, worried that she "might not 'know what to do'" with her first baby after it arrived. Should "'hot weather babies' wear flannel?" she solicited her mother by post. Well into the twentieth century, middle-class American women like Frances tended to see birth and childcare as the most powerful of intergenerational bonds. How many little dresses should she make? Some grandmothers could be outspoken. In the New York City of 1901–02, thirty-six-year-old Annie Winsor Allen got letters from her mother suggesting that her husband should not share the bedroom with her and their newborn. "I almost wish I didn't know the details of your *squalid* living," wrote her mother, invoking middle-class expectations about separate rooms. "I never heard of such a thing except in a . . . tenement house." Fresh air, and the appropriate degree of heat in the baby's nursery, also came in for her comment.[17]

The particular savvy of granny or lay midwives was that of practice and talent, the same kind of cunning intelligence cultivated by ships' pilots or carpenters or politicians. I recollect the few pages "On the Child" in Jane Sharp's 1671 *The Midwives Book*. Sharp was documenting female know-how in an early modern world of custom and continuity, the carrying on of usual ways. Don't keep a baby awake "longer than it will," she reported, "but use means to provoke it to sleep, by rocking it in the cradle, and singing Lullabies to it." Also, "carry it often in the arms, and dance it." Don't let it "suck too much at once, but often suckle it" to help digestion. Alternate breasts when you nurse. This is as close as we can now get to the spool of information handed across seventeenth-century English generations, senior female knowledge so continuous as hardly to need unspooling into black-and-white type.[18]

Lay midwives gave out baby know-how well into the twentieth century. (They became known as "traditional" midwives whenever and wherever modern medicine and regulation reached.) Lancashire mothers, who called these white-aproned visitors "handywomen" or "missus," preferred lay to medically licensed midwives because they were friendlier and less starchy. Among Jewish and Italian immigrants to New York, as the nineteenth century turned into the twentieth on the Lower East Side, the advice of midwives drew upon long-standing ethnic traditions. Letitia Serpe, an immigrant from the Adriatic port city of Bari, recalled that the midwife wrapped her first child in swaddling "so that her legs would grow long and straight," and that babies were fed on demand.[19]

For several generations across the early twentieth century, grannies and handywomen incorporated medical hygiene into older forms of knowing, modern sterilization meeting mother wit. In the expanding 1890s London suburb of Cricklewood, where there were plenty of young married couples, the practice of the midwife Mrs. Layton incorporated ideas from local doctors. Meanwhile, women among the Issei, the first generation of Japanese immigrants to the United States, took their advice from Japanese-trained midwives who blended tradition and medical innovation. Having a midwife was *atarimae*—what is common, proper, usual, natural—and especially valuable, as young immigrants had usually left both mother and mother-in-law at home in Japan. A bold and imposing Seattle midwife such as Toku Shimomura or Sawa Beppu showed how to clean a baby properly or recommended Lysol as a good disinfectant. In immigrant communities in particular, midwives could be *the* voice of seniority.[20]

In San Miguel County, New Mexico, a place of foothills, plains, and rust-colored mountains, thousands of Hispanic American women learned from Jesusita Aragon, from the 1920s through to the 1970s. Jesusita's know-how came down through older Spanish midwives and her grandmother, as well as from a midwifery class she took in the local town. Eating beans makes for gassy breastfed babies. Wrapping a baby in a big spare handkerchief can support its neck, unless the baby wants "to move and stay out." A woman in Red River was able to nurse a baby that she had not birthed by drinking beer and "put[ting] the baby to suck" for a few days. Chamomile tea is good for a weak, sickly baby. Keep short, clean nails.[21]

"What both grandmothers advise" can encapsulate all of what's shared from one generation to the next—not just the senior know-how of a mother's mother or an aunt or an older neighbor but also the "cunning intelligence" of traditional midwives and healers. Most often, the knowing that was shared was practical and on the ground, decidedly empirical, more shown and done than spoken. I miss my mum terribly. I am the one who has chosen to live so far away. I can't blame her for the distance, but I do mind it.

"The doctor's careful and scientific instructions . . . stories the nurse relates"? In 1942 the Aldriches pictured a world in which hospitals had nurseries with "usual feeding times," and the first visit to the doctor's office was an expected event: a world in which professional expertise, including how-to guides, was utterly routine. Yet this widespread medicalization of knowing was in fact new. Even during the decades turning from the nineteenth to the twentieth century, and well after scientific how-to guides started instructing literate women with well babies to consult medical experts, quite possibly half of American women, for example, did not receive professional medical advice or care. That included the people of Onnie Lee Logan's Alabama world. Doctors and nurses, clinics and pamphlets were a late game in town, sometimes welcome, sometimes not.

The "wellness check," which brings me back to our doctor's office, originated in the second and third decades of the twentieth century. Dr. Franklin is bluff, calm, pragmatic. She soothes: some parents do find the second six months more challenging. With some babies, the sleep deprivation accumulates. Weight, length, ears, throat, tummy. Keep going with the reflux medication; let's adjust the dose to his growing size. Keep breastfeeding. She treats me as if I'm intelligent, and while we're in the office, I feel I am, too. Is this a mirror effect, I wonder, just like the mirroring we do with the baby? I stick my tongue out at him, and he sticks his own out, right back at me. He smiles, I smile.

In Otis Burger's New York, the professional expertise came in many forms. Hospital staff had taught her how to make up formula and sent her home with records of height, weight, formula, and schedule. A doctor had remarked that something was "too complicated to explain," which felt to Otis like an extension of "the patronizing attitude of many men toward women." A nurse on a home visit had an unwelcome "social-worker attitude." A "nice woman doctor," on the other hand, was helpful and supported a switch to bottle-feeding on demand—what Otis, in an unsteady mix of terms, called a "demand schedule." Meanwhile, her husband reading Dr. Spock aloud—the first edition of 1946, with its friendly iconoclasm—provoked "whoops of joy." Otis found the mechanics of care to be entirely more important than she had expected. Eventually she came to practice what she thought of as reasoned observation, an effortful dialogue with what "the books say." "Modern woman," she remarked, "is not as lost as many experts seem to think."[22]

There is a long middle-class and elite history to this kind of picking and choosing among medical expertise. A century earlier, in the 1840s, the social reformer Elizabeth Cady Stanton "read everything" she could on the subject of caring for a child. She found that "one powerful ray of light illuminated the darkness; it was the work of the Scottish phrenologist Andrew Combe on 'Infancy.'" Come the scientism of the late nineteenth century, and such picking and choosing could appear as an urgent obligation: writing to *Babyhood* magazine, one mother reckoned that "constant reading and study of such literature" was "the mother's profession." Unlike what I hear from Dr. Franklin, much of the advice came in decidedly authoritarian tones, suggesting that mothers were incapable of safely acting alone. As Otis's aunt told the story about scheduling and tears, she had asked, rhetorically, "If the doctor *told* you to do it, wouldn't you be afraid to do something different?" But obedience was not exclusively the case. In the 1930s, Marion Marks, a schoolteacher's wife from a "pretty well-situated" African American family, organized her baby's feeding according to scheduling recommendations. But she never woke a baby for a 2:00 a.m. feed: "I would never wake up a baby to feed them because to me it's silly to wake up a baby to feed it when the baby was all right. I just couldn't see it." Her doctor concurred: "Well that was marvelous . . . you should teach [the] rest of them to do that."[23]

Spock's particular brand of expertise was taken to be both comprehensive and less authoritarian than the rest. His opening line in 1946 was, "You know more than you think you do." One Oxford mother, a graduate who had her first baby in 1948, remarked, "Dr. Spock came along and that was pretty sensible." Another declared, of the late 1950s, that

"Dr. Spock was sort of the source of all knowledge then." A third echoed Otis Burger's experience remarkably directly: earlier generations had been "brought up in the old-fashioned style of you leave the baby to cry, you know the pram down the garden, it's got to learn." But she was doing it differently: Spock "was right at the forefront of thinking about child upbringing." An army wife living in Fort Leonard Wood, Missouri, thought Spock "was wonderful. Especially for a new mother away from home who doesn't have her mother to run to every time something new arises."[24]

From browsing the childcare manuals, I remember the slim late-nineteenth-century and twentieth-century maternity pamphlets aimed at the urban and rural poor, pamphlets with such titles as *Infant Care* or *The Canadian Mother and Child* that invoked clinics and social workers and public health officials. How did their target audience navigate expert medical advice?

In the heyday of the U.S. Children's Bureau, which issued *Infant Care* to some twelve million readers, ordinary women wrote hundreds of letters seeking advice from professional government employees. "People here in the mountains raise them very rough and call mine a *book* baby," wrote Mrs. H. S. of Virginia in the winter of 1917: please send advice about loose bowels. "I nurse her regularly," she elaborated in terms that echoed prescriptions in *Infant Care*, and "give her an outing every day." (Perhaps the infant is being overfed, came the reply.) From New Mexico in 1924, Mrs. N. F. asked how to keep her three-month-old baby from sucking her thumbs and fingers. "I have her hands pinned down but as soon as I unpin them she sucks them and she should have the use of her arms. I put mittens on her and she even sucks them." (Answer: put small splints of wood on the child's arms or pin elastic between the child's sleeves and the bed so she can move her arms but not reach her mouth.) Mrs. C. S. of New Jersey found her baby a puzzle despite having *Infant Care* to hand; was her formula correct? (Heed your physician, and pay no attention to other advice, which "though meant in the kindest spirit, undoubtedly can have no scientific value.")[25]

But in Onnie Lee Logan's black Alabama, public health officials and doctors were absent or ignored. There was a Maternal and Infant Clinic in the 1930s and 1940s, before the dismantling of government aid, but this was Klan country. Poor black people, she reckoned, preferred a midwife, as the clinics were run by whites. They were afraid of white doctors. In retrospect, she connected this to a history of medical experimentation on enslaved people. The Alabama Bureau of Maternal and Child Health would have concurred with Onnie Lee's assessment that their clinics did not reach much of their population. In 1944, their statistics suggest, 12 percent of women attended their clinics. When Margaret Smith of Eutaw had her babies, she drily observed, women "didn't go by what the doctor said too much, 'cause there weren't any doctors." Contemplating the situation in Alabama in 1955, a Marengo County civil rights activist spelled it out: "Blacks were permitted to hold only the menial jobs, domestic workers and common and ordinary laborers . . . In the whole state of Alabama we probably had less than five black doctors."[26]

In other communities, medical expertise did not hold a torch to older forms of knowing. In 1950s Bethnal Green, London, a Mrs. Banton compared what she knew from her mother to "the Welfare": "I take more notice of my Mum . . . She's had 8 and we're all right. Experience speaks for itself, more or less, doesn't it? If you're living near your mother, you don't really need that advice." She added: "When I was in hospital they taught me how to bath him—you're supposed to lay him out on your knees on a towel. But as soon as I got home, Mum said, 'Don't bother with doing it like that. Just put him in the water and wash him.'"[27]

M doesn't want to be laid out on anybody's knees. Now that he can sit up alone, he holds himself comically vertical, sideways-glance-catching, grinning.

"Suggestions . . . by friends"? At the community center, a woman with tight, curly brown hair is voicing a dilemma. Her kindergartner needs to be walked to the bus stop, but that's exactly the time that her baby goes down for his first nap. Can she leave the baby in his crib for ten minutes? A dad asks if there is a neighbor who can walk the kid. But most of us are new to this business and don't have much to offer. Sarah is not yet here. My usual friends, the long-standing friends, are at work and on a different daily schedule, a contrast that feels humbling even as my workplace leave ticks down.

I can hear M if he is crying from anywhere in the house and halfway down the garden, I think to myself. The street, no. But even at seven months, he wakes up if a door scratches or slams, so I've not tested that out much.

Distinguishing the particular role of friends from that of mothers and aunts, neighbors and grannies made little sense in Onnie Lee Logan's Alabama. Her world of community and family did not create a set-apart circle of peers of the same generation. Among the many women she advised over a long career, the particularity of "suggestions by friends" may have been most familiar to her racially mixed clientele in the 1970s and early 1980s. By those decades, the gains of the civil rights movement had brought rudimentary clinical care to poor black communities, and those who benefited from Onnie Lee's knowledge included young white women of the counterculture. These "white girls," suspicious of the professional diktats of doctors and nurses, found her through word of mouth from friends and peers, other hippie types with the same bell-bottom values. (The doctors did not like the competition: "When I started doing a whole lot of white girls, nice outstanding white girls, then that's when they started complaining," Onnie Lee said.)[28]

The particular category of "friends" as peers who share knowledge and experience emerges when generations, and generational change, are most markedly visible. (The notion of a generation, meaning people living at the same time and marking out youth from older cohorts, developed in the early nineteenth century.) Having friends as peers involved many in the 1940s, but not, quite, Otis Burger. She was not only a tomboy but a self-declared "lone wolf." Although she had former college roommates, attended parties, and visited a peer out in the suburbs who had baby twins—all hallmarks of generational connections—she appears not to have been the type to have close women friends to draw upon.

"It is important that members should express themselves freely in regard to their own trials, that they may sympathize together, and receive the aid of each other's experience in difficult cases," ran *Newcomb's*

Manual for Maternal Associations in 1840. The most visible history of knowing through "suggestions by friends" is surely that of mothers' clubs. Members of American evangelical "maternal associations" between the 1810s and the Civil War were just one example. Such groups shared instructions for "the government and training" of children from infancy. Many also established how-to libraries, mixing different kinds of know-how. Imagine the minds of children as easily turned this or that way, like water, ran the discussions. In Utica, New York, the constitution written by club members made explicit a sense of sibling generation, distinct from mothers, grandmothers, and aunts. Each mother should "suggest to her sister member such hints as her own experience may furnish, or circumstances seem to render necessary." Sisterhood was the favored metaphor, self-disclosure and sympathy the currency of connection.[29]

In nineteenth-century Britain, ordinary urban women met together in some numbers, usually under the auspices of middle- and upper-class patrons with a strong sense of parish responsibility. In 1890s Kilburn, in London, the usual number of club members ran into the three hundreds—a worrisomely high figure for the organizers, who wished personally to inculcate Victorian values of Christian motherhood and the sanctity of home life. More usually, London clubs met as sixty or seventy women, which must have offered plenty of opportunity for conversation among lower-class peers. Participants showed up especially often in the winter, for church halls and schoolrooms had warm fireplaces. The proceedings usually opened and closed with a prayer and lasted two or three daytime hours, while husbands were at work. The larger meetings offered childcare. Young mothers might be sent away with penny publications or extracts from improving books, as well as whatever needlework they had stitched from the discounted fabric swatches. We know neither whether the books got read nor of the conversations the women held with one another, sewing or with babies on laps. Occasional later commentary suggested that some "respectable" women left the clubs because of all the "gossip and cadging."[30]

My father, a descendant of this community, would have had his own tart opinion about the improvement books. In his healthier days, he liked to remember showing up to "improving" meetings with his socialist mother, there for the mug of hot tea and the sandwich, the hall packed with neighbors, and his mum's shoulders heaving in repressed laughter at all the do-gooding.

"We formed a club of just friends," recalled Marion Marks of 1930s Philadelphia, who helped form a club of upper-middle-class black mothers. These women, of the same age, from families of physicians and dentists, funeral directors, and teachers and business owners, were otherwise scattered to the four corners of the city. Their Tot Club "brought [the] children together." In Garfield, Wisconsin, community women ran a "Better Babies Club," with some encouragement from a county nurse.[31]

In the 1950s, a Catholic club of like-minded women became the La Leche League. Nursing was on demand, not scheduled; childrearing was a special vocation; and good mothering fostered trust and security. The feminist collective that wrote *Our Bodies, Ourselves* two decades later liked the knowledge printed in the League's *Womanly Art of Breastfeeding*, if you could get past the sickening stuff about how a woman's role was to bear and raise children. Playgroups and living cooperatives of their liberationist ilk tested out forms of mothering set determinedly against the bad old days. In mid-1970s London, Terry Slater had flashbacks to her childhood with her mum and got unwanted advice from her rather than the intuitive warmth she preferred. Learning about babies happened in Terry's housing cooperative.

Coming together among peers spelled no particular orientation about babies, no invariable stance about stringency or spoiling. But it may have stoked a distinctive, shared sense of generational moment over the continuity of handed-on tradition, of gossip and sympathy and the latest, all carried in distinctly youthful tones.[32]

Memories and white-coated experts, midwives, seniors, friends, and peers—there are several distinctive modes for a person to come to know about mothering. In any one life, or moment, they can be present or absent. They can be accepted, ignored, rejected, or adapted. They can be exceeded, as in the cunning intelligence of "traditional" midwifery. They can be institutionalized in the offices of a clinic or at a mothers' club or in a community hall. They can be channeled by new media. In the 1940s, the same Oxford readers who thumbed through Dr. Spock's index could also have listened to Donald Winnicott preach his crackly brand of "good enough mothering" on the BBC, before chatting to the landlady or heading out to a Women's Institute meeting.

The Aldriches were making a particular point about their own mid-twentieth-century moment: sources of knowledge are multiple. They must be selected among. The marginalia-scribbling mother, reading their book after 1946, could have a moment of recognition. *That's exactly it!* For the authors and for that individual mother, this generated a "cloud of confusion": a problem, a dilemma. The broader point is more neutral: knowing about babies is always syncretic. More and less deliberately, coming to know how to mother invariably entails weaving together observation, and know-how, and doing. That weaving together, the fact of the syncretism, gets propelled to the surface by generational shifts or by sharp rival claims to expertise or innovation. That's when it appears most noticeable.

As far as I can tell, there are no past times of simple tradition or purity of form. In seventeenth-century England, Jane Sharp reckoned that not all mothers did the same thing—one woman might know one thing, another might know something else. Among the early-twentieth-century Navajo, who celebrated grandmotherly knowledge, Helen Claschee found her relative to be a bad example. It's convenient to call knowledge "traditional" when it passes out of use or needs fixing in place or supplanting by expertise. Tradition is a label both of scapegoaters and celebrants. But in no time and place was knowing what to do completely a given, or uncertainty a complete absence.

At the community center, the woman with the kindergartner and the baby still has no answer to her dilemma about the school bus. The conversation has drifted elsewhere, interrupted by one person's diaper change and a baby's cry, and unsteered by my sheepish silence. The curly-haired woman is a devotee of the Dr. Sears books, but this is not the kind of help they offer. My friend Sarah arrives.

17

Back and Forth

Passing the baby back and forth. Handing the baby over and walking away for the day, the night, the season. Receiving the baby. Hearing an infant tended in the next room, or being overheard. Or not hearing the infant— cry, call out, laugh—at all. Knowing who in the household, among its immediates, is protecting the baby from the winds of ill fortune.

The first time I handed the baby over for an hour, he slid half asleep into the sling. The soft purple fabric stretched across Gaury's back. I adjusted a wrinkle. "You know exactly where we are if he's unhappy when he wakes up!" The experiment promised regular babysitting: a chance to do a spot of work, pay some bills, be a couple, feel "normal."

We know Gaury through friends who are leaving town for the year. She is a student who needs the cash, a sister of older siblings, a baby lover, a half stranger briskly made privy to my most intimate life. In 1960,

The New York Times thought babysitters were for suburban couples to head out to the movies or bowling on a Saturday night. The term was then in common use and some three decades old. The decline of domestic service after the Second World War and then the arrival of the modern teenage girl—evolving through the streetwalking Victory Girls of the early 1940s and then the bobby-soxers of the 1950s—made for one particular version of passing an infant (or older children) back and forth.[1]

Passing the baby back and forth has entailed kin and non-kin, lengths of time both short and long, mothering by other names. The first time I did it, and now again as I write at this quieted desk, I notice the exchange of feeling, the triangulation of care. The purple sling takes on the scents of Gaury, baby, and me.

In the spring of 1846, Emeline Spaulding was one among many youngish women to chance her hand at life out west. She was a former Lowell, Massachusetts, mill girl, with blue eyes and stately posture, whose new husband intended to farm on the Illinois prairie. They were joined by Emeline's sister Lucy, her younger by seven years and a fond letter writer to their family back home. On the overcrowded stagecoach, Lucy envied her sister's baby. He cried most of the way through the Allegheny Mountains, the only member of the extended family able to express his discomfort at being packed in like sardines.[2]

When employed at the Lowell factories, the two sisters had begun work at 5:00 a.m. in the summer and at daybreak in the winter, with half-hour breaks at seven and at noon. For a spell they had shared the same clattering textile machine in front of a sunset-facing window. These had been the novel rhythms, din, and hum of nineteenth-century industrial life. Once in Illinois, the two women shared a kitchen in a whitewashed cabin, the care of baby George, and a view of wheat fields, cattle, and Looking Glass Prairie, so named for its mirror-flat surface. They had exchanged what Lucy called the "half-live creature" of the factory machine for a fully alive infant. There was a rocking chair, where they got him to sleep, as well as a stained wooden table big enough for six chairs, a rag mat by the cooking stove, and a shelf for the water pail in the corner. That's more or less all there was in the room, barring the fireplace and a patch curtain hung against the one unplastered wall.

The useful younger sister played by Lucy was something of a given role, even as sentimental ideas of motherhood took hold among sufficiently well-resourced early-nineteenth-century families. People of "middling" and less fortune, admitted the author of the 1831 *Mother's Book*, cannot take on complete care of an infant: "Other cares claim a share of attention, and sisters . . . must be entrusted." Emeline's sister already knew how to play the part. At around thirteen or fourteen years of age, after many months of Lowell mill work, Lucy had been sent back to the salty coastal air of Beverly, where another married older sister had two small children who needed tending. Like Emeline, Lucy was bookish; she had read Charles Dickens's *The Old Curiosity Shop* with "the baby playing at [her] feet, or lying across [her] lap, in an unfinished room given up to sea-chests and coffee-bags and spicy foreign odors." In Illinois, she looked for a job as a rural schoolteacher: white women on the frontier were usually missionaries, teachers, or wives.

Two years later, between teaching posts, Lucy performed the same service for Emeline once again: George had died, but the next baby, Lottie, routinely turned to her aunt rather than her mother. Emeline's household had moved to Woodburn, a frontier town, where Emeline's husband had dropped farming to become a minister. The cabin had been switched for a cottage. Emeline organized the women of the small brick church into the Woodburn Congregational Sewing Society. Caroline Kirkland, a witty and incisive writer about Western life whom the young women read before their Illinois migration, reported that every woman had to be her own seamstress, as well as nurse, cook, chambermaid, waiter, and schoolmarm. Emeline was pregnant again.

Whatever letters Emeline might have written about her relationships with her babies and her younger sister have not survived. Lucy's letters to their mother and other sisters reveal most about her resulting view of the "domestic happiness" of married life. "I should like tending the babies well enough," she wrote in 1850, but when it came to washing, baking, brewing, and mending, her patience would take "French leave." The letter added, "I don't know how I could ever get along with all your cares."

Lucy Larcom never married. You can read her family correspondence in her *Life, Letters and Diary*, published in 1894, because she went on to become a well-known poet. (The male editor rushed past the factory work and the sisterly roles in favor of Lucy's religious commitments and great literary success.) Of Emeline, Lucy liked to reckon that there "never was any break in our affection."

Such scenes of extended family sharing a single household, with their female caregivers passing off a baby, prove remarkably various. Sometimes the passing goes up and down a sibling order, sometimes the passing crosses generational lines. In the Irish Catholic slums of Liverpool, in the early 1950s, the usual pattern was for a woman to take her husband home to live with her mum; rarely did the couple with an infant rent a house of their own. There were plenty of illegitimate babies, too, whose young mothers stayed on living at home. All this can be read, between the lines, from the fieldwork of a small team of social psychologists who were interested in environmental stress and personality development. Outsiders saw these Liverpudlian streets as full of delinquency and vandalism, but most families had lived there for at least two generations, and few wanted to move away.[3]

I wish I could overhear the conversations about the bread and jam and margarine that were usually out on the kitchen table, the plastic table cover needing a wipe, or how recently the chimney was swept. I wish I could gather the many unspoken presumptions that helped such extended households run: that whoever's down first in the morning lights the kitchen range, that a pot of tea stays warm in the oven. I wonder when the baby got a first taste of jam tarts or dumplings or meat and gravy. Most households had a cooked hot meal at teatime; upon whose lap was the baby sitting when she had "tastes"?

In one kitchen–living room, a Mrs. U (so recorded by the psychologists) picked up her daughter Ella when she whimpered and put out her arms to be lifted. Sometimes Mrs. U held the baby with one arm and went around with the duster in the other hand. Even though the chimney had been swept two months earlier, the wind blew smoke back into the room.

These terraced houses were originally well built, and they were kept clean, but by the 1950s they were often damp and in need of repair. Children played outside in the bombed-out gaps of the street, turning craters left by Second World War bombs into makeshift playgrounds. A pram stood in the corner of the room. Ella slept in it during the day and at night. Which woman of the house rocked the pram to help her fall asleep? Or did they leave her to cry? In some extended households the older woman became known as "Mother"—the children having heard her called this—and the birth-giver got known as "Mum" to tell them apart. Perhaps we should call this "extended mothering."

In another house, Joyce, Eunice's illegitimate baby, got a bath every day. Eunice's mother gave all the younger children baths at least three times a week, sometimes four. To do this, they had to boil water on the kitchen range and then give the baths in front of the fire. When a cake of toilet soap was thrown into a white enamel bath, the mother remarked, you could beat up the water and make it quite soapy, just as if there were soap flakes in it. Larger baths were made of tin. In another household, one young woman reported, "My mother does all the cooking for me and my children. She's a very good cook even though she's 78. I do all the washing." Given the habits of large households and shared care, I'm not surprised that the visiting social psychologists found that babies were weaned early. Propping a bottle in a pram or a bed—the habit they routinely observed—could be done by a "mum" or a "mother."

In these households, and in caring for a baby, the extended family took precedence over relations with neighbors or friends. Eunice was probably not on visiting terms with her neighbors, though she did give away the baby's outgrown clothes to a woman whose husband had walked out on her. The caregiving was flexible and knitted into other expectations about life, family, and love. In another terrace, Molly, age twenty, had an illegitimate baby to care for, but she still got to go out to the dance hall. She described herself as mad about dancing.

The psychologists diagnosed that the pattern of life in these slum streets was matrilocal, even mother-dominated, "if such a label were considered to be useful." Their fieldwork was dominated by the words of older mothers—the women whose children were fully grown or in school rather than the younger band of new, married or unmarried mums. Of the younger women's relationships with their mothers, I surmise gratitude, dependence, complicity, resentment, fear of separation, and strength. I doubt such ties were straightforward. But whatever the emotional texture, the evidence suggests that rarely did they break.

These mum-mother relationships weathered bad temper, disputes over money, and illegitimate babies. They handled usually being broke at the end of the week. The psychologists reported that the relationships foundered only if a young woman entered prostitution or married across racial lines. Unfortunately, these researchers had no interest in those local families involving parents of African or West Indian descent, so I cannot follow these discarded young women as they navigated 1950s Liverpudlian society with their biracial offspring.

In the Mexican Spanish that Gaury speaks at home, a babysitter is *niñera*. She has words in both languages. Head to the plains of northern Saskatchewan in 1988, and no Cree term for babysitter comes quickly to mind. When in that year several Cree women were interviewed about their lives between the two World Wars, one described her grandmother as "the only 'babysitter,' as they are called, that I ever knew." She was talking to another Cree woman, so the borrowing of an English term—a babysitter, "as they are called"—owed a debt to the vocabularies and expectations of nearby white Canadians. Grandmotherly care was routine, even primary, in the extended families of many twentieth-century Native nations. Sometimes a first or later child would be entirely adopted, a habit also not unusual in 1950s Liverpool.[4]

In Alberta, when Emma Minde's first child was M's age, she had been living at Hobbema for less than two years. In 1928 birchbark canoes were still in occasional use, their hulls so fragile that occupants did not wear shoes. Seaplanes had started to appear in the sky. Emma was newly married, in the Cree reservation's Roman Catholic mission, and living in the household of her husband's parents. Her main recollection was the quiet stress of an arranged marriage into a family she did not know: "At times

I had a difficult time, since I had not been used to the things they taught me, I never said anything, I was going to try to listen, I tried to please the people I now had as relatives." Younger female family members were expected to live communally. Their older counterparts gave counsel. Reticence and self-control were important Cree values.

Breastfeeding was usual, a birth mother's own task. Glecia Bear, another Plains Cree, recalled that a baby was "held while suckling, you kissed it and held it and you unbundled it" from the moss bag. (She was withering about the young women of the later twentieth century who dumped their babies on grandmothers to be fed with cow's milk or formula.) Sometimes babies were cross-fed—on the arrival of twins, for example, if a relative could not nurse both. In 1928 Emma Minde likely gathered moss for the beaded bag alongside her new mother-in-law, Mary-Ann Minde, just as she collected firewood or sewed flour bags into underclothes. Perhaps Mary-Ann Minde shook out the used moss and placed a new supply—crushed, reddish, absorbent—between the baby's legs. Or perhaps Jane Minde, Emma's husband's aunt, did so. She, too, was close at hand in Emma's childbearing years.

By 1928, sometimes the "traditional" Cree moss was replaced by cloth diapers. In winter months, Emma Minde recalled, some Cree women washed diapers inside by hand before going "outside and throw[ing] them high up to freeze." The challenge was to not get cold; laundering was sweaty work. Familial laundering at the marsh was easiest in summer months, the wet cloth thrown on willow bushes drying quickly. "There was lots of laundry when you had children," Emma said, laughing, but walking into the marsh on a hot day could feel like play. "I used to think, 'I am having a picnic.'" Did you use to take food along? asked her interviewer. "Sometimes, when we were there for a long time."

In Emma's reminiscences Mary-Ann Minde and Jane Minde both appear simply as "Mrs. Minde." They are, in Cree terminology, *nisikos*, a single word used to capture "my father's sister, my mother's brother's wife, my mother-in-law, my father-in-law's brother's wife." One of these two women may have been expected to sleep with the baby during weaning: ready with warm soup, perhaps a broth of scrapings from buffalo hide, when baby Theresa woke and searched for Emma's breast. Or perhaps that person was one of Emma's younger sisters-in-law, such as eleven-year-old Justine.

The voice of Emma's reminiscences is funnier and more confident than the shy, even silent, woman she portrayed herself as being when she lived with the two Mrs. Mindes. Emma Minde went on to raise three daughters and then a granddaughter in turn, a *nisikos* carrying forward Cree habits of multigenerational, extended mothering.

Had I been at Emma Minde's interview in 1988, I might have asked for stories about Cree ancestors or the contemporary reservations near Hobbema. Similar and long-standing traditions shaped the experiences of mothering in many Native nations. Or, drawn into a conversation, I might have raised the subject of the extended mothering in the polygamous households of seventeenth-century Miami- and Montagnais-speaking peoples, the earlier inhabitants of a similarly harsh northern climate.

Among these seventeenth-century peoples, too, new wives usually traveled to their husband's families, often at considerable distance from their own. Perhaps they also traveled in quiet trepidation. Occasional European observers tended to agree that polygamy could make for either marital harmony or strife in Native families. One of them reckoned that Indian men often married sisters because the presumption was that the women would get along better. Another noted that many men had two wives who lived in "quite harmonious manner, although not relatives." A Montagnais dictionary entry compiled by a disapproving French priest translated the sentence: "I will not marry a man who already has a wife."

Having being raised in a mix of early-twentieth-century Cree and Catholic ways, Emma Minde might have observed the pastness, the sheer unfamiliarity of seventeenth-century polygamy. Cree leaders once practiced polygamy, too. But perhaps the conversation would have pivoted, turned, to the shared caretaking that was one outcome, or perhaps even a female incentive. Holding, feeding, and tending were shared among adult women. Being able to raise many children in such a cold and forbidding climate was crucial to the strength of a household. In seventeenth-century Miami phrasing, unlike in twentieth-century Cree, "mother" and "maternal aunt" were exactly the same word, a remarkable fusion of terms for an identical thing.

When I first read the term "othermothering," I need to say the word aloud to get its cadence exactly right, to find a pause between "other" and "mother" sufficiently long for the term to make sense, but not so long that they disconnect. The word sounds out into the empty house.

It's not a word from the past, but only from the end of the twentieth century. Patricia Hill Collins, the distinguished black feminist who coined it, smashed "mothers" and "others" into a single verb. She wanted to capture the full-blown mothering of others' children, to honor and to analyze habits of care unrecognized by the mainstream.[5]

I am made to think again of Alabaman Onnie Lee Logan. In the 1930s, the future midwife raised the child of her husband's daughter from an earlier marriage, from babyhood to age five. (Of the baby's birth mother and that relationship, I know nothing. I just know these facts: from birth to five.) Beyond her husband's blood ties and perhaps the impulse to love, deep historical explanation for Onnie Lee's othermothering comes from West African origins and the survival tactics of black people during and after slavery.

Imagine the enslaved Winney Jackson, eighteen years old, on the cusp of a century two hundred years before. She was a chambermaid for Anne Ogle Tayloe at Mount Airy, one of the largest plantations in Virginia, with nearly four hundred enslaved people farming wheat and corn. John Tayloe, a fourth-generation slaveholder and an energetic entrepreneur, wanted to be elected to Congress. Winney's husband, Harry, twenty years old, was their coachman.[6]

Where Anne Tayloe went, Winney Jackson went, too, as did Harry. Come the winter, that was to Annapolis and then to Washington, D.C., leaving behind Winney's first child (and later a second and a third). Winney switched the black spaces of Mount Airy—kitchen, blacksmith's, carpenter's shop, slave cabins, main-house passageways, pathways through fields—for the tight city lot and back stairs of a town house, where her movements were summoned by a bell.

The shop books, work logs, and slave inventory that reveal what we can know about Winney do not mention who took care of her infants in absentia. Perhaps by night it was her sister Phillis, a textile spinner. Perhaps by day it was one of the adult women who survived John Tayloe III's massive slave sale of 1792, when the two sisters were children.

Mid-April to mid-October, Winney lived at Mount Airy. Mid-October to mid-April, she lived in the city. Six or seven other enslaved domestic servants made the hundred-mile crossing between plantation and city twice a year. Their movements were echoed, amplified in miniature, by the hundreds of field slaves whose quarters were repeatedly moved between the eight farms strung out along thirty miles of the Rappahannock River. Families were stretched, torn, broken, sometimes repaired.

Owing to forced relocations or long hours, a mother's presence to a baby might be flimsier than the stick jutting from a cabin wall to hold a shelf or the wooden board over a storage hole in the center of the earthen floor. Hence Aunt Phillis. Hence "aunt."

Enslaved people called "aunt" those adult women who nurtured children not their own: Aunt Katy on a plantation near Fayetteville, North Carolina; an Aunt Comfort and another Aunt Katy in Maryland; an Aunt Mandy in Georgia; an Aunt Catherine in Kentucky. In *My Bondage and My Freedom*, one of the most famous slave narratives of the nineteenth century, Frederick Douglass pictures one of the Aunt Katys cutting thick slices of bread for children in the plantation kitchen and sometimes favoring her own. Douglass's mother gives Aunt Katy a fiery lecture about caring properly, even if a child had offended her, a scene he found "instructive and interesting."[7]

Othermothering looks long and meandering on the page, a lengthy verb for an activity that continues into the present. In the beginning, women in West African societies shared childrearing duties alongside agricultural tasks, extended family groups being more important than nuclear units. In the seventeenth to nineteenth centuries their enslaved descendants survived in part by extending mothering beyond kin. They made a community norm of mothering by other female kin and non-kin, redescribing who was an "aunt," which continued post-emancipation. The doing of the verb carried on past the coinage of the word "othermother" near the end of the twentieth century.

Looking out from Cincinnati in 1990, Patricia Hill Collins saw othermothering in her own African American community. White middle-class mothers, she observed, assume that mothers take almost complete responsibility for childrearing, treating it as an occupation. She reported, by contrast, what black domestic worker Sara Brooks had said about a neighbor's aid: "She kept Vivian and she didn't charge me nothing either . . . I reckon it's because we all was poor, and I guess they put their self in the place of the person they was helping." Passing back and forth, handing over, evoked hardscrabble empathy from othermothers for "blood mothers."[8]

When Gaury heads out with M on her hip, I usually walk to a corner near the back of the house. Absent bright baby plastics and cottons, the wooden desk and chair have a sepia quality. *A Room of One's Own*, Mondays, ten until twelve, and then Wednesdays during the same hours.

Virginia Woolf cared a good deal about how books get written. Motherhood, she lectured in Cambridge in the late 1920s, has its genres—the novel and nonfiction prose rather than the play or the poem—because less concentration is required for the former. I'm reckoning even less concentration: the anecdote, please.[9]

Woolf could write, and write fluently and long, not just because she was childless but because she had servants. That grants me an odd relationship to her insights. My father's aunt, so he told me before the stroke, worked as a maid for Rebecca West, one of Woolf's Bloomsbury circle. The aunt was a char, a skivvy. What my dad wanted me to know was that West's family was literary and unconventional—she and her son's father, H. G. Wells, also a writer, were not married. Like so many working-class people who lived around domestic service, my dad hated the class hierarchy bitterly but held slim pride in the family association.[10]

Woolf's voluminous diaries, if not her Cambridge lectures, reveal altercations with servants as well as affection, exasperation, and feuds.

Giving and receiving orders could be brutalizing and estranging, or exasperated and belligerent, hostile and needful, devoted, cool. Surely at least as various a range of experience accompanied the babies who were also handed over with orders in other early-twentieth-century households; surely such a range also marked earlier interactions between seventeenth- or eighteenth-century employees and employers, intimate and intermittent interactions and delegations that we can discern even less easily.

The vocabulary of domestic service was like that of cloth, a nomenclature of hard, close usage. For delegated mothers across the centuries there was nurse, nurse-girl, nursemaid, mother's help, as well as the more common maid-of-all-work, domestic, char, and skivvy. In the further rungs of service—silver not cloth—add upper nurse, lady nurse, nursery governess, and nanny. *Nursie! Mammy! Girl!* spoke one side. In reply: *Missus, mum* (short for ma'am) or, perhaps under the breath, *piker* (the 1920s American term for a mean employer).

The archetypal figure of live-in infant care in Woolf's early twentieth century was not the posh nanny, but the nurserymaid or housemaid. An Alice Fisher, say, of Lower Broughton, youngest girl in a large family, her father a joiner from London, her mother from Wales. The family Alice Fisher served were "Scots folk"—a tall, dark mother, whom she almost never saw, and a parson. In exchange for half a crown a week, Alice did what she termed "everything," which seems to have meant keeping each child clean, fed, taken to the park in the pram, bathed and washed and put to bed. Alice was interviewed in her old age, when domestic service was no longer at the heart of most Englishwomen's lives.[11]

"I never remember her getting up to them when they used to cry a bit in the night," she observed, "but when I'd say in the morning they were a bit cross she'd say well, I never heard them. They didn't want to hear them—I was getting half a crown a week and I had to do all the lot."

Half Wednesdays and Sundays after chapel were time off, the main moments of passing back and forth. Once a child could walk, Alice remembered, it might "come trotting after me." The mother "said—here that doesn't look like a very good advert for your mother—for her you see. I used to let them have a bit of—you know—scrape off sort of thing." (The food in the house was pretty dismal.) "I'd say hurry up before your mother came." What did she call you? "I don't like to tell you when kids was crying . . . I call off some bad words." Otherwise, Alice.

Across the Atlantic in those same early-twentieth-century decades, nursemaids interviewed by Martha Haygood Hall in New York, Boston, and Chicago described other scenes of passing back and forth. Most of the nursemaids were young and single. Many were immigrants fresh from Germany, Sweden, Ireland, or England. Turnover was high—every two months, every five months. Staying a year was exceptional. Hall captured the maids in unguarded vein; she was a former nursemaid turned sociology student, and she knew their world of meeting in the public park, taking meals with the other servants, being on call at night, and marcelling their hair to get the pencil-size waves just right.[12]

"We get along," "I want good feelings," "She has a grudge against me," "She likes me all right, and I think she is really as nice a lady as you would want to see anywhere" went the relations between nursemaid and mother. Kathie told Martha of "thrusts" and hurts, a mistress fuming over socks that need washing. "The mother didn't seek my advice about the children—our hours didn't coincide somehow—she was out when I was with the children and vice versa. So naturally I couldn't talk to her about the children, though I frequently wished I could. Then when she did try to help, it was a hindrance."

The German-born Lisa worked for a "Mrs. F.," who was away more than typical mothers. Mrs. F was jealous "because of the baby's love for me. He had a special way of showing his affection for me, by beating a little tattoo with his foot when I picked him up. His mother came into the nursery once, and said, 'Sometimes I envy you, having the baby so fond of you. He hasn't any special "ways" with me.' I wanted to tell her it was because she was away so much."

"I didn't get on very well with the parents," reckoned Anna, "but the baby loved me and I love him, and he would do anything for me."

In trying to capture the emotional dilemmas of these delegated mothers, and perhaps of her former self, Martha Hall borrowed a two-decade-old phrase from Virginia Woolf's acquaintance, the English poet Rupert Brooke. They were "wanderers in the middle mist," those who "cry for shadows, clutch, and cannot tell / Whether they love at all, or, loving, whom." Brooke had been thinking not of nursemaids and infants, but rather of betrayed or ambivalent or cutoff adult love. These relations were confusing, needy, and truncated.

Before this early twentieth century, the emotional tenor of passing a baby between mother and servant is largely lost to us. The wife-and-mother authors of baby manuals offer mainly prescriptions for frictionless delegation. Scenes and feelings mostly surface where delegating fails, when hands fail to go properly to the task. There's Frances Parkes's 1825 lady-mother who, on hearing a baby cry unusually long in the middle of the night, goes to the nursery and finds the nurse drunk on the floor.[13]

Or there's her 1865 counterpart, Eliza Warren, who, on heading out to give a forgotten note to the laundress, comes upon her infant son and baby carriage in a working-class yard. A gaunt pig roots haplessly about in the baby wraps. The wind is cold and cutting. Inside the house is a remarkable scene of chain delegation. Hester, the "girl," is visiting her grandmother, who makes a living looking after the children of working-class women. The scene is written to horrify elite readers: the girl is cast as a lump of cunning and seeming ignorance; Warren the lady-mother is breathless with anger; the baby trembles and goes white.

Occasionally, very occasionally, there's a glimpse from the other side, from a servant. Mary Ann Ashford, still not yet seventeen, was employed by the wife of the headwaiter at Garraway's Coffee House in London at the turn of the nineteenth century. That's the same time as Winney Jackson was waiting on Anne Tayloe in Mount Airy and Washington, D.C. Perhaps, as with Mary's last employer, the baby had particularly "taken" to her. This mother wanted Mary "to nurse the child, and do everything that was laborious." The *Life* Mary composed forty years later tells little of the actual passing back and forth, and more of the skills denied her that might have allowed her to move into better employment: "All that required any art or knowledge, she not only would not let me do, but would send me out of the way, with the little boy, while she did it herself." Nursing the child—tending, taking care of—was seemingly low on the scale of marketable know-how.[14]

Twenty-first-century evolutionary anthropologists, I already know, reckon that all caregivers become attached. Birth does not determine caring, though the blast of hormones can intoxicate; holding is the thing. In many twenty-first-century circles, healthy attachment is the fulcrum on which infant care turns. What choice is to reproduction, bonding is to care— the wished-for given, what is to be protected.

Passing our baby back and forth certainly takes a species of kind and mutual cunning, a staging of ease, with determination hovering just out of sight. Gaury plays the game exquisitely, but the stakes of second best are higher for K. Our asymmetry, forged in milk and leave, visibly rankles. We glare and silently bicker over the baby's head or, better, raise eyebrows and tilt a nod at a smooth success. Equality is elusive, winking at our attempts to have things just so for the baby, and for us.

"I hope K gets his just due," remarks an older male colleague when I mention writing this book. The comment skids, judders, behind his departing back.

About fathering and the history of baby care, we are still relatively uninformed: There has been caring about infants, for certain, but caring *for*?[15]

Caring *about* appears readily. Nineteenth-century middle-class fathers, for example, were encouraged to invest in their tender offspring. In 1860 John Wesley North, a frontier lawyer and businessman, tended not to be home with his wife and sister much, but Ann North wrote of their eight-month-old daughter, "As soon as her father comes in the house, she begins to spring, reach towards him; laugh, squeal, and halloo 'bra!, bra!'"

Caring *for*? As far as I know, there is a single seventeenth-century image of a father holding a baby, one that requires looking to Amsterdam, 1661. It's clearly nighttime, and winter. Firelight glows across wooden flooring, the legs of a wicker-bottomed chair, the top corner edge of the fireplace, the man's full-length bed robes, and the infant's dangled left arm. A solid chamber—wood paneling, four-poster bed, leaded windows, low cradle with blankets pulled open—is in faint shadow. The father is stepping toward the fire, pacing perhaps or approaching the light to see if something is wrong. The hold is awkward. The large baby is pulled into his left side, yes, but otherwise held away from his body.

I can't tell if the awkwardness belongs to the father or to the artist. Or perhaps the holding away is for perusal. The man looks steadily, intently, into the infant's face. Either the father is doing well enough, or the mother is too tired, unperturbed, or unwell to care; she sleeps, unmoving, beneath unruffled sheets.

My best guess is that there are rich pockets of male caring for infants, but they are stitched along broken and hidden seams of history: among the less economically secure of small nineteenth-century middle-class households, perhaps, where expectations of invested fathers—caring *about*—met an insufficiency of servants and female kin. Or where isolated necessity compelled: in rural father-and-mother homesteads, when a mother was unwell or birthing again. Or where anomaly or eccentricity allowed. In 1928 the gray-goateed, formerly muckraking journalist Lincoln Steffens, a first-time father at sixty-three, reported the pleasures of minding the baby—the "menial tasks of the cradle"—to self-respecting young men who were otherwise out to make a name for themselves.

In mid-twentieth-century Britain, where caring *for* gains the earliest hard evidence, the newspapers were full of discussion of the "family man": the proud father who pushed the pram on a Sunday morning while his counterpart, the loving mother, got on with cooking the lunch. This was seen as a novelty. Ray Rochford, a father in working-class Salford, was scornful. A bloke pushing a pram was "unthinkable"; "you'd be a laughing stock." The slurs trailed: "you big Jessie" (1930s Edinburgh), "under your wife's thumb" (1950s Nottingham). But another man remembered pushing his daughter around the village and taking her into the local pub. "Oh yes he could change a nappy and I mean in these days that was something, because fathers didn't really take much interest," remarked a Scottish woman of her husband in the 1940s. Such involvement was helped along by shorter working days compared with those of their fathers' generation. Listeners to the popular radio program *Woman's Hour* on January 4, 1949, heard the presenter Joan Griffiths conclude a discussion: "So all fathers should learn how to fix a baby comfortably in a nappy without sticking a pin in him and learn lots of useful things like how to hold the baby the right way up." I'd need to hear a recording, not read a transcript, to know exactly the tone of that last phrase.

By the end of the twentieth century, the involved dad—still only cast as helping out, but certainly more present—was becoming widely visible. Leaflets for fathers appeared at prenatal clinics with titles like *It's Your Baby Too*. When mothers in Avon, England, were surveyed about paternal involvement—"help"—in infant care, their positive answers rose from about a third for the 1950s to more than three-quarters in the 1990s. The favorite task, they itemized, was bathing the baby.

Perhaps, thinking of 1661 Amsterdam, night held its own particularities, wherever bodies lay close and more sleep was an incentive. (Or so it can seem, a little hopefully, to the mother of a big baby who craves the confection of a better night.) In the late 1830s the Massachusetts-born Alabama lawyer Lincoln Clark sat up at night with his infants when they could not sleep. Mrs. West, born to farm servants in 1921 Aberdeenshire, Scotland, agreed in a 1988 remark that a good husband "helps in the house," but: "Never in our day, never. He might rock the cradle at night but that would be all."

Or maybe the particularity of the night is wishful thinking on my part. The housemaid Alice Fisher, who worked for the thrifty Scottish parson and his dark-haired wife, went on to marry a mailman and had a one and only child. At night she'd take the wakeful baby from the crib into the bed and "put her between us. She'd go off then." About later in the night, Alice reported, "No, not him get up. She used to be in the cot at the side—she'd yell her head off."

So a best guess at rich pockets of fatherly caring *for* may be an overstatement. The past societies I research typically depended on rigid and often incompatible expectations of male and female behavior. Older children came in and out of fathers' responsibility, but babies stayed in the arms of mothers, sisters, aunts, grandmothers, and female slaves and servants. That's in the details starting in the seventeenth century, whether among West African communities, or Native American nations, or in English towns and villages.

This year, I wonder about pronouns on my syllabus. For the first time,

I add, after the pause to isolate my gender from everything else: she/her/hers. The LGBT center on campus is renaming itself LGBTQ+. But fourteen women and no men answer our carefully gender-neutral babysitting ad on the university website.

K is a historian too. In the skid of these unending releases, there's barely a moment to ask for his sense of fathering past and present. In our handing forth and back, or upon arrival in the playground after disappearing out of sight, is he a "new" father, a mothering father, or some radical or menial being with a wilder gender?

Asking who holds the baby displaces the birth-giver or mother from the pure center of many settings. Sometimes she is nudged to one side, sometimes she passes almost entirely out of the frame. The "nuclear" of family is buffered or buffeted, or explodes into a welter of other family and household forms. Hierarchies appear close at hand, or they are the tasked hand—sibling order, senior family authority, class background, racial privilege, labor relations.

On one hand, holding and nursing a particular infant does not invariably flow from birthing: see surrogacy, adoption, wet-nursing, domestic service, communal caregiving. On the other hand, until at least the mid-twentieth century, caring *for* was exclusively associated with women. Could there be any more conservative history of sex and gender?

The fact that babies could be fed by bottles, starting in the nineteenth century, failed to usher men decisively into mothering. The long century's pause between the arrival of formula and the possibility of equal parenting suggests that expectations about women and men have been more metal-plated and hard-edged than technology. It has been simpler to separate femininity from maternity, showing that women are other than mothers, than to separate out mothering from women.

And yet. Today my local hospital has a policy for when a trans man gives birth. A Winnipeg trans man can work as a La Leche League counselor. In the twenty-first-century here and now, as I stand waiting for Gaury and the baby to get back, birthing and nursing are loosening, untethering at the edges, from people called women. A new trans history layers itself onto the late-twentieth-century innovations of involved fathers and women's liberation. Definitions of sex and gender remain muddled and uncertain, in play.

Twice a week at the sepia desk, I ready myself for the return to work. Jotting, taking notes, I am always listening for the baby's return with Gaury, anticipating her taut, musical narrative of events to him, the voicing of their arrival at home, to me. *Here we are now. There's the door handle. Hold on a minute.* I notice wanting their return, my desire to stretch into research punctured and truncated, the preparation for returning to teach always incomplete.

18

Paper Flowers

At the life-point of mothering, most people, in most times and places, are working. Even the prosperous 1950s homemaker, with her first (then second, then third) infant and suburban house, was cleaning, cooking, shopping, and balancing a budget, her own mode of providing. Leisure has dominated the lives of only a few. Exclusive maternal absorption in a baby has been the situation in relatively few cases.

It bears repeating, keeping strong and simple. At the moment of becoming a mother, the life-point of mothering, most people work. What changes are just the forms of the work and their location—how and where the activities of mothering get undertaken, juggled, squeezed, enjoyed, in and around everything else.

It's a peculiar strain of contemporary guilt that fuels the much-reported tension between stay-at-home mothers and "working" mothers. That guilt cannot trickle down from much precedent: not from Native generations, nor farm women, nor enslaved peoples, nor new immigrants, nor those below the employing classes. The guilt derives, I am reckoning, from Victorian sentimental fantasies of exclusive maternity that depended on domestic servants for everything else, and from theories of mother-baby attachment that have overlooked the presence of other householders, and from rare historical periods when economic prosperity and a single family wage seemed like a norm.

The guilt is relatively unfamiliar to me. It takes a while to hear it other than individually, biographically—as a feeling idiosyncratic to this person or that person. My London grandmother scrubbed steps to earn a little extra, taking her donkey stone and water down the street. My mother worked "for the family," as she put it, the emphasis carefully placed not on career, but on providing an income. Though no women's libber, she told indignant stories about men who treated her as "just" the secretary in the company she started with my dad, stories laced with contempt for male belligerence. There just weren't reference points for *not* working, though I am hazy about when, where, and how she combined work and early childrearing.

Once some of the women from the community center start heading back to their workplaces, guilt shows as an unhappy response to short maternity leaves, unhinged weekly hours, economic recession, and employer expectations of the employee as a breadwinner with full support back at home: to a forbidding set of economic structures beyond any one person's control. Six weeks off, then a return to a forty-plus-hour week. Or a guiltily grateful two or three months. My own fast-disappearing leave—almost nine months when you add a summer to a semester—looks extremely generous by American standards, okay by British standards. I tighten my hold on my big baby.

I channel nerves and ire into historical curiosity. I look not for the pasts of maternal guilt bobbing through past prescriptions about motherhood. Nor do I look for the story of modern labor legislation or activism, the effect of nineteenth-century industrialization. Former laws and

policy debates tread too far from the short view in front of me, the sod-
den absorption in how a person managed with an infant at hand.

I look, rather, for the history of getting on with it, of working at the
life-point of mothering. I staff my imagination with the "mustn't grum-
ble" maternity of my grandmother in the Peabody buildings, London's
East End. It's hard not to romanticize a woman I never met. What I do
know is that Edith Knott left school early because her parents needed her
to earn; completed the *Times* crossword in five minutes, except where
Latin or Greek was needed; had dark hair and a short temper, and liked
her Guinness; protested against the Fascist Oswald Mosley; and loved my
dad with great intensity and flair.

I don't know whether Edith Knott would have counted what I do for
a living as "work," though I like to think my chances are in part her leg-
acy: that *Times* crossword, my dad's love of words and arguing, his approval of strong-willed daughters. Perhaps she would have shared his sneer
at middle-class ways, or at teaching and writing rather than doing.

Most of the time, unromantically, unsentimentally, there's getting on
with it. Of mothering and working—in some fashion—together.

Thus comes the moment when my rhythm stutter-steps away from that
of the baby. Suddenly, from one September day to the next, I am back "at
work." On this first morning, I nurse him in the half-light on awakening,
the early hour partly illuminated by the red numerical glow of a bedside
clock. He sinks against my body, sighing, drifting into a doze. At my
shoulder, his head rolls into the nape of my neck. At 6:20 he crab-crawls
to the door frame, looking for corners and steps.

Nine months of age. For some weeks now, the two-and-a-half-hour
gap between naps has started to give us a rhythm that more closely re-
sembles a regular adult life. That is: long enough for a spontaneous deci-
sion about what might happen next, in place of the nurse-and-go readiness
to get something done. Leisurely enough to head out for an errand and a
picnic, both, at the weekend. Now I will be teaching, and K will not; I will
be hurrying home and he will already be there. The everyday shape of his

leave from our workplace will contrast to my rhythms and habits with a younger, smaller baby.

This day I choose shoes whose laces I tie, both hands being free. My step on the pavement lands eighteen pounds more lightly, as if the road is sprung and I am a prepubescent gymnast. M usually sits against my left hip, on the heart side, so the novel symmetry initially feels lopsided. My wave hesitates, persists. His wave is plump, naive. He and K converse, one pointing the other to a different room: I turn away.

The manila folder waiting on my office desk has a set of lecture notes to be used again. It's a survey course, a grand sweep of human history. There's a distinct economic thread running through, as I recall. First there was a household economy in which "home" and "work" were the same place. Then mass markets developed, and "homework"—making goods at home for the mass marketplace—got added to the household economy. Then industries developed, factories were built, and the household split into "home" and "work": the separate workplace and all its legislation was born. Household economy. Then, homework. Then the separate workplace. Overlapping pasts, each with a distinctive context for working— and, surely, mothering.

At main issue in giving a history to mothering and working is their location in the same spot, or their separation into "home" and "workplace." The where of the baby and the where of the rest of the work. "Mothers' work in relation to childbearing," as one group of reformers wrote in appalled awe at the lives of early-twentieth-century Montana farm women.[1] "Military operations" my mate Myfanwy calls it: tin soldier on the line, making shelter, rationing out, planning offensives, trudging hillocks, noticing what worked before, getting up and doing it all over again.

In the small rural communities of seventeenth-century England, such as Odiham or Chishill or Nazeing in the southeast, feeding, cleaning, and swaddling an infant was combined with preparing food, or tending the hearth, or spinning, or boiling water, or brewing and distilling, or straining and sifting a remedy. Spinning could be done just outside, the wheel pulled into doorway or lane, to take advantage of the light. Streets were mainly female spaces in the morning, with menfolk returning from the fields at lunchtime. Sometimes itinerant traders vended cloth and tobacco, or a neighboring farmer stopped to sell meat. Coins and barter changed hands.[2]

This is one example of the household economy at the life-point of mothering. The main work happened in and around the household. Much of that work was designated as usually female or usually male. Mothering and working were *collocated*, a coolly abstract and unfleshy verb for such close-at-hand improvisation. They happened in the same place.

Working inside an Odiham house or at a Chishill threshold did not accomplish all the necessary providing. Other tactics entailed bringing a baby along, taking a baby with: when making hay, or herding cattle, or fetching a husband from a drinking party, washing rags in a water ditch, visiting the bailiff, tending to cattle in a barn or to a swarm of honeybees, picking turnips, checking cabbage, or assisting a neighbor about to give birth. A baby had to be carried, and feet trod unpaved roads in handmade leather boots. A healthy big baby who can totter, like mine now, surely struggled to be put down, to explore mud or leaf or verge.

Leaving a baby unattended for a short while was also a habit in these seventeenth-century English villages, most usually among small or poor households—those without older children or a servant to keep an eye out. Perhaps a mother was going to the woods to fetch swine, or heading to the mill to grind a little flour, or fetching water to rinse yarn, or taking a husband his food. It was easier to leave an infant briefly unwatched when it was still small and easily immobilized.

On a cold day in these villages it was better to work an herb garden with the baby inside. Smaller babies were usually fed first and then swaddled and put to bed. On the coldest days, such a baby would be put near the hearth and the fire left as safe as possible—covering the burning matter with ash, sometimes, or placing wet logs between the fire and the baby. Improvising could extend to turning a chair upside down, tying the baby to the chair legs with its swaddling bands to form a kind of cloth frame, and placing both near the hearth. Sometimes there was a feeding horn that could be fastened onto something steady, so that a bigger baby could eat by itself.

During harvest warmth, a baby could be placed in the shade of a tree. On finer days in Nazeing, the wives of local farmers and craftsmen did their knitting on the village common. Suffolk women walked and spun, walked and spun, with a rock and a distaff in their hands. Once a week, the local market offered other provisions and foodstuffs. Agricultural laborers, male and female, who needed to work for wages or payment in kind, bought their bread and beer from local victualing houses. Arriving at both subsistence and infant nurture was hard for them: wages were too low even to support a single child, and many ended up on poor relief.

The homesteaders of early-twentieth-century Nebraska or Montana might have recognized some dimensions of this household enterprise. But life in homesteading Nebraska was more isolated than on seventeenth-century Nazeing Common. A Nebraskan farmwife juggled a baby with milking and churning to make butter, the care of poultry and the kitchen garden, and the gathering of whortleberries and cranberries. There was plenty of outside labor, too: planting, weeding, cultivating, haying, and harvesting. Some also took care of large numbers of livestock. Travel by wagon into town afforded fewer options than walking to an early modern English common or market. There was nowhere for a woman and her baby to be. Pool hall, saloon, post office, blacksmith's shops, these were male spaces.[3]

What dominated the logistics of providing for her similarly isolated contemporaries in Montana or Colorado was the distance from house to spring and whether or not a husband usually hauled water in barrels by team. Sometimes it was a woman's job to feed and water the livestock; sometimes that was the role of a hired hand or a husband. The summer heat challenged. A baby might be left a brief daytime while in a root cellar, as the coolest place. The trick in managing all the work, firsthand accounts suggest, was always to be the first up in the morning—a new wrinkle on the particularities of maternal sleep.

The sea tuned certain household economies to tides and wind more than to chill and sun. In pre–First World War Golspie, Scotland, a fishwife like Betty Sutherland used one foot to rock the cradle on the living room's dark flagstone floor. Flagstone was terribly cold, unlike the wood flooring underfoot in her other rooms, but this room was where cooking happened in the fireplace and where boots and oilskins trailed wet salt. The front door was usually left unlocked. The road outside tracked the shape of the shoreline, but Betty usually just walked across to her kitchen garden and the North Sea just below. Caring for the baby happened, with the help of older Fishertown relatives, alongside carrying her husband above the water to his boat in the morning's very early hours, in order to keep him dry; tucking rotting seaweed around potato roots as fertilizer; gathering cockles and mussels and baiting the husband's fishing line; preparing fish for smoking; and gathering fir cones for the fire.[4]

Betty sold the fish to local Golspie golfing hotels and to crofters each morning. The weight of a full creel, hoisted on the back, bent the body forward. The creel's rope cut into the upper arm, leaving distinctive marks. Fish were exchanged for eggs or oatmeal, perhaps kept in a wooden butter cask, or for money, the load of the creel slowly lightening. In summer, Betty trod the Golspie road in canvas shoes with rubber soles, like gym shoes. Heavier shoes were worn beneath her long skirts in the winter.

All this household labor was generally too much for a husband and wife who had no older children, so a widow or a young boy or girl from another family could be paid to help gather the bait and prepare the lines each day but Sunday.

Betty Sutherland bought tea, butter, sugar, and wheat flour in Golspie. A pram could be left outside a shop with the baby inside. Most of the rest of what was needed was provided by the household's labor: line fish like haddock, flounder, and turbot; netted fish like cod; catfish that was ugly and unsalable but tasty to eat; salt herring; potatoes, turnips, and cabbage from the garden; and eggs from the hens. Betty cooked oatcakes on a griddle suspended over the fire by a hook attached to a chimney chain. They kept fresh in a tin for several days even in sea-damp weather, at least according to the memories her son and daughter-in-law shared with a visiting anthropologist.

At my workplace, old competencies snap back into place. Grown-up greetings repeat along the corridor. Shortcuts to get things done spring familiar. Feeling qualified and able juxtaposes with squeezed time and lowered energy. I press the fatigue away from my head and into my gut to the extent that this is possible. The dilemma of mothering and the contemporary workplace, I read, is the tension between being treated equally as gender-neutral and being recognized as having particular skills. Or needs. Hurrying home from the university in the late afternoon means missing out on the good stuff—the public talks, the reading and writing groups.

With the emergence of mass markets and industrialization in the nineteenth century, "workplace" came to mean not simply the different environs where a person worked but, much less casually, a new kind of location, the premises of a company or a business, such as a factory or an office in which employees drew a salary. But for someone at the point of mothering, the more consequential nineteenth-century effect of the mass market was initially "homework." Not homework as in school exercises, but homework as in making goods for the mass market within your own four household walls. Homework contrasted with factory or office work and with housewifery. Homework added wages to a household income, the influx of cash letting a person buy manufactured goods made elsewhere.

Folding paper flowers was among the most common forms of homework in the Italian tenements of early-twentieth-century New York City. Artificial flowers were known locally as "the Italian trade." One young Italian woman with a big baby, surveyed around 1913, earned the exceptional wages of $8 to $12 a week, income equal to that of her husband, who was a porter in a saloon. Before marrying, she had learned the paper-flower trade in a factory shop, so she was fast and skilled. Her mother-in-law was on hand to do the housework and some of the baby care, leaving her free to work without interruption. The flowers she got from her contractor were made abroad and then branched or bunched in her home. "Sometimes I can make $1.50 and sometimes $3.00 a day," she calculated. Work stretched the day's length. "You can't count home work by the day, for a day is really two days sometimes, because people often work half the night."[5]

In a more typical scene among these Italian tenements, a homeworker with a single small child earned about a quarter of her household's income. The white box from the factory tipped its contents onto the table. She could sit at the table and work even while nursing. A larger baby could hold itself up, leaving both hands free. Or the homemaker could stand once the baby was back in the wooden slatted cradle. For one particular gross of 144 flowers, the least skilled detail involved picking apart the petals, then separating the stems and dipping an end of each into paste spread on a piece of board on the kitchen table. The most skilled detail was slipping the petals up the stems. A violet of three petals, one velvet and two silk, might earn six cents a gross. Rent got paid first, then food, clothing, and insurance. The white box was carried back to the factory, usually within walking distance, by its string. Getting more reliable or better-paid work might entail befriending a foreman, or avoiding the place where he did not speak your language, or swapping one contractor for another. You had to be savvy.

Neighbors conversed in Italian. Their older children fetched new boxes from the contractor. Among these New York tenements, other kinds of homework were common. Cracking open nuts. Eyeletting boots. Rolling cigars. Wrapping sweets. Sewing doll's clothes. Embroidering stems of flowers onto dress waists. Beading shirts. Crocheting bedroom slippers. Tufting bedspreads. Stitching neckties. Carding safety pins. Assembling garters. Finishing men's coats. Lace pulling. Tag stringing. Making artificial jewelry, baby bonnets, feathers, and spaghetti. Yet more kinds of homework were concentrated in different cities or regions. In the nineteenth century, palm-leaf-hat making and lace making in New England, chair caning and coverlet weaving in the southeastern United States, button making in Iowa, handkerchief making in the Chinatowns of California, cigar and sack making in London's East End, woolen tailoring in Leeds. In the twentieth century, homeworkers undertook home knitting in Vermont, assembled electronic subcomponents in central New York, and tailored raincoats in Manchester.

Homework rang changes to older family economies. An Italian immigrant mother in New York City may have grown up among the household economies of the Sicilian peasantry, raised to the labor of fetching water or washing at a lake, river, or public fountain, and of cooking, sewing, weaving, and spinning in the summer heat. The fingers on her left hand may have been protected with *cannedda* when she first learned to scythe just outside. In her New York City—or for homeworkers in Vermont or Manchester—waged and unwaged labor now intermingled in the same place, the working day stretching or contracting according to economic rhythms imposed from outside as well as from within the household.

One kind of heir to the homeworking women of the Italian tenements might be Mrs. Lee, a Chinese homeworker in the New York garment industry of the 1970s. Speaking in Cantonese, she recalled in 1989 that the restaurant earnings of the baby's father paid for only half their rent. Mrs. Lee worked at home because there was no one else on hand to take care of their child. In the 1970s, as in 1913, homework was more poorly paid than other kinds of waged income. Homework was *jyu tauh gwat*—pork neck bones, nutritious but with hardly any meat, and thus slim pickings compared with "soy sauce chicken," the Chinese garment industry slang for easy work.[6]

Mrs. Lee reported her logistics to a Southeast Asian–born scholar and activist: a babysitter was costly; she'd have only $10 a day left if she had to pay for one. At home, she remarked, if the baby was awake, "I could only do auxiliary work not involving the use of the sewing machine, such as turning corners and trimming. But when she slept, it was my turn. I would drive myself at full speed. All at once, I would finish my household chores and the part of sewing that would do harm to my baby." The machine stayed on for lunch (pizza, or a bowl of Chinese instant noodles, whatever she could grab). The most frustrating moments were when work had to be rushed back to the garment shop: the baby might cry in her bed, but there was no time to go to her.

The "part of the sewing that would do harm"? I am rushing to finish reading the interview even as the clock ticks to 4:50, 4:52. That Mrs. Lee's baby cried in her bed makes my breasts hurt, press with overdue milk. Empathy makes me wince, too, with a sense of better fortune. The dilemmas of working and providing are surely where the interests of those mothering can be at greatest variance, can be most materially pitted against each other.

Mrs. Lee. Perhaps she was thinking of a near accident, when her daughter was crawling on the floor. She nearly put her fingers in the sewing-machine wheel. Logistics, providing, improvising: "From that time on, whenever I had to sew when she was awake, I circle my machine and myself with an iron screen wrapped with bumper pads," to stop her from getting dangerously close. Military operations, tin soldier on the line.

The grand historical narrative about the rise of mass markets and factories appears in week ten of my current lecture series. That will be November, when the baby turns eleven months.

The lecture is titled "The Rise of the Market Economy," and illuminates that change through the story of shoe manufacturing in New England. In the seventeenth and eighteenth centuries, my notes explain, a village shoemaker made rough custom-made shoes in his kitchen or shed. Then, changes in transportation—the extension of roads, the building of canals, the laying of railway tracks—made a mass market possible for the first time. Merchants got involved, and contractors commissioned homeworkers to sew precut uppers, which were then "bottomed" with thick sole leather and pegs in an artisan's shop. These shoes could be sold farther afield than those of the village shoemaker: unlined work shoes, called brogans, were made for enslaved men and women in the South or the West Indies, for example. Finally, shoemaking was mechanized in factories, their top floors dominated by cutting and stitching and their basements crammed with heavy, steam-powered machinery. Factory chimneys stretched higher than New England church spires. An old world of households in self-sufficient communities gave way to a new world of river-strung factories; barter and local markets gave way to wages and manufactured goods.

What if I view New England shoe manufacturing from the history of working at the life-point of mothering, from my novel vantage? I reopen the historian Mary Blewett's 1988 *Men, Women, and Work*, the standard account of the production of shoes on the Eastern Seaboard.[7] At the beginning, shoemaking was a male artisanal craft, and other householders obtained their shoes through local barter—for butter, cheeses, beeswax, tallow, or cider, say, or for the promise of labor such as combing flax or wool, husking corn, or harvesting onions. The bartering and laboring often entailed female work within the household, the kind of work routinely done by those mothering infants.

Next, "homework" for the mass market was undertaken, in particular by women with children. Robert Gilman, a traveler through Lynn, Massachusetts, in 1797, remarked that the New England small town "supplies even the Southern States with women['s] shoes for exportation. The women work also." By the early nineteenth century, New Englanders had coined the term "shoebinding" for the specifically female labor of making holes in the leather upper with an awl; sewing up the back, front, or side seams; putting in the lining; binding the top edges; and sometimes adding hand-worked eyelets or designs. Shoebinding took two hands plus a new tool called the shoe clamp. The homeworker in her kitchen did not straddle a bench, like the old village shoemaker, but held the clamped shoe between her knees to free both hands for an awl and a needle. In 1836 Sophronia Guilford was given a new pair of shoe clamps by her soon-to-be husband, Charles Fisher. For homeworkers also undertaking childcare, the work could be slow. Sophronia's contemporary Hannah McIntire, who had two small children on hand, took eleven months to finish binding four lots of shoes, or about 240 pairs.

Then, in the middle of the nineteenth century, full-scale industrialization spurred a separation of male workplace from female home. Respectable female work was reconstrued not as wage earning, but as domesticity and mothering. The steam-powered shoe factory made homework far less available and largely excluded those who were mothering. Shoes could now be completed within a single building, mostly finished by unmarried and childless young women who left their homes to work ten-hour days stitching shoes by machine. Some of them organized the first national union for women in the United States, the Daughters of St. Crispin. The factories churned out new styles: a high-buttoned shoe

225

for women, for example, made of imported serge cloth that was less costly than leather, or later novelties such as a croquet shoe of black glove kid with a rosette and buckler, or a buttoned walking shoe with pink kid trim. A New England woman at the point of mothering, such as Mary Young, a cordwainer's wife who had one small child in 1860, was left taking in factory workers as boarders or accepting the decreasing and then disappearing wages of homework.

Thus the story of New England shoe manufacturing until the 1880s. Exactly what happened to those new mothers of infants in the last part of the story is hard to discern. They do not appear in Mary Blewett's account of fights and strikes over factory conditions, nor as a particular object of concern for visiting reformers. The small numbers of wives who did work in the shoe factories—during the economic depression of the 1870s, for example—tended not to board with children, suggesting that any children they had were older and being cared for elsewhere.

The times I forget my child are most strongly marked by the moments that follow, in which I suddenly think of him again. Now he is napping, hopefully, his arms flung over his head and his face turned toward the swirling blue, red, and green paisley patterns of a cotton blanket. Now he is staggering through the fallen leaves in the park, confronting the hillside, his father stooping over to grasp each hand and the pair appearing as a mess of limbs and triangles.

Holding a job in a separate workplace, for a person at the life-point of mothering? Providing, strategizing, allocating, and improvising in scenes of dislocation rather than collocation? Dislocated scenes require considerable forward or formal planning, and the navigating of particular workplace cultures. Being in the workforce has come labeled as economic necessity or as a way to earn pin money or—only very recently—as a career or vocation. I am here, so I describe it to myself, so that I can still be here in two years, in five years.

Formalized childcare came in the workplace's wake: day nurseries, day care centers, preschools, aftercare. Such institutions were initially for the "benefit of working women compelled to leave their homes and go out" to work, as one concerned philanthropist and founder put it. Among the earliest was an infant day nursery established in Kensal New Town, London, in 1873, and known locally as "the Screech." Factory reformers were appalled by the sight of malnourished babies, fretted over high infant mortality, and saw such institutions as the solution. Later, local municipalities and private companies got in on the act.[8]

An 1880s study of London mothers working in commercial power laundries found that half left their infants in the care of relatives, a third used neighbors as babysitters, and about 14 percent used a day nursery, these being few in number. Middle-class reformers and working mothers did not invariably see the relative merits of neighbors and nurseries in the same way. Childminding neighbors knew they needed to preserve a good reputation. "Getting a bad name" as a childminder was terrible in a working-class neighborhood. "Maybe somebody would look after two or three," recollected a working mother of the early twentieth century. "It had to be a reliable person. You often came to the point where it would be, 'Oh, not her' kind of thing, and this was bush telegraph in the mill, you know. The deaf-and-dumb language was fantastic."

1946, Hollywood, Los Angeles. Juanita Loveless had worked in an aircraft factory in the early and patriotic years of the Second World War. She was a single mother, the father being one of those flighty types who bragged about avoiding work in the war effort and skipped town. After her baby was born, Juanita waitressed in one restaurant and then another, a Greek steak and chophouse: "I used to take her in a basket and put her in an office while I worked." That was hard, so for a while she lived "in homes where they took care of the baby while I worked . . . It was very, very common for two or three mothers and babies to share a home." Or, as she explained to an interviewer in the 1980s, "some widowed lady had a home and would rent rooms to mothers with children, and then they'd hire a colored maid. There were so many babies then that it was like a business or a profession. People got together, rented a house and rented a housekeeper. I did that for a few years. That's how we made it." She joined the Waiter and Waitresses Union.[9]

As Juanita looked back on 1946 from the 1980s, she also observed Los Angeles in her current decade. She missed stronger unions and was not so sure that her Spock generation had made the right choices for their babies. She supported "women's lib," with qualifications, and remarked that you "almost have to have a two-family income to survive—if you're going to buy a house, have furniture and clothes, and bring up children."

1956, Brixton, London. Thelma L—the researcher does not reveal her full name—was a middle-class Methodist immigrant from Jamaica, one of a wave of Caribbean migrants encouraged to come to Britain as workers. Thelma found a job as a power machinist for a central London garment firm and made extra money dressmaking at home on the side. Her baby, Gloria, was cared for during the day—"given out," in another migrant's parlance—at the local London County Council day nursery. As many other Caribbean migrants found, the English weather was trying. Some found English people ignorant and insensitive. "You don't know where you are with them," another Brixton immigrant remarked, "unlike the States where there is a colour bar and that's that." Most hoped for a better chance at education and economic improvement, but arranging childcare was a novel challenge. Jamaican habits of othermothering contrasted with life in London: the extended "family unit" of the Caribbean versus "no grandmother or aunties, [being] completely alone," as one Brixton inhabitant put it.[10]

Nineteen sixties North Lancashire in a decade of rising living standards. For the previous generation of working-class families, grandmothers had typically helped out as paid childminders, releasing mothers for paid work and gaining a little extra cash for themselves. Now there was a rising social expectation that babies were a mother's sole responsibility. Peter Craig's, a mail-order firm in Preston, arranged a special short evening shift for mothers of small children. Other mothers found occasional cleaning work in a pub. Mrs. Burrell worked as a part-time secretary in a school. She took her first infant to the school in a pram "and it worked very well. If she was a bit grizzly they used to let me come home with her. My hours were very flexible. I could work it just the way I wanted, so I used to do most of my work when she was having her sleep." The improvising continued as the baby grew: "then she got to the crawling stage and to the toddling stage, and the headmaster then he made a big play-pen in the middle of his office; so we put her in that."[11]

Mrs. Burrell's story shoots forward into her baby's "running about stage," into what I count out as my next summer. "One day she ran out and rang the bell before it was time for end of lessons. So I thought, right, this is the time she should be going to play-school. So I used to take her to play-school and then go back and do my hours while she was there." The paradox, for part-time working women like Mrs. Burrell, was that the relative prosperity of that decade had lowered cultural acceptance of this kind of managing to make ends meet.

The conventional story of recent economic change suggests a world loosened from earlier times. The globalization of big companies has propelled deindustrialization. Increasing levels of female employment, including for mothers with babies, have become a distinctive feature of contemporary economies. A recent U.S. assessment calculates that more than half of women who have children under age one are in the workforce. (Such assessments do not count trans men caregivers or stay-at-home fathers. Nor do such statistics offer any information about othermothering or delegated mothering.) The increasing female participation in the formal waged economy has come alongside an overall improvement in living standards, yet also a rise in inequality.[12]

To this story of recent decades might be added the enduring presence of past ways, as well as a fuller definition of "working." For any one person reckoning with work at the point of mothering, the long reach of the past comes from the individual circumstances they inherit from family background and race or class, and the privileges or disadvantages (mainly, for women, disadvantages) that have accrued to gender and other identities, as well as deep-rooted and recurring dilemmas of the dislocation or collocation of working and mothering. Maybe economists might figure out how to count mothering as work as well as love? Maybe the many labors of mothering can be made visible and valuable here under late capitalism?

I overhear bits and pieces of conversation about working that recall and rework details from seventeenth-century Nazeing or late-nineteenth-century tenement New York. On her two-person farm, Arwen adjusts the patterns of an agricultural household economy, the roles divvied out now less by expectations about what men or women usually do than by preference and by skill. The schoolteacher who returned to work at the same time as I did wonders about leaving her job and maybe her nursery place to start a business at home. No overheads, and she can sell everything online, she surmises, a novel kind of "homework."

Nine months old, ten months, eleven. I phone again about nursery waiting lists, looking for the match of a place to how old the baby will be and which month K's leave will end. The workplace crèche—the term debuted in the 1970s, alongside feminist activism—is full. Within ten minutes' drive there are family day cares, in which a woman takes children into her own home; not-for-profit day cares run by churches or temples; and commercial nurseries. Their acronyms had circulated at the community center, from which I have now disappeared: BDLC, PDO, CCC. More on my mind, though, are the immediate logistics: the yellow Post-it note on my office door that announces that the occupant is busy for ten minutes, as the breast pump grinds within. Whether or not our still-refluxy baby will relent to take a bottle. How long to continue K's habit of bringing the baby to me to nurse between classes. Where to find the evening energy to prepare for the next class and to start applying for research funding again.

My steps on the seventh-floor corridor each workplace morning are quiet and even. I get absorbed. Three hours later, the baby pads in on soft scuffed leather, his giggle turning impatient. The latch onto me is so quick it is almost ferocious.

19

An Oak Dolly Tub

Fast-forward two years and cross the Atlantic. The baby, now a toddler by modern terminology, talks in short, stocky phrases just as sleep returns and the sentences in my own head start to lengthen. All done, he says. No like it. Here we are. Weaning has not lowered the intensity of his gaze in mine. The scar beneath his eye, made by unkempt newborn nails, has begun descending his cheek.

Early infancy had been a slow time warp, in which nothing quite settled. So much had happened, often too much and all at once. The baby's reflux, now long past, had sometimes taken me apart. Now mothering is starting to feel familiar, and other events intrude lightly upon the marking of time, interweaving with the baby's growth and the demands of work: moving back to England for a year of research, hoping for a second child. "It had been one of those suspended times," wrote Jane Lazarre in

The Mother Knot of 1976, "when you need to stagnate in your external life so that all of the new things which have begun to root in you can grow in peace for a while, not bothered by still newer demands."[1]

The history of mothering settles into me, too, awes and steadies and compels by turns. Those many verbs so remarkably dependent on time and place and person: conceiving, miscarrying, carrying, birthing, lying-in; and then, with a different range of characters, hearing tears, holding, seeing, smelling, being interrupted, sleeping, not sleeping, feeding, not knowing, seeking to find out, passing back and forth, providing . . .

And using stuff. For a new pregnancy is sending me on a mental journey through our North American attic. The three of us have been installed in a small terraced house in this English town for a month or so, finding our way to new routines, registering with a doctor's surgery, unpacking sabbatical research notes, scoping the surrounding streets for children my son's age. But the maternity and baby gear are boxed up across an ocean— an archaeology of baby objects, if you like, with the Moses basket left perched at the top of the attic steps. What is needed, again? And what pasts of mothering do objects reveal, given that tools shape us even as we use them?

Wherever there is mothering a baby, there is always some stuff. The avalanche of objects today is partly an effect—like almost everything else in our homes and on our persons—of the rise of mass consumption. For a hundred years, the ready-made infant clothing industry has suggested that babies require particular colors. (The first industry trade journal of 1918 recommended pink for boys. The apparent certainty of girl-pink and boy-blue did not solidify until the mid-twentieth century.) Today, the most expensive consumer objects are people substitutes that serve to replace delegated mothers. Well-resourced nineteenth-century and early-twentieth-century homes had not needed baby swings. The nursemaid carried and soothed and entertained the baby.[2]

The stuff for babies I like to think of as mothering tools. They can be clever and apt, or they can be maldesigned and unkind. Invariably these objects express and shape relationships—between a caregiver and the tool, or between a caregiver and an infant, or perhaps between mothering and other kinds of activities or desires. In 1970s London, Pauline Diggery, a market researcher, was put off from getting a papoose, a kind of soft carrier, because she wanted to "feel like a woman" again. The most revealing of the historical tools is the stuff from back when there were few written texts left behind, from where the remaining words about mothering are least in number and objects can, retrospectively, tell the most.[3]

Large mothering objects sometimes end up in museums or paintings, as the kinds of tools that are not easily crumpled or dropped or overlooked. Native cradleboards that once carried infants, sturdily securing head and limbs, became collectors' items in such places as the Smithsonian National Museum of Natural History in Washington, D.C., or the Pitt Rivers Museum near the end of my bus route.

Dakota women of the 1830s were well used to making and using all kinds of carriers, from knife sheaths to pouches for tobacco pipes. In 1835 one woman carried her infant in a red, cream, and black ornamented cradleboard. The baby faced outward, feet resting on a piece of wood attached to the bottom of the flat wooden backboard. Two wide strips of deerskin, completely covered in porcupine quillwork, wrapped her completely within a rawhide cover. The largest and coarsest quills came from a porcupine's back; they had been flattened by being worked between the teeth and then dyed. Images of Wakinyan, the Thunder Beings who controlled the weather, the clouds, and the rain, decorated the board beneath. Feathers, shells, and cones hung off the board's bow-shaped top for the baby's amusement. As tools go, this was solid, even heavy, and certainly the most substantial mothering item in Dakota use. The cradleboard pressed aesthetic creativity and spiritual welfare into the simple act of carrying.[4]

Living in permanent summer villages and smaller winter groupings along the Mississippi and Minnesota rivers, these Dakota moved frequently, relied on wild foods, and were often engaged in warfare. A cradleboard could be suspended from a bark lodge pole or from the bough of a tree while a mother cut wood, or be balanced by another child in a similar object on the other side of a pony. George Catlin, the aggressive collector and traveler who purchased the board from the anonymous Native woman in 1835, described her taking it down from her back in front of him. An oil painting from the period by Seth Eastman, a United States Army captain once married to a Dakota woman, shows a summer scene of a woman working the pale interior of a hide, her female companions close at hand and a sleeping baby leaned half upright in the cradleboard at several steps' distance. The woman's hair is loose, her hands press firmly into the tanning tool, and her gaze skates with faint, distracted concern over the infant's head.

Ojibwe people living around Lake Superior in the early twentieth century had a verb exclusively for swinging the cradleboard up onto a person's back. Once in place, a leather strap around the chest or forehead held the board against an adult's back for walking. These red and blue cradleboards, too, were solid affairs, maybe some twenty-four inches in length, with a curved piece of wood at one end for the child's feet and a hoop at right angles above the other end. The hoop was good for holding a blanket in winter or a thin cloth against the sun in the summer, as well as for attaching the leather carrying strap. A person might put a child to sleep by resting the cradleboard on her toes in front of her as she sat on the ground, rocking it by moving her feet from side to side. Ojibwe hopes that the child would grow straight and vigorous were expressed in the cradleboard's uncompromising shape and in the care taken to secure the child's arms, legs, and back.[5]

The use of a cradleboard shaped mothering as more than just a means of carrying or containment: it was an artistic object, spiritual charm, sleep aid, and instrument of character formation. The last potential use, and surely its most prosaic, was spelled out in the Navajo term for the object—literally "baby (his) diaper." Before cloth or disposable diapers became popular in the Arizona desert, older Navajo women gathered the delicate bark of the cliffrose plant for mothers to place under the infant and between its legs. Indeed, the desert cliffrose was so strongly associated with the cradleboard, or perhaps the cradleboard with the useful cliffrose, that they came to be identified by the same name.[6]

The first object I gather—I'd forgotten the trick, until necessity reminds—is a rubber band. Twisted in a figure eight between rivet and buttonhole, the band furtively holds up a shrinking pair of jeans on a pregnant waist. The minimum of what should be gathered for a baby in 1797, according to local charities in Buckingham and Essex, was three sheets, two blankets, one "leathern sheet" (presumably for the damp mess of labor), two bedgowns, two nightcaps, three bed shifts, three children's caps, three children's shirts, one cotton wrapper, one flannel wrapper, and "a sufficient quantity of small articles"—perhaps further scraps for diapers. Broth and beer caudle might also be needed for the confinement. The lying-in woman got to keep one of the charities' caps and one of the shirts and some of the flannel for the baby; the remaining stuff was washed for reuse by someone else. In London a century later, to be nice and respectable when the nurse came for the birth, a woman saved up a pair of clean sheets, clean pillowcases, and little odds and ends such as a belly binder for the baby and a back flannel made of flannelette to keep its bottom half warm. The next generation added a supply of rubber diapers to such a mental list.[7]

Perhaps there were also objects of comfort among these "small articles" of 1797 and the later little odds and ends? The smallest maternal objects to have left traces of past use tend to be means of amusing or soothing an infant, such as the bronze rattle with small bells, with a fitting for a suspension on top, that was recovered from a 1664 shipwreck off the Shetland coast. (The ship was the Dutch East Indiaman *Kennemerland*, a reminder that toys have long been objects of trade.) Less affordable versions, made in coral or silver, appear in elite portraits of the period. To seventeenth-century European understanding, coral warded off the evil eye, and the smooth, solid, even surface was good for teething.[8]

More maternal objects are lost to us: the sucking bags or sugar rags used to keep infants content, for example. A small rag from an old shirt might be filled with bread, milk, and sugar and given to a child for "nour-ishing and composing it" (observed of poor European mothers in the late eighteenth century). Or "sugar with a little bread or pounded cracker . . . tied up into a bit of linen" was "kept in the child's mouth sleeping or wak-ing" (the early-nineteenth-century United States). Or there were the small objects known alternately as comforters, dinky feeders, dormels, and titties: what contemporary Americans call pacifiers and Britons call dummies. I recollect a stubby red plastic teething device that always seemed too large for M's mouth, and his frantic fondness for chewing on the corner of my shirt or a soft toy.[9]

Most objects are lost entirely, of course. Dozens of black children were born on Oakley Plantation, Louisiana, between 1840 and 1950, but ar-chaeologists recovered no specific hints of mothering tools for infants among the shards of jam jars, doll's heads, tobacco pipes, oil lamps, and toothbrushes. The possible exception is an English "Britannia" penny with a pierced hole, lost through a gap in a cabin's sloping floorboard, which may have been given to Silvia Freeman as a birth coin in 1855. Rural black people throughout the South wore pierced coins to ward off evil. Some-times the coins were tucked into the toe-end of a shoe. At other times, they were placed around the neck of a teething baby.[10]

Cradles, cribs, and cots feature among large mothering tools, but as West-ern objects they were rarely gathered by travelers or anthropologists, and as maternal objects they were not regarded as museum-worthy. Place them next to Native cradleboards, to illuminate a comparison, and they seem most forcibly to express mothering as primarily stationary and domestic. The Western cradle rocks, and the cot or crib does not, but neither item was designed to carry a child from place to place, as Na-tive women did, or to contain an infant during communal work outside. The wooden slatted crib, in my American home, had never stirred from its corner.[11]

In the same half decade that Seth Eastman was painting the Dakota tanner, the Northumberland watercolorist John Henry Mole captured a nineteenth-century scene of a rural Englishwoman minding a baby. She is sitting by an interior hearth, hair neatly parted, knees set steadily apart, and the baby nursing on her lap. The recently vacated cradle tips away from her and toward the viewer: a substantial hooded wooden contraption, loaded with blankets, affixed to two semicircular rockers. A pair of wooden knobs or finials, smooth from use, protrude from the top of one end. This basic shape had been known since before the seventeenth century and could be carved out of wood or woven from wicker or lime twigs. The woman's gaze rests lightly on another child praying at her knee. Sun catches at a pale blanket, the woman's hair, and the children's flowing white clothes. The artist's gaze is approving and sentimental.[12]

Unlike a Native American cradleboard, which was typically crafted and decorated by female relatives, such a wooden cradle was usually made by a male joiner or carpenter or a father, the product of a differently gendered division of labor.

As with cradleboards, using such a wooden cradle first entailed swaddling a child firmly in place. Mothering was a matter of shaping and molding an infant's body. One method was to place the infant on the lap, drawing the legs out straight and then winding the swaddling bands securely around the legs, feet, and torso, stopping beneath the baby's arms. With the second band, the infant was wrapped from fingertips to shoulders, and the third, the stay cloth, bound forehead and shoulders. The result was a firm package, like a loaf of bread or a turtle in a shell. This bread-baby was next laced into place: many English and American cradles, though not that pictured by the Northumberland watercolorist, had holes or pegs along the top for lacing. If the cradle did not, the baby could be restrained by tucking the bedclothes under the mattress.

The finials protruding at the end of the cradle were useful as an aid to rocking, or perhaps for winding wool or to allow swaddling bands to air. The cradle even occasionally came with an occupation attached: wealthier households hired a "rocker" to keep the baby quiet and content. In some quarters, rocking the baby served to regularize sleep. In 1732, the minister's wife Susanna Wesley described having laid her infants in their cradle awake and rocking them to sleep, "and so they were kept rocking until it was time for them to awake." The process was described simply: "This was done to bring them to a regular course of sleeping, which at first was 3 hours in the morning, and 3 in the afternoon; afterwards 2 hours, till they needed none at all."[13]

An air of pleased nostalgia clings to John Henry Mole's watercolor portrayal: in 1852, rural England was transforming rapidly under the impact of industrialization, but the woman minding the baby seems to reflect older, implicitly simpler times. If so, however, the absence of swaddling bands, usually associated with the world of the rocking cradle, was crucial. From the middle of the eighteenth century, physicians and middle-class parents took a dim view of what became seen as the cruel and confining mistake of the swaddle; Mole's watercolor baby, fat and happy, sprawls across its mother's lap in loose-fitting clothes. One much-read nineteenth-century commentator, Mrs. Beeton, complained in the same breath about the habits of "Indian squaws" and of "our grandmothers." The Native American (or Polynesian or Inuit) habit of strapping a baby on a board, termed "backboard dressing," was cast as antithetical to modern notions of freedom and exercise. The unhealthy "mummying" of children by Englishwomen a hundred years earlier was declared even worse. Mrs. Beeton's scorn webbed through a list of sternly hyphenated swaddling cloths, the rejected tools of an earlier era: chin-stays, back-stays, body-stays, and forehead-cloths, as well as rollers, bandages, girths, and strings.[14]

Exit mothering by swaddle, and the rocking cradle disappears, too. Many immigrant and working-class communities retained the cradle. But for nineteenth-century middle-class consumers, the flat bed and then the crib or cot was the thing. Mothering meant allowing a baby its physical freedom and independence. The dilemma would be in guiding, or leaving, babies to figure out daytime sleep, and in keeping them safe.

The late-nineteenth-century crib developed high sides to stop the newly mobile child from falling out. An illustration from *At Home* magazine in 1881 shows small children in crisp white bonnets playing in their drop-sided cribs. The Acme Company promised that their crib of 1901, with its very high sides and tightly spaced spindles, was entirely accident-proof. Sometimes a hinged side meant that the child could be easily lifted in or out, a clever trick that eventually gave way to the modern form of the sliding side.

I remember the many hours of patting my eighteen-month-old back to sleep, the thin top rail of the crib pressing awkwardly against a rib as I hung over, eyes shut against the dark. Either the object, or my own design, was entirely flawed. In 1986 the poet Anne Winters reached out of her nighttime window for a metaphor, reassuring and calm, that would have made little sense to a nineteenth-century Dakota tanner or to her English peer seated by a rocking cradle, but speaks to me: hanging above the cradle like a planet, she notes, recognizes, the dark space between her and the baby. The baby is like a planet, also, one planet loving the other.[15]

So I never liked our crib much, and its absence I mind little. Our new next-door neighbor, in fact, offers to lend us a Moses basket with a separate wooden frame, an object that would evoke an earlier wicker cradle if you added a rocker, thickened the mattress, and deleted the consumer safety standards. As I project ahead, the details matter terribly, all over again. Some of my confidence, and many feelings, repose in the objects left behind in the attic, even if I am less nervous this time around. Will this new basket fit between bed and wall, and can the whole thing be propped up at an angle if the next baby is colicky? The rocking can be outsourced to a chair at the foot of the bed. Or maybe, like last time, the baby will largely end up in bed with us.

Many useful objects, such as my rubber band, do not announce themselves as maternal tools and only show themselves retrospectively by chance remarks. The "little end of a small new wax-candle" might serve in place of a coral teether (1653 London). A feather stuck on a finger with some honey might amuse, or "a basket of poppies from the garden" might make a baby "drowsy" while a housewife got her work done (noted, without further remark, in early-nineteenth-century Ohio). In the Irish countryside of the mid-twentieth century, a glass Guinness bottle might prove as adequate as something specially designed to feed a baby: "You're in the country and the [baby] bottle might fall in the fire, an open fire, and it's plastic, and you mightn't have too many of them," explained Nina Brady. "And the child is crying: you've got to feed it."[16]

Mary Siddall, a coal miner's daughter whose children were born in the 1920s, mentioned to researchers that she put her "little ones" in a dolly tub—a tallish pot that squatted on the ground on a flat bottom and was used for soaking, soaping, and rinsing clothes. Placing a child in the dolly tub while she worked helped teach him to walk: "I used to put him near the door to see the traffic passing through near the house. He'd play for hours in that tub. So that's what learnt him to walk as well, 'cause he couldn't bend down so much, you know, in a tub. I used to throw him one or two little bits of toys and his little bread tin and a paper." Sometimes dolly tubs were made of galvanized metal, sometimes wood. Mary Siddall's was oak. Her anecdote reminds me of the wooden standing frames of seventeenth-century England and the colonies, which encouraged babies to stand upright, or, better, the hollowed-out sections of tree trunk, smoothed on the inside and upper edge, that improvised the same device. The difference in the objects resides in their primary intent. Seventeenth-century standing frames were motivated by moral anxieties about crawling, which to contemporary English eyes looked worrisomely like going on all fours like an animal, a new member of mankind reduced to bestiality.[17]

Other objects have improvised a place for the baby to sleep: an "old clothes basket" with a handle (the genteel British Northerner Ellen Parker, traveling from Selby to Colne in 1817 to visit her great-aunts and not wishing to be confined to the nursery). The "family clothes basket" (a Boston tenement around 1906). A "cracker-box," though easily overbalanced, or a pallet (a 1903 Georgian farmstead). A banana box, with brown paper between the blankets for extra winter warmth (early-twentieth-century Lancashire). An old drawer, with flour bags restitched for pillow slips (South London in the same decade). A "fly-proof, kiddie-coop type of baby bed" fabricated by a Southern tenant farmer of the 1930s. A piece of stiffened leather hooked over the saddle horn, if there was no cradleboard (reported in the 1940s of the "old days" among the Gros Ventre people of Montana).[18]

Some objects allow tradition and improvisation to coexist. Cradleboards remained in use among members of the Navajo even as their homelands gave way to reservations and their ponies gave way in the later twentieth century to pickup trucks. Harried Navajo mothers of the 1970s, many living in newly nuclear families, found that a baby bottle could be tied to the hoop or propped up against it so that a baby could feed itself.[19]

With my intense, refluxy baby I had come to be typical of a certain twenty-first-century moment concerned with "natural," gentle mothering, by way of a purple fleece sling that kept him pressed softly into me—neither swaddled for a cradle or cradleboard, say, nor dressed loosely and placed independently in a crib. That fleece was at once a well-crafted tool, a middle-class consumer object and a nod, at least by the manufacturer's marketing department, to "traditional" cultures in which babies are supposedly held continually and cry far less. (The anthropologist Margaret Mead may have smiled wryly at this. Some non-Western cultures, yes; others, no. In 1972 she described the Mundugumor people of Papua, New Guinea, as actively disliking children, hanging their babies in rough-textured baskets against the wall, and scratching gratingly on basket exteriors at the sound of tears.)[20]

The first time around, in the months-long blur of keeping M upright and walking the garden path, the fleece manifested as utter, felt necessity. I'm not suspicious of that fierce need in retrospect, but I have noticed that around this town, strollers rather than slings are much more frequently the norm.

On the morning I go into labor a second time, a new friend and I are walking through a flea market outside a football stadium. Our toddlers—she has twins—are on their balance bikes with K at the park. Kate and I pick through nearly new baby clothes: newborn, one to three months, three to six months. Goodness, they are small. The cotton clothes cue developmental expectations. All-in-ones for the hapless newborn. Knee patches for the crawler. I try somewhat vainly to recall what happens at one month, at three months. Here I go again. One vendor, a grandmother fiercely jiggling a baby on her knee, talks over the head of a sullen teenage daughter to recommend sleep training. Lines of empathy tangle, the contractions pull at my attention, and a chance to chat disappears. A good omen flashes on the way out: the bright green dragon, complete with sewn-in mirror and Velcro flowers, is entirely identical to the soft toy we have at home.

20

Yard Baby, Lap Baby

Dowager babies, they were called. In small Victorian terraces like our sabbatical rental, built as "two-up, two-down" and later extended by modern bathrooms, kitchens, and middle-class mortgages, this was the term for the child displaced by an arriving newborn.

Dowager baby? A dowager widow slept alone after her husband's death, benefiting from the inheritance of some title or property. She was a dignified figure of loss and gain. A dowager baby, rather, was kicked out of its mum's bed, no longer the smallest and most dependent object of her attention. For those working-class Victorians who spoke the phrase aloud, in a time of large families, the term was surely a promise and a warning. Having a "dowager baby" meant mothering a new baby and forcing—offering—greater independence upon the older child.

My last glimpse of my displaced dowager, before I once again disappear into labor's hard work, is framed by the cat flap at Kate's house. Home from the park, M peeks through in the small triumph of arrival. Hey, Mama! I rode the whole way! My heart aches for him, for our intimacy, the feeling riding flotsam on the waves of contractions. Just yesterday I noticed that he counts from one to ten in Midwestern English, and from ten to twenty in Oxford English, all hard "t"s and taut precision. He belongs here too, now, and I am about to upend his world.

Birthing in a Victorian terraced house and then in a maternity unit run by midwives is an altered prospect. I lean over the brick garden wall, house-side and belly hidden, with feet set and face turned toward the sun. People cycle past. Early contractions, again. Maybe a birth without pain relief, again, if I am lucky. Kedi, a doula with the same brown hair as Molly and my mum, arrives in time to drive us up the hill to the maternity building: "I told you it would be quicker this time around!" She's tall, taller than I am, and built to take a person in her lap, with the kind of strength and calm I imagine to have belonged to experienced seventeenth-century midwives. But I won't need a lap: faucets to a birthing pool are being run. I don't exactly know how I climbed inside. But I do know that a newborn can be covered in white vernix, unrubbed off. That he can arrive, into my own hands, in a dozen or two dozen smooth, swift pushes. Up through the water's surface to me. I'm not even ready for birth's second ending, and here you are. Not "again" at all, but entirely fresh, with a new face on.

Several days after the baby's arrival, when we are all awake in the house, the dowager climbs on my lap, chanting and rocking: me and you, me and you, me and you. We are a four-square family, suddenly, its three older members in small shock, alliances shifted, orbiting the Moses basket.

Rambling through the gateways of speech, M's fictions are as telling of his preoccupations as his fair reports. Possibility makes for truth. Another family, the dowager tells me at the preschool door a few days later, has *five* small babies. His eyes blare open in emphasis. As we walk home, he grasps my hand and I do not need to stoop. At least I thought I didn't, but carrying a newborn in a sling shows me otherwise. We proceed at a tilt, off plumb.

The "double shuffle" is how the middle-class American Elizabeth Cabot termed it in 1861. Occasionally, just occasionally, the archives reveal this caring for a new infant alongside the growing firstborn. The counting out of a new baby's time has run alongside older children's markers as weaning or walking, or coming into speech, or reason, or memory. I pursue these pasts, the former ways in which people have talked of continuing to raise small children while adding a new.[1]

Past language offers a whole series of phrases, hints at preoccupations that suggest the variety of terms for both the double shuffle and the larger, growing child. Speakers of Assiniboine, a Native language of the North American plains, inherit a term for an infant who is prematurely weaned because of his mother's pregnancy with a new child, or for a baby (so the definition continues) who has a sibling born before a year has elapsed since his birth. This is the Assiniboine coinage for the dowager, their distinct version of sibling proximity and the effect of a new baby's arrival.[2]

Until the late nineteenth century, English speakers might describe a recently weaned child as a weanling, a term also often associated with learning to walk. The novelist who wrote the wildly popular *Lorna Doone* in 1869, who liked historical romances set in the past, imagined a character tottering into an Exmoor farmhouse like a weanling child. Weaning and walking, I have found, were also tightly associated in other cultures. Observers of Tlingit peoples in early-nineteenth-century Sitka, Alaska, remarked that "the mother nurses the infant until such time as he begins to walk" (Kyrill Khlebnikov, the manager of the Russian American Company in 1817–32), or the "child is suckled until he can walk" (Frederick Lutke, a naval captain).[3]

In the 1930s American South, the next-to-youngest child in a white tenant farm family was neither a dowager nor a weanling but a "knee-baby." The term conveys size, verticality, and a small autonomy—the baby who was too large to be swaddled, neither lying nor sitting but standing at an adult's side. There's a certain lack of ambivalence. The expected pattern, once a family was significant in size, was for the knee-baby to join with the rest in adoration of the youngest. Sometimes, a visitor remarked, knee-babies regarded the newborns as their especial property, since they were more closely associated with the mother and her new child than were the rest. When one mother was lying in after childbirth, her knee-baby pulled up a chair and sat there. He "feels proprietary rights because of this sentinel duty," the visitor recorded.[4]

Or in rural Georgia of 1946, in another turn of phraseology, a black midwife referred to one of "her" mothers with "a lap baby and a yard baby." The mother, Lou Della Garland, or Ludy, returned to live in town because she could not stay out at Poison Lake with two babies while her husband, Hal, was gone to the war. Hallelujah Garland had left just after cotton picking. The story of the lap baby, the yard baby, and Lou Della was recounted by the midwife and set down on paper by a public health nurse. Hal's old uncle stayed with mother and babies, chopping wood, tending the cow, and plowing with the mule. Lou Della got an army allotment from the government and kept up the payments on their property. "She keeps her and the babies and Foolish John [the uncle] with rations and clothes, but she doesn't waste none of her government money. And she keeps her house clean and raises a fine garden."[5]

I pause to let the phraseology come alive. The midwife describes the yard baby on a hot 1946 afternoon, playing in "the good clean garden dirt and wearing a leaf apron Lou Della made out of leaves from the chinaberry tree by the garden fence." Chinaberry leaves are lacy and dark green, with strong stems good for threading and a musky smell. The lap baby stood "in a big cotton basket set in the shade." Now and again Lou Della took the lap baby out of the basket "to rest it, and played with it and the [yard baby] a little while."

Dowager, knee-baby, yard baby, lap baby. These terminologies suggest that sibling rivalry is an expectation in many cultures—among Assiniboine speakers, the Victorian laboring classes, the Tlingit, my own—but not all. Tell that to my dowager, who races to the chair before I can sit to nurse, or tries to wheedle his backside next to mine as I sit with the new baby in my arms. The dowager tries to cover the newborn in stickers; he pats the baby's head and looks for some kind of collegial reply; he protests in the night, hearing the cries, then wants to kiss the baby better. V. He says the newborn's name softly, and I know we have chosen the right one.

The newborn? He is steady and open and content, that's my initial impression. The first baby was all storm and sensitivity and in need of my intent protection. This new child is a creature I don't yet recognize; he is calling forth mothering I have not yet known. Once, I walked on eggshells. Now, not so much.

For some time before this arrival I had been looking not just for the phraseology and vocabularies but for the scenes of the double or multiplying shuffle, for new living infants alongside a growing first.

Sally Williams, near Fayetteville, North Carolina, the early 1820s. She carried both children into the plantation rice fields with her, taking a long walk over fences and pastures and sycamore trees. Sometimes the older, Isaac, was securely fastened to her back and the baby brother tucked in her dress in front, tied inside. Other times she rolled up the front of her skirt and fastened it to make a resting place. Sally wanted neither to leave the infants in her cabin in the slave quarters nor to lay them down in the fields by the side of a fence or along a ridge, where a snake might crawl over. She was seventeen years old, tall, with a body shaped by five years' field labor. Her husband, Abram, was enslaved on a neighboring plantation, her slave mother worked as a waiting maid elsewhere, and her father had been sold away. At noon, the meal that supported her nursing and her field labor was bread, meat, and boiled rice.[6]

December 1849, the East Coast of the United States. Augusta Knapp's husband, Gideon, has been trying his luck in the California Gold Rush. "I am alone all day," she wrote briefly in her diary, "and still I cannot say I am lonesome. I sit with the children, and read a great deal. I should not say I am alone, when I have two such sweet children." She adds, "I fear I am often impatient, when they interrupt and bother me:—children will."

There are many more nineteenth-century diaries and letters like this, with scenes of the amplifying interruption of one, two, more.[7]

February 18, 1899, Wynn's Mill, Georgia. Magnolia Le Guin, one half of a small-time farming white couple, picked up a small memorandum book: "I purpose to write down such things as I find sweet pleasure to me I wish to retain in here." She had a three-year-old and a baby just turned one. Askew, the older, had weighed ten pounds. "One of the 'best' babies— slept lots. Was very quiet. Amused himself. Often left him with Lil or Jane Miller"—even as young as three months, Magnolia remarked. Jane Miller, called "Aunt Jane," proves to be a black washerwoman and family "help"—the "Aunt" designation surely the inheritance of local habits of othermothering. The newer infant, Fred, took a month to reach ten pounds. At seven months he had one tooth and could not sit up alone. At the diary's beginning he could stand holding on to chairs, had eight teeth, and could say please, Mama, Papa, and kitty. Unlike Askew, Magnolia recorded, Fred wouldn't easily be left. Askew talked early and unusually clearly; Fred's early speech was "a little slow and long in a kind of musical tone." The unfolding diary, kept in an odd assortment of long, narrow ledgers and farm account books, portrayed small babies as the most demanding: Magnolia had "no time of my own till babies can walk."[8]

Dorset, 1902. The nanny to Viola Bankes slept with baby Ralph, who as the firstborn male on the massive English estate of Kingston Lacy was welcomed with roasted oxen, bonfires, and fireworks. A nursemaid now cared for his older sister, Viola: a sudden downgrade from the nanny. The double shuffle among the delegated mothers of aristocrats was shaped by expectations about gender and status as rigid as the children's starched clothes or the brass bells of the servant quarters.[9]

Violet Harris, in working-class Lambeth, mid-twentieth-century London. "When I had my Lena," she recollected, "I had to have the other poor little darling—was no age—on the bed with me all day, you know, crying. There was this other little one . . . getting more notice than a tiny born baby." Closely spaced siblings like these were a fading norm in her community.[10]

Nottingham, the 1960s, during the height of working-class habits of baby scheduling. Many women got more flexible with a second child. A cabinetmaker's wife reckoned, "With Jane I was very routine-minded. I went to the clock. If she was asleep, I woke her up. But I changed my mind over Paul; I was more relaxed from the start, having had one, I suppose. You don't worry so much." I recognize the lowered worry. As individual women became more experienced, attitudes toward scheduling often trended in the same direction: emigrants among the English who moved to the coal town of Wonthaggi, Australia, were also more likely after the first baby to adapt once-strict routines to suit themselves.[11]

Mid-1980s London. Jean Radford, one of the very few twentieth-century mothers to write openly about adopting, reported on the arrival of a second infant. Her daughter, birthed in 1980 to an "English mother and a Caribbean father," had been clamoring for a sibling. Jean had been pessimistic: she and her partner were too old and too white, and the policy on transracial adoption had recently shifted in favor of black adopters. But a phone call and the arrival of a three-month-old boy changed everything: "It's another chance, another miracle, we feel chosen." This time around was more challenging. The baby took the separation from his foster mother very badly, he cried incessantly, and the daughter suggested they send him back—she had had in mind a baby for herself, not a demanding rival for her parents' love and attention.[12]

In late 1980s eastern Kentucky, where more than half of two- to four-year-olds were still sleeping in close proximity to their mothers, some were moved to their own bedrooms on account of a newborn. Other reasons included "it was time," "the bed was too crowded," or "we couldn't get any sleep and we both work and need our sleep." Feelings about a child's bedroom exit ranged widely: "I was very worried and checked several times during the night"; "I was afraid of fire or that something awful would happen to him"; "I missed him"; "Good"; "Relieved"; and "I try to sneak him back with me whenever I can."[13]

Usually K goes to M in the night. I'm relieved, in this renewed fatigue. I miss them both. But my ears and body are most attuned to the baby's sounds.

At his three full years of age, my dowager has acquired what seventeenth-century English people thought of as the second stage of man. In the stages of the early modern life cycle, at least as pictured for boys and for elites, the first was shown as a swaddled baby and the second appears as a small curly-haired child playing with bat and ball or hobbyhorse. Infancy. Then the greater competencies of childhood.[14]

Among seventeenth-century English people and New England colonists, mothers might ask such small children to undertake very light work. Thomas Shepard, born around 1604 and later a colonist in Massachusetts, was age three when he was sent to keep geese. The presumption of competence is shared in other times and places: in the fishing village of pre–Second World War Golspie, for example, where a three-year-old might be sent to collect the fir cones that smoked the haddock, or to gather the eggs from the henhouse or winkles from the beach for the next shipment to Billingsgate. A small fisherwoman's child might make himself brose for breakfast, which needed little preparation: pour hot water over oatmeal, perhaps with a little butter or salt.[15]

The seventeenth-century Jesuit missionary Paul Le Jeune was appalled that Algonquian peoples considered young children incapable of wrongdoing and refused to punish them. The comment tells us as much about early modern European expectations of very small children as about Native ways.[16]

Enslaved mothers of the nineteenth century usually weaned their offspring at between two and four years of age, a habit that corresponded with West African weaning practices. (The cornmeal-based, low-protein diet that replaced breast milk did not.) Planters discouraged this late weaning and rarely "allowed" breastfeeding after the first year. The slave children forcibly separated from their mothers were usually considerably older than two, three, or four, however. (Nine to twelve seems to have been an especially likely time, I learn.) I pause over this bald fact: during the 1850s, in response to growing antislavery activism in the North, several Southern states, such as Alabama, made it illegal to sell away children under five, a softened legal provision among the many laws that enshrined slavery. So: usually, but not invariably, older.[17]

Being judged capable has often mattered more than exact numerals.

Among early-twentieth-century Ojibwe people, a child's age was not typically counted in years. A toddler (my lingo, a term used by English speakers since the early nineteenth century) might be described as "just old enough to remember" or "before it had any sense." The Ojibwe age of reason, according to a Western anthropologist, was four or five.[18]

As a child comes into hearing stories, and into speech, the particularity of time and place surely amplifies. Most bedtimes I still read to M. About the tiger coming to tea. Or the cat, Mog, disturbing a nighttime burglar—another tale from my own childhood that entails a teapot and a shared cuppa, the burglar standing around with a friendly policeman and Mog's human family. K finds the stories perplexingly English. Stories are how children come into culture, gain words and contexts of their own.

In the last decade of the eighteenth century, the enslaved New Jersey mother of Peter Wheeler, jogging him on her knee, told him stories of his African-born great-grandfather coming to America in chains. Across generations, Catawba adults warned small children of Wild People who sneaked babies from cradles at night, or touched clothes that were left out to dry.[19]

Even very small children give precise voice to the world they feel and witness. A Victorian child asked about death: When God takes good people to heaven, does he pull them up with a rope? Pity the seventeenth-, eighteenth-, and nineteenth-century delegated mothers, those many servants who hated being told what to do by small children. The nursemaids of 1920s Chicago and New York heard: "You know you are paid to keep me happy." "You'd better come on and read this book to me." "What are you anyway; you are only a maid; I don't have to do what you say." Or "You have nothing about me," meaning, according to the nursemaid's interpretation, "you have no right to tell me what to do." Babies, though hard work, did not insult.[20]

The older children in the nursemaid's care, I notice, had an impact on the infants. "Baby sometimes picks up Muriel's tricks," remarked a nursemaid called Jean. "Sometimes baby calls me She—hissing out, 'Sh—she did so and so.'"

I sit in a café on the main road, with V bound against my chest, his smell in my nostrils. I smuggle warm coffee sideways into my mouth. (Don't consume hot drinks over the baby's head.) This baby yawns theatrically when he is tired, and after a few weeks he bats at his eyes. He turns calmly within and away from the world, an impulse I recognize. That's where we start to find each other.

21

Navigating the Times

Life on life's terms, not my own, is how one of the café-goers, a bank teller, wryly casts the months of tending her baby. Her baby doesn't nap much and wakes at the slightest noise. She's not complaining. Her voice has the be-positive tone I know from my own upbringing, what the maternal philosopher Sara Ruddick called "resilient cheerfulness." We navigate the times that we inherit from the past, and the babies that we have been given, in our own ways.[1]

The Baby Café—the term belongs to the National Health Service—is part baby-weighing clinic, part lactation center, part social hall. The people I encounter here with V are mostly first-time mothers. Many of the babies are older than those I saw at the community center with my first child, maternity leave lasting longer in twenty-first-century Britain than in the United States. The café is open to many comers: the daughter of a

Pakistani immigrant first employed in the local car works, a graduate student at one of the universities, the neighbor who works at the supermarket, a lawyer whose household is one of the many that are gentrifying the surrounding warren of Victorian terraces and 1930s semis. I'm here, sometimes to check V's weight, sometimes for myself, sometimes to be someone else's Sarah. Across the room, someone is handing around a petition.

Navigating these months of infancy—and for me they are short months, slow in the living but rapid in the disappearance—is most often a matter of managing and getting along, of living on life's terms. Caring for an infant is hard work. Holding a baby often takes two hands. Those mothering very small children are especially unlikely to be game changing in politics, making revolution, pursuing reform, or creating literature and art. Perhaps they come to those activities later, with new insights or energies, priorities or skills. Susan B. Anthony, the energetic and childless nineteenth-century women's suffragist, chided her married comrades to free themselves from the constant tasks of childrearing so they could do more work for the cause. Adrienne Rich kept an angry and tender diary during her children's infancy in the 1960s, but it took until 1976 for her to publish the lengthy and rabble-rousing *Of Woman Born*.[2]

The petition arrives at the bank teller and me. Government cuts threaten the county's Baby Cafés. Can we please sign, asks the woman behind the clipboard. Sometimes navigating the times is more than living on life's inherited terms. Sometimes navigating infancy and the times includes seeking to change the present—to defend or protect, or to advance or create something. I think of the artist Jenny Saville's immense charcoal figures on the museum wall, how in switching paint for charcoal she reprised the past and reinterpreted maternity. Like "flying," she remarked of having her babies. In front of me now, the baby held by the woman with the clipboard arches his back and grabs toward V's face, just missing.

The past is always in the present, and the present keeps moving on. How have those mothering most actively navigated their times?

———

Perhaps the best-known form of actively navigating the times is loud, collective organizing, the deliberate and visible reimagining and remaking of the world as it is.

In Jewish East New York in 1917, Clara Shavelson had a three-year-old son and an infant daughter. She was thirty years old and theatrical in style, the kind of person who liked to talk, sing, and argue. As a younger woman, she had led a shirtwaist makers' uprising, organizing in the workshops of shirtwaist manufacturers and being blacklisted for her efforts. Now she worked part-time in a tie shop and lived in Brownsville, Brooklyn, a suffragist, a mother, and the wife of union man Joseph Shavelson, whose activist Jewish family had emigrated to the United States after the failed Russian Revolution of 1905. Brownsville was a long-standing Jewish immigrant ghetto and a hotbed of political activism.[3]

Clara Shavelson's contemporaries thought of her as a spark plug. She took her small children to meetings, organized a strike to prevent rent increases, and became well known as a "soapboxer" even in a neighborhood where there were many other speakers. In 1917 New York City, rent mattered, as a moratorium on building during the years of the First World War had led to a severe housing shortage, and families who could not pay their rent had almost no chance of finding other quarters. Inflation, meanwhile, was eroding the quality of life for many American workers. Anti-eviction protesters patrolled the streets of Brownsville and wore banners advertising the rent strike in Yiddish and English.

Clara's primary cause was housewives' unions: she thought that organizations of housewives, focused on consumer and housing issues, could become as important to the working-class struggle as industrial labor unions. One observer, Sophie Gerson, recalled, "There were no loudspeakers. You had to have pretty strong lungs. But it was the passion and conviction with which she spoke that got people's attention." Gerson added, "She had a simple motto . . . You speak the truth, she said, and people will listen."

Shavelson's actions while her children were infants helped lay the foundations for the 1930s housewives' movement, a campaign that tried to create sturdy political organizations through which working-class mothers could make themselves heard. As one activist explained, pushing and amplifying the maternal ideology of the day, their place might "be in the home but the home is no longer the isolated complete unit it once was. To serve her home best, the woman of today must understand the political and economic foundation on which that home rests—and then do something about it." Like Clara, this activist recognized no boundaries between public and private life, nor between caring about her own children and the children of others. The American housewives' movement of the 1930s, though little known today, would come to stretch from New York to Seattle, from Richmond, Virginia, to Los Angeles and hundreds of small towns and farm villages in between, demanding a better quality of life for mothers and their children.

Clara Shavelson was loud and visible, publicizing her mothering and her activism in the same breath. A rather different form of navigating the times with an infant is quiet resistance, or impassive rejection.

Starting in 1896, and especially in the decade of the 1910s, the U.S. Office of Indian Affairs sent field matrons to southwestern Colorado to "uplift" and "civilize" the Native peoples living on the Southern Ute Reservation there. Acculturation, ran the civilizing logic, must include changing Native modes of infant care. The Ute should live in houses as nuclear families, with the mothering undertaken by younger, "progressive" women, well-versed in scientific housekeeping, consumer goods, and hygiene. This agenda was encapsulated in the exhibits displayed by matron Josephine Belt in 1917. There were home-sewn baby clothes, baby and toddler food, a crib with a fly screen, and a playpen, as well as demonstrations of how to bathe babies or to give them boiled water. Also on display were "unsuitable items," from pacifiers to "cheap candy." Belt's lectures listed cradleboards among the improper objects.[4]

Some Ute people viewed the presentations and attended the lectures. They showed up for homemaking contests and created exhibits of beaded infant clothes for fairs. Reading between the lines of the OIA's records, however, one can see that the repeated complaints about "reactionary squaws" and the lack of progress suggest that Ute women also continued to mother in egalitarian extended families: sharing childcare, running farms, rearing livestock, gathering and processing wild foods, and carrying the frowned-upon cradleboards. Many had no interest in moving from tepees to permanent dwellings with curtains and cribs. A few useful new sanitation practices did take hold, as did a readiness to take advantage of such labor-saving devices as sewing and washing machines, especially when they could be won as prizes in OIA contests.

At best, from the vantage point of the field matrons and their superiors, there was selective borrowing; at worst, there was active resistance. By 1920 the matrons had disappeared, the civilizing program having ended in failure.

A final form of actively navigating the present is underground creativity, the kinds of activities that leave the least evidence behind for a curious historian.

Fast-forward to 1980, Seattle. Maidi Nickele began helping lesbians to become parents soon after she herself was able to conceive. Around the time her son Jordan was born, she started to expand the grassroots, word-of-mouth urban network that had enabled her to get pregnant. She had learned of a woman who worked at a local women's health clinic who helped another lesbian to inseminate herself. Now Maidi asked gay men to be donors, and delivered sperm to other lesbians who wished to become pregnant. Eventually she held "Make a Baby" classes on insemination and parenting at the Seattle Lesbian Resource Center.[5]

In 1980, the existing bias against lesbians, and against unmarried women, held that they would not make fit mothers. Doctors expressed what they called medical ethical problems with inseminating lesbians or with assisting with children being born out of wedlock. Maidi estimates that in the six years after 1980 she aided in about twenty inseminations that led to births. Given the many other babies born to local lesbian couples, she assumed that others, too, were clandestinely assisting lesbians to conceive. These underground networks forged connections between gay men and lesbian women, based on a shared appreciation that reproductive freedom mattered to both groups' civil rights. Maidi found that unlike heterosexual men, gay men made good donors, as they did not find anything objectionable about lesbians becoming mothers. The gay men she asked, she remembered, were excited about "helping create families even if they weren't part of that family."

The past is always in the present, and the present keeps moving on. Sometimes the raw materials of mothering get amplified, spilling into realms that we name politics, or activism, or historical change, or the defense of tradition.

At the Baby Café, the bank teller is heading out, with a short smile directed at V and me. Freeing a hand, I sign the petition and read the small print about what to do next. It is easier to attend a protest with an infant strapped on your front than with an older child who can discern adult worries, who can read a slogan.

The historical materials I garner offer no manifesto for the carrying and caring of an infant. Perhaps I am not the manifesto-writing type. I am wary of a politics grounded in the authority and experience of mothers, maternalism looking like feminism for conservative times. But I might be wrong about that. Switch the noun to a verb, the identity of "mother" to the act of "mothering," and the prospect looks rather different. A defense of caring under late capitalism, uttered by caregivers of every persuasion—adoptive, biological, and employed; female, male, lesbian, gay, trans, and the rest—could be a wide coalition indeed. The twenty-first century keeps shifting under our feet.

22

The End of the Night

The new baby is no longer so new. He just slept "through the night." That marvelous phrase may not mean a full eight-hour adult stretch, but I do feel rested, startlingly clearheaded, ready to move mountains. I woke up with the birds' chorus, moments before the sound of the first grunt as V swung his body upright. It is half past six on a darkish morning. The leaves of the oak tree are unfolding against the bedroom window. When I walk to the crib, he points to the nursing chair with one arm and to a stack of new diapers with the other, pleased by the day and by his mastery of our usual habits.

Small rituals accomplished, I set the baby down on his feet and he heads at great pace down the corridor. Shhhh, don't wake your older brother. Early light streams in through the hall window, turning the baby into a blanked-out silhouette of determination, topped by a halo of fuzz.

For a split second, he is everychild: small, unmarked, outside culture and history.

But, of course not. There are no everychildren any more than there are everymothers—just the verbs for mothering, a grabbed-at pile, each with its own distinctive history. I'm glad for them: to know that carrying and caring have their own histories, that maternal sleep has its own history. That mothering is plural and specific to time and place and situation. Finding these histories has felt as consequential, this last while, as knowing about congressional debates or parliamentary legislation.

Historical forgetting leaves holes in the fabric that binds us. Things that seem natural only by force of repetition too easily take on a false status. Appeals to old, mistaken certainties, or to universals, stand uncorrected. How things are now too readily becomes how things were and should always be. It's not healthier to forget, to lose the past: historical remembering makes matters bigger and more open-ended.

For a split second, the streaming light outlines the baby's silhouette and stretches his shadow toward me along the wooden floorboards. Then he turns back to check I am coming, too, nose wrinkling, and beckons me into our morning.

Acknowledgments

Many people helped midwife this book. Roman Krznaric and Kate Raworth encouraged me to write for a wider audience. Rebecca Carter, my London agent at Janklow and Nesbit, saw potential in an idea, played editor *avant la lettre*, and brought me into the orbit of her excellent New York colleague Emma Parry. As I started writing, Arwen Donahue, Jennifer Fleissner, Alexandra Shepard, and Barbara Taylor read chapters and steered the book's form and content. Their fellow-traveling means a great deal to me. I would not have ventured into first-person writing without Barbara Taylor's precedent.

Archivists and librarians, in person and at a distance, helped in the process of research: at the Indiana University Archives; the Kinsey Institute Library; the Library Company of Philadelphia; the Lilly Rare Books Library; the Vere Harmsworth Library, University of Oxford; the Wells Library of Indiana University; the Wylie House Museum; and Yale University Library. So too did awards and fellowships from the New Frontiers for the Arts and Humanities to the College Arts and Humanities Institute,

Indiana University, the Rothermere American Institute, the University of Oxford, and the Centre for Writing, Oxford.

Many scholars and writers supplied information or insight or read individual chapters, including Judith Allen, Edward Baptist, Norma Clarke, Nick Cullather, Faramerz Dabhoiwala, Konstantin Dierks, Toby Ditz, Leslie Dunlap, Mary Fissell, Wendy Gamber, David Henkin, Martha Hodes, Lara Kriegel, Greta LaFleur, Jen Manion, Cecily Marston, Amrita Chakrabarti Myers, Seth Rockman, Aaron Sachs, Sina Salessi, Russell Shorto, Susan Sleeper-Smith, Christina Snyder, Micah Stack, David Thelen, Merry Weissner-Hanks, and Ellen Wu. Audiences at the Center for Eighteenth-Century Studies, Indiana University; the Raphael Samuel History Centre; the Johns Hopkins University; and Yale University challenged and extended my ideas. In the voices of friendship, so, too, did Amy Dillard, Jesse Eisenberg, Sarah Hurwitz, Emily Jones, Judy Klein, Myfanwy Lloyd, Elaine Monaghan, Helene Neveu Kringelbach, Anna Strout, and Karen Woody.

Sally Alexander, Nikki Brown, Marie Deer, Susan Gubar, Nancy Shoemaker, Steve Stowe, and Jodi Vandenberg-Daves each read the entire first draft with their own specialisms in mind, catching mistakes and making suggestions. They also proved, as I had guessed they might, to be acute readers of the whole. In London, Venetia Butterfield at Penguin placed faith and excitement in the importance of the topic. At Farrar, Straus and Giroux in New York, Sarah Crichton worked her remarkable editorial magic.

Written with one and then two small children on hand, the book depended on other caregivers and friends as much as intellectual help. Georg'ann Cattelona, Stacey Decker, and Molly Mendota were three among many attached to Bloomington Area Birth Services, a rare and much-missed institution. Gaury Alfaro stuck around even when the baby had reflux and the mother was novice and needy. The preschools of Gan Shalom and SS Mary and John provided warm and caring communities for one or both toddlers. Emily Pike has long showed what a "family-like" relationship means, not just to both my children but at least as much to me.

My two children prompted the occasion and the concerns I explore here. Inspiring and impeding the writing have proved to be more or less the same thing. Along the way, they have imagined their own versions of this book and given them a title: *A Tale of Two Boys* and *Babies to the Rescue*.

Before our children were born, my partner offered that they take my last name. That offer signaled a determination to egalitarian parenting as well as to love that he has fiercely upheld. The writing of this book, and much else that is good in my life, could not have happened without his grand generosity. The book is dedicated, with great love, to the three of them. I write, here, only of my own experience, and not of theirs.

A Note on Method

A history of maternity, verb-led, based on anecdote, and composed in the form of a first-person essay may seem like a novel proposition. At times, in the sleepless alternation of mothering and doing research, it seemed that I had conjured up the method and form entirely from scratch. I was feeling my way as a new mother and as a historian together. I was having conversations in doctors' waiting rooms and at bus stops more often than with my colleagues. I first came across the scholarly term "matrescence"—the process of becoming a mother—in the popular press. Later, however, I teased out and formalized the method. For there are historians' genealogies in which such an account can be placed, other lineages that help such an enterprise make sense. My approach emerged, as methods usually do, in the ply between questions in the present—What is the history of maternal sleep? Was Joan Wallach Scott worrisomely correct that we should avoid investigating what most set people called "women" apart?—and the available sources.

Why anecdote? The anecdotal method I pursue here has three distinct origins. The first—to point out that there is a weighty but not continuous lineage—is a tradition of historical writing that emerged in the seventeenth century and took anecdote as a means of exploring private lives and inner worlds. This was in contrast to conventional preoccupations with the doings of important men. As one seventeenth-century commentator observed, usually historians considered the actions of "Men in Public." They did their duty by depicting men "as they were in the Army, or in the tumult of Cities." But the new historians tried "by all means to get open their Closet-door," to perceive people "in conversation," and to be a "Witness of their inward Life, and . . . at the most private hours." While most historians told political narrative, now some recounted anecdotes of personal talk and inner experience. The commentator even coined a clunky name for these openers of closet doors: anecdote-grapher.[1]

The second point of origin for my use of anecdote is the highly fragmentary, piecemeal quality of the traces of mothering left behind from former times and places. The residual archive of childbearing and infant care is so spotty that historians working on North America and Britain before the twentieth century have repeatedly remarked upon it. About otherwise loquacious Puritan New Englanders, Ruth Bloch observed, "We know next to nothing about actual child-rearing practices." Amanda Vickery agreed, of the Northern English elite of the eighteenth century. Here, she wrote, evidence is at its most fragmentary, and we can know little. Taking a longer view, Anthony Fletcher noted the "sparse documentation of motherly practice" among the English upper and professional classes between the beginning of the seventeenth century and the First World War. It is not hard to sense the frustration. We "know surprisingly little" about childcare, writes Linda Oja, and the relevant sources have "irritating blanks and uncertainties." But small shards and occasional nuggets *do* remain, exactly as many historians have unearthed on their way to other quarry: the aside in a letter, the scene in a travel account, the detail in a slave narrative or a plantation business account, the incidental information in a court record, or, into the modern period, the short report in anthropological fieldwork on a Native reservation, or the brief testimony in an oral history or sociological survey. Anecdote is a way of recasting such shards and nuggets of evidence, of turning absence into presence, what's mentioned *en passant* into the main drama.[2]

The last origin for my method is a theory of maternity in the twenty-first century, most precisely articulated by the psychoanalyst Lisa Baraitser. "Motherhood lends itself to anecdote," Baraitser explains, because of the "constant attack on narrative that the child performs." A small child continually breaks into maternal speech. The mother's personal narrative is "punctured at the level of constant interruptions to thinking, reflecting, sleeping, moving and completing tasks." Thus rejecting narrative as a useful starting point, Baraitser turns to anecdote as the basis of interpretation. She casts the state of being interrupted as mothering's key condition.[3]

I take anecdote to have, then, a kind of valuable status for making knowledge: produced by maternity in the present, available in the scattershot archive of the past, and with a sturdy lineage in historical writing. Certainly there is tension between these points of origin. The sense of interruption that characterizes much contemporary parenting is neither universal nor transhistorical, for example, but has its own particular history. Nor is maternal interruption the sole explanation, or even the main reason, why the archive of mothering runs mainly to anecdotes. But observing these three points of origin illuminates the crucial point. Let's think of anecdote as neither bare nor incomplete, but exactly what is needed. A historical interpretation can reside in the slow accumulation of a trellis of detail. Juxtaposing, contrasting, pausing over, and serializing anecdote can make for a full historical interpretation by comparison and accretion.

Why verb-led, and in first-person form? Verbs have a particular relationship with anecdotes, of course. An anecdote typically shows a scene unfolding, a person or people in some action: doing, being, feeling, thinking. Verbs are invariably about how we use or inhabit time: to fish cod, to till a field, to carve spoons, to type a report, to have sex, to watch an infant. Some verbs for mothering are common and experienced specifically (quickening and birthing, in the case of pregnancy, or making provision, in the case of an infant). Others are more highly particular (handing a baby over, in the case of larger households, say, or bottle-feeding, among possibilities for infant nourishment). The verbs change, or they come with changing activities and meanings attached. Following verbs allows us "to pluralize and specify" mothering, to use Eve Kosofsky Sedgwick's apt phrase. Or, to place a different emphasis, thinking in verbs helps to diversify and to particularize what is otherwise easily mistaken as purely natural or biological, necessary or mundane.[4]

Pluralizing and specifying by verbs responds to two hesitations that have shaped much of what historians of women, gender, and sexuality have set out to learn in the past forty years. The first is the uneasy assumption, voiced for example by Linda Pollock, that the tasks of bodily nurture and protection of an infant are transhistorical. Exactly because they reappear in each century, she suggested, they are not worthy of consideration.[5]

The second is the clarion call issued by Joan Scott in 1987. Historians of women, she influentially argued, should move beyond studying only women, lest they remain in a "subdepartment," unable "to point out [their] relationship to History or to the rewriting of History" and tending falsely to confirm that "women belong in a separate sphere . . . which underscores, indeed legitimizes, the existing lines of sexual difference" and inequality. Why sequester oneself from historians' big stakes? Why emphasize women's distinctiveness from men? At the very core of notions of sexual difference, reproachfully physical, pregnancy and infant nurture can seem guilty as charged. In pluralizing and specifying by verbs, I borrow a confidence from queer scholars such as Sedgwick that bodily practices in the past were remarkably various and are worth recapturing. Queer history provides the tools for returning to precisely that which has been most normative in relation to sex and to women. I also borrow a confidence, from present-day queer parents who have made public their experience, that such embodiments retain this remarkable plasticity.[6]

Writing while doing, composing in the first person, I have found, can be complementary to this verb-led approach: not necessary, but not incidental either. In so doing, I walked through a door opened and held ajar by dozens of earlier feminist historians' acknowledgments, prefaces, and introductions. On my bookshelves, an account of motherhood in "outcast" London begins, in sentences that remain deeply moving, with the historian losing a seven-year-old child to a brain tumor. A history of American childbirth recollects the "spark" of a family story of a harrowing taxicab ride during labor.[7] Such books typically open the door to a first-person approach in the framing materials, and then close it for the main analysis, which is presented in carefully distanced tones. Objectivity was the means by which women of all stripes first claimed their place in the history profession—a familiar convention, a necessary stance to join the club. Yet historiographers also remind us that objectivity has not been the only commitment in historical writings, and feminists persuasively challenge the presumption that male generations of historians have written adequately or objectively.

I wanted to see what might happen when the door is held open from the very beginning to the very end of a book. Researching as I carried and then cared for first one and then a second child made me want to reconnect the often separate histories of sexuality and maternity, pregnancy and infant care. Writing in and with my own doing of mothering helped me stay with topics I would otherwise have found dull or weird, such as damp cloth, or overlooked, such as sleep. I bumped into both solace and disidentification in learning the ways of former worlds, making me attentive to how a sense of the past may have shaped earlier people's perceptions of what they were doing, and newly aware of tastes and blind spots from my own lineage in the white British working and lower-middle classes. I became grateful for 1970s women's liberationists' coinage of "ambivalence" as the sine qua non of mothering, rescuing darkness from Victorian-style sentimentality, mainly for the precedent thus set for writing directly and sustainedly about maternal experience. I was unsurprised that contemporary essayists on being with an infant—Maggie Nelson, Sarah Manguso, Rachel Zucker, Trevor MacDonald—gave me a sharper sense of the present from which I was viewing the past, as well as distinctive dimensions of sexuality or whiteness or gender or temperament. Most especially, I was viscerally aware of mothering as a kind of work, a labor of love, an activity always being carried out among other activities.

I came to want to leave an image of the historian that contrasts with the tweedy caricature of popular culture, or the semi-heroic figure of the historian-as-detective blowing dust from a torn and fragile manuscript, any of his dependents tucked out of sight. Doing history, like mothering, is a form of embodied labor.

Notes

The spelling and punctuation of quotations have been modernized where necessary. The main purpose of the notes is to identify the sources of citations in the text and to point to useful secondary reading on important themes. Full details of sources are given at their first citation in every chapter. The *Oxford English Dictionary* (*OED*) is cited from its online edition (www.oed.com).

Prologue

1. Anthony Fletcher, *Growing Up in England: The Experience of Childhood, 1600–1914* (New Haven, CT, 2008), quotation at 95.
2. Ann Oakley, *From Here to Maternity: Becoming a Mother* (Harmondsworth, UK, 1979), 42–43 (Hartley), 44–45 (Brady).
3. M. Inez Hilger, *Chippewa Child Life and Its Cultural Background* (Washington, DC, 1951), 5; [Charlotte Teller Hirsch], *The Diary of an Expectant Mother* (London, 1917), 74.

4. Oakley, *From Here to Maternity*, 51–52; Sharon Olds, *The Sign of Saturn Poems, 1980–1987* (London, 1991), 8–9.

5. The phrase originates in Eve Kosofsky Sedgwick, *Tendencies* (Durham, NC, 1993), 25.

6. Jenny Saville, *Study for Pentimenti III (sinopia)* (2011).

1. Mothering by Numbers

1. In adopting an interpretation, form, and focus of its own, this book nonetheless builds on some of the most important scholarship on the histories of women, gender, and motherhood in Britain and North America since the seventeenth century. I benefit especially from Jodi Vandenberg-Daves, *Modern Motherhood: An American History* (New Brunswick, NJ, 2014); Katy Simpson Smith, *We Have Raised All of You: Motherhood in the South, 1750–1835* (Baton Rouge, LA, 2013); Angela Davis, *Modern Motherhood: Women and Family in England, c. 1945–2000* (Manchester, UK, 2012); Rebecca Jo Plant, *Mom: The Transformation of Motherhood in Modern America* (Chicago, 2010); Jacqueline Jones, *Labor of Love, Labor of Sorrow: Black Women, Work, and the Family, from Slavery to the Present* (New York, 2010); V. Lynn Kennedy, *Born Southern: Childbirth, Motherhood, and Social Networks in the Old South* (Baltimore, 2010); Marie Jenkins Schwartz, *Birthing a Slave: Motherhood and Medicine in the Antebellum South* (Cambridge, MA, 2006); Stephanie Camp, *Closer to Freedom: Enslaved Women and Everyday Resistance in the Plantation South* (Chapel Hill, NC, 2004); Mary E. Fissell, *Vernacular Bodies: The Politics of Reproduction in Early Modern England* (Oxford, UK, 2004); Laura Gowing, *Common Bodies: Women, Touch and Power in Seventeenth-Century England* (London, 2003); Theda Perdue, *Cherokee Women: Gender and Cultural Change, 1700–1835* (Lincoln, NE, 1998); Amanda Vickery, *The Gentleman's Daughter: Women's Lives in Georgian England* (New Haven, CT, 1998); Elizabeth Roberts, *Women and Families: An Oral History, 1940–1970* (Oxford, UK, 1995); Evelyn Nakano Glenn et al., eds., *Mothering: Ideology, Experience, and Agency* (New York, 1994); Eileen Boris, *Home to Work: Motherhood and the Politics of Industrial Homework in the United States* (New York, 1994); Barbara Duden, *Disembodying Women: Perspectives on Pregnancy and the Unborn* (1991, Cambridge, MA, trans. 1993); Ellen Ross, *Love and Toil: Motherhood in Outcast London, 1870–1918* (London, 1993); Valerie Fildes, ed., *Women as Mothers in Pre-Industrial England: Essays in Memory of Dorothy McLaren* (Abingdon, UK, 1990); Sally G. McMillen, *Motherhood in the Old South: Pregnancy, Childbirth, and Infant Rearing* (Baton Rouge, LA, 1990); Sylvia D. Hoffert, *Private Matters: American Attitudes to Childbearing and Infant Nurture in the Urban North, 1800–1860* (Urbana, IL, 1989); Elizabeth Roberts,

A Woman's Place: An Oral History of Working-Class Women, 1890–1940 (Oxford, UK, 1984); Laurel Thatcher Ulrich, *Good Wives: Image and Reality in the Lives of Women in Northern New England, 1650–1750* (New York, 1982). Many further materials on particular themes appear in the notes.

My thinking benefits, too, from theorists of maternity, especially Lisa Baraitser, *Maternal Encounters: The Ethics of Interruption* (Hove, UK, 2009), and Patricia Hill Collins, *Black Feminist Thought* (1990, repr. New York, 2000); queer scholars, especially Maggie Nelson, *The Argonauts* (New York, 2015), and Valerie Traub, *Thinking Sex with the Early Moderns* (Philadelphia, 2016); and the contemporary memoirists and essayists cited in ch. 1, n. 8, and ch. 16, n. 1. The latter expand a women's liberationist tradition of maternal memoir (treated in this book as an archive) owing especially to Jane Lazarre, *The Mother Knot* (Boston, 1976), Adrienne Rich, *Of Woman Born: Motherhood as Experience and Institution* (New York, 1976), and essays in Alice Walker, *In Search of Our Mother's Gardens: Womanist Prose* (San Diego, 1983).

See the "Note on Method" for discussion of the verb-led, anecdotal, first-person approach to the historical interpretation made here.

2. For this and the next paragraph, on seventeenth- and eighteenth-century birthrates, see C. Dallett Hemphill, *Siblings: Brothers and Sisters in American History* (New York, 2011), 21; Susan E. Klepp, *Revolutionary Conceptions: Women, Fertility and the Family Limitation in America, 1760–1820* (Chapel Hill, NC, 2009), 41–54; Pamela Sharpe, *Population and Society in an East Devon Parish: Reproducing Colyton, 1540–1840* (Exeter, UK, 2002).

3. On the overall fertility transition discussed in this section, see especially Klepp, *Revolutionary Conceptions*; Herbert S. Klein, *A Population History of the United States* (Cambridge, MA, 2004); Karen Oppenheim Mason, "Gender and Family Systems in the Fertility Transition," *Population and Development Review* 27 (2001), 160–76; John R. Gillis, Louise A. Tilly, and David Levine, eds., *The European Experience of Declining Fertility, 1850–1970: The Quiet Revolution* (Cambridge, MA, 1992).

4. Klepp, *Revolutionary Conceptions*, 87 (Hopkins), 116 (Fisher).

5. Ibid., 207 (Atlee), 88 (Bowen).

6. Robert S. Lynd and Helen Marrel Lynd, *Middletown: A Study in American Culture*, 131 (Muncie, IN, 1929); Miriam Glucksmann, *Women Assemble: Women Workers and the New Industries in Inter-War Britain* (London, 1990), 160–75, 231, 234, 248 (Doris Hanslow, a pseudonym); Mass Observation, "Women's Reasons for Having Small Families" (1945), 4 (London streets).

7. Kim Anderson, *Life Stages and Native Women: Memory, Teachings, and Story Medicine* (Winnipeg, 2011), 41 (Cree); M. Inez Hilger, *Chippewa Child Life and Its Cultural Background* (Washington, DC, 1951), 4.

8. Rebecca Walker, *Baby Love: Choosing Motherhood After a Lifetime of Ambivalence* (New York, 2007); Chitra Ramaswamy, *Expecting: The Inner Life of Pregnancy* (Glasgow, 2016), 7; and alternately, Rebecca Solnit, *The Mother of All Questions* (Chicago, 2017); Sheila Heti, *Motherhood: A Novel* (New York, 2018). For choice as a widespread modern notion, see Daniel T. Rodgers, *Age of Fracture* (Cambridge, MA, 2011), 10–11.

9. For this paragraph and the next: Hugh Cunningham, *Children and Childhood in Western Society Since 1500*, 2nd ed. (Harlow, UK, 2005), 95, 173.

10. Carol Karlsen and Laurie Crumpacker, eds., *Journal of Esther Edwards Burr 1754–1757* (New Haven, CT, 1984), 191; Narcissa Whitman to Stephen Prentiss, May 8, 1845, *Mrs. Whitman's Letters* (Salem, MA, 1893), 167.

2. Generation

1. Frank D. Prager, ed., *The Autobiography of John Fitch* (Philadelphia, 1976), 37.

2. Philip Larkin, "Annus Mirabilis," *Collected Poems* (London, 1988), 167.

3. For this and the next six paragraphs, see Simon Szretzer and Kate Fisher, *Sex Before the Sexual Revolution: Intimate Life in England, 1918–1963* (Cambridge, UK, 2010). The names given here were assigned by the researchers. For the quotations, see esp. 203, 76, 281, 276, 321, 338, 276 (Phyllis); 304–306 (Doreen); 310 (Dora); 150, 192 (Penny); 322 (Eleanor); 304 (sitting back); 1 ("two arms"); 310 ("have a bath").

4. Scholars confirm the general stereotypes about the Victorians. See Stephen Kern, "When Did the Victorian Period End? Relativity, Sexuality, Narrative," *Journal of Victorian Culture* 11 (2006), 327–28, but also Peter Gay, *The Bourgeois Experience: Victoria to Freud. Volume 1: The Education of the Senses* (New York, 1984). Samuel Johnson, *A Dictionary of the English Language*, 2 vols. (London, 1755).

5. The approach and evidence for early modern England are owed especially to Valerie Traub, *Thinking Sex with the Early Moderns* (Philadelphia, 2016), esp. ch. 7, esp. 180–82, plus 371–72 n. 50 (play), 371–72 n. 50 (the wordy courtesan), 377 n. 130 (dictionaries); Sarah Toulalan, *Imagining Sex: Pornography and Bodies in Seventeenth-Century England* (New York, 2007), esp. 62–91; as well, more generally, to Faramerz Dabhoiwala, *The Origins of Sex: A History of the First Sexual Revolution* (London, 2012).

6. On theatergoers, see Andrew Gurr, *Playgoing in Shakespeare's London* (Cambridge, UK, 1987).

7. Hera Cook, *The Long Sexual Revolution: English Women, Sex, and Contraception, 1800–1975* (Oxford, UK, 2005).

8. Claire Langhamer, "Afterword," in Alana Harris and Timothy Willem Jones, eds., *Love and Romance in Britain, 1918–1970* (Basingstoke, UK, 2015), 249 (vocabulary); April Gallwey, "Love Beyond the Frame: Stories of Maternal Love

Outside Marriage in the 1950s and 1960s," in Harris and Jones, eds., *Love and Romance*, 100–123, 105–106 (Walker); Kathleen Kiernan, Hilary Land, and Jane E. Lewis, eds., *Lone Motherhood in Twentieth-Century Britain: From Footnote to Front Page* (Oxford, UK, 1998).

9. Cissie Fairchilds, *Women in Early Modern Europe, 1500–1700* (Harlow, UK, 2007), 142 (Essex); Ann Kussmaul, *Servants in Husbandry in Early Modern England* (Cambridge, UK, 1981), 44 ("had to do"); Adrian Wilson, *Ritual and Conflict: The Social Relations of Childbirth in Early Modern England* (London, 2013), 11 (Parker); Tim Meldrum, *Domestic Service and Gender 1660–1750: Life and Work in the London Household* (Harlow, UK, 2000), 100–110.

10. Philip D. Morgan, "Inter-racial Sex in the Chesapeake and the British Atlantic World, c. 1700–1820," in Jan Ellen Lewis and Peter Onuf, eds., *Sally Hemings and Thomas Jefferson: History, Memory and Civic Culture* (Charlottesville, VA, 1999), 52–86; George P. Rawick, *The American Slave: A Composite Biography* (1941, repr. Westport, CT, 1972), iii, 194–95, quoted in John D'Emilio and Estelle B. Freedman, *Intimate Matters: A History of Sexuality in America* (New York, 1988), 101 ("shell corn").

11. Harriet Jacobs, *Incidents in the Life of a Slave Girl, Written by Herself*, 1861, repr. with an introduction by Jennifer Fleischner (Boston, 2010), 52–61, 80, quotations at 52 ("property"), 78 ("perilous").

12. *Philosophical Transactions of the Royal Historical Society* 89 (1799), 162; Ellen Lewin, *Lesbian Mothers: Accounts of Gender in American Culture* (Ithaca, NY, 1993), 48–49.

13. Traub, *Thinking Sex*, 371 n. 45 (terms for male and female emission); Thomas Laqueur, "Orgasm, Generation and the Politics of Reproductive Biology," in Catherine Gallagher and Thomas Laqueur, eds., *The Making of the Modern Body: Sexuality and Society in the Nineteenth Century* (Berkeley, 1987), 110; Ann Rosalind Jones, "Heterosexuality: A Beast with Many Backs," in Bette Talvacchia, ed., *A Cultural History of Sexuality in the Renaissance* (Oxford, UK, 2011), 35–36 (inside out); Emily Martin, *The Woman in the Body: A Cultural Analysis of Reproduction* (1987), 27 ("same genitals").

14. [Jacob Ruff], *The Expert Midwife, or, An Excellent and Most Necessary Treatise of the Generation and Birth of Man* (London, 1637), 63.

15. James Marion Sims, *Clinical Notes on Uterine Surgery* (London, 1866), 369, quoted in Angus McLaren, *Reproductive Rituals: The Perception of Fertility in England from the Sixteenth to the Nineteenth Century* (London, 1984), 27; Margaret Jarman Hagood, *Mothers of the South: Portraiture of the White Tenant Farm Woman* (1939, repr. New York, 1972), 118.

16. Jennifer Evans, *Aphrodisiacs, Fertility and Medicine in Early Modern England* (Woodbridge, UK, 2014); Frances Harris, *Transformations of Love: The Friendship*

of *John Evelyn and Margaret Godolphin* (Oxford, UK, 2003), 256; McLaren, *Reproductive Rituals*, 45 (frequency).

17. Lewin, *Lesbian Mothers* (Ithaca, NY, 1993), 51–52 ("wanted," "always loved"); Mary O'Donnell et al., "Alternative Fertilization," *Lesbian Health Matters!* (Santa Cruz, 1979), 49–63; Laura Mamo, *Queering Reproduction: Achieving Pregnancy in the Age of Technoscience* (Durham, NC, 2007).

18. Francis Rosnin, "Heterosexuality," Gert Hekma, ed., trans. Joanna Oseman, *A Cultural History of Sexuality in the Modern Age* (London, 2014), 27–47; Rebecca L. Davis, "Inventing the Normal Heterosexual in the Twentieth-Century United States" (unpublished paper). My thanks to Professor Davis for sharing her paper with me before publication.

19. Traub, *Thinking Sex*, 181–82.

20. On the Miami, see James Madison, *Hoosiers: A New History of Indiana* (Bloomington, IN, 2014), 11; and more broadly, see Mark Rifkin, *When Did Indians Become Straight?: Kinship, the History of Sexuality, and Native Sovereignty* (New York, 2011). On same-sex unions, see Emily Skidmore, *True Sex: The Lives of Trans Men at the Turn of the Twentieth Century* (New York, 2017), esp. 19–20, 37–42; Jennifer Manion, "The Queer History of Passing as a Man in Early Pennsylvania," *Pennsylvania Legacies* 16 (2016), 6–11, quotation at 9; and also Rachel Hope Cleves, *Charity and Sylvia: A Same-Sex Marriage in Early America* (New York, 2014).

21. Carroll Smith-Rosenberg, "The Female World of Love and Ritual: Relations Between Women in Nineteenth-Century America," *Signs* 1 (1975), 1–29, quotations at 4–5.

22. Leslie Reagan, *Dangerous Pregnancies: Mothers, Disabilities and Abortion in Modern America* (Berkeley, 2010), 15 (Coley); Mary Chamberlain, *Growing Up in Lambeth* (London, 1989), 89 (Baxter); Hagood, *Mothers of the South*, 123–24 ("tobacco"); Jacques Guillemeau, *Child-birth Or, the Happy Deliverie of Women* (1612), quoted in Mary E. Fissell, *Vernacular Bodies: The Politics of Reproduction in Early Modern England* (Oxford, UK, 2004), 152 ("delight").

3. Finding Out

1. Linda L. Layne, "Why the Home Pregnancy Test Isn't the Feminist Technology It's Cracked Up to Be and How to Make It Better," in Linda L. Layne, Sharra L. Vostral, and Kate Boyer, eds., *Feminist Technology* (Chicago, 2010), 90; Sarah A. Leavitt, "'A Private Little Revolution': The Home Pregnancy Test in American Culture," *Bulletin of the History of Medicine* 80 (2006), 317–45.

2. Laura Gowing, *Common Bodies: Women, Touch and Power in Seventeenth-Century England* (New Haven, CT, 2003), 112.

3. On uncertainty, see, for example, Barbara Duden, *Disembodying Women: Perspectives on Pregnancy and the Unborn* (1991, Cambridge, MA, trans. 1993), 160–62; Patricia Crawford, "The Construction and Experience of Maternity in Seventeenth-Century England," in Valerie Fildes, ed., *Women as Mothers in Pre-Industrial England: Essays in Memory of Dorothy McLaren* (London, 1990), 17; Sally G. McMillen, *Motherhood in the Old South: Pregnancy, Childbirth, and Infant Rearing* (Baton Rouge, LA, 1990), 28; Jane Sharp, *The Midwives Book, Or the Whole Art of Midwifry Discovered*, ed. Elaine Hobby (New York, 1999), 81–82; Nicholas Culpeper, *Directory for Midwives*, 2nd ed. (1650), quoted in Mary E. Fissell, *Vernacular Bodies: The Politics of Reproduction in Early Modern England* (Oxford, UK, 2004), 152 ("Shoe").

4. Linda A. Pollock, "Embarking on a Rough Passage: The Experience of Pregnancy in Early-Modern Society," in Fildes, ed., *Women as Mothers*, 43.

5. For this and the following two paragraphs, see Sharp, *Midwives Book*, 81–84; Duden, *Disembodying Women*, 62–66.

6. Angus McLaren, *Reproductive Rituals: The Perception of Fertility in England from the Sixteenth to the Nineteenth Century* (London, 1984), 46. Additional information on Boyle from Wellcome Library catalogue. Sharp, *Midwives Book*, 83 (worms, spots); Stephen Wilson, *Magical Universe: Everyday Ritual and Magic in Pre-Modern Europe* (London, 2004), 119 ("sprouted").

7. Fissell, *Vernacular Bodies*, 33.

8. Layne, "Why the Home Pregnancy Test Isn't the Feminist Technology It's Cracked Up to Be," 89–90.

9. Sandra Steingraber, *Having Faith: An Ecologist's Journey to Motherhood* (Cambridge, MA, 2001), 19.

10. McMillen, *Motherhood in the Old South*, 29 (Thomas); Edward Maunde Thompson, ed., *Correspondence of the Family of Hatton*, 2 vols. (London, 1878), i, 54 (Lyttelton, 1667); Amanda Vickery, *The Gentleman's Daughter: Women's Lives in Georgian England* (New Haven, CT, 1998), 99.

11. Kim Anderson, *Life Stages and Native Women: Memory, Teachings, and Story Medicine* (Winnipeg, 2011), 43; Ellen Ross, *Love and Toil: Motherhood in Outcast London, 1870–1918* (New York, 1983), 104, 106.

4. Week Ten, or Eight Weeks Gone

1. Sandra Steingraber, *Having Faith: An Ecologist's Journey to Motherhood* (Cambridge, MA, 2001), 14–17.

2. Barbara Duden, *Disembodying Women: Perspectives on Pregnancy and the Unborn* (1991, Cambridge, MA, trans. 1993), 75–76.

3. Elaine Forman Crane, ed., *The Diary of Elizabeth Drinker: The Life Cycle of an*

Eighteenth-Century Woman, 3 vols. (Boston, 1994), i, 99, Feb. 6, 1763; Sarah Blank Dine, "Diaries and Doctors: Philadelphia Medical Practice, 1760–1810," *Pennsylvania History* (2001), 413, 418–19, 434.

4. Sylvia Plath, "Parliament Hill Fields," *Collected Poems* (London, 2002).

5. Kathryn S. March, "Childbirth with Fear," in Susan E. Chase and Mary F. Rogers, eds., *Mothers and Children: Feminist Analyses and Personal Narratives* (New Brunswick, NJ, 2001), 171 (1990s Nepal); Linda L. Layne, *Motherhood Lost: A Feminist Account of Pregnancy Loss in America* (New York, 2003), 247–48 (1980s Jordan).

6. Crane, *Diary of Elizabeth Drinker*, i, 109, Sept. 19, 1763 (Howell), and Dec. 3, 1763 (James).

7. Laura Gowing, *Common Bodies: Women, Touch and Power in Seventeenth-Century England* (New Haven, CT, 2003), 121.

8. Duden, *Disembodying Women*, 62–66; Barbara Duden, *The Woman Beneath the Skin: A Doctor's Patients in Eighteenth-Century Germany* (Cambridge, MA, 1987, trans. 1991), 162–70.

9. Angus McLaren, *Reproductive Rituals: The Perception of Fertility in England from the Sixteenth to the Nineteenth Century* (London, 1984), 39; Lyndal Roper, *Witch Craze: Terror and Fantasy in Baroque Germany* (New Haven, CT, 2004), ch. 6, esp. 135.

10. Gowing, *Common Bodies*, 114 ("ten children"); Elaine Tyler May, *Barren in the Promised Land: Childless Americans and the Pursuit of Happiness* (New York, 1995), 21–23; Laurel Thatcher Ulrich, *Good Wives: Image and Reality in the Lives of Women in Northern New England, 1650–1750* (New York, 1982); Susan E. Klepp, "Revolutionary Bodies: Women and the Fertility Transition in the Mid-Atlantic Region, 1769–1820," *Journal of American History* 85 (1998), 920; Crane, *Diary of Elizabeth Drinker*, i, xi (housekeeper).

11. *Pennsylvania Packet*, May 11, 1787, July 10, 1787; *Pennsylvania Evening Herald*, Oct. 27, 1787.

12. May, *Barren in the Promised Land*, 127–36, 140 (Taylor); Paul Alexander, *Rough Magic: A Biography of Sylvia Plath* (New York, 1991), 256; *OED*; May, *Barren in the Promised Land*, 11.

5. Quickening

1. Gladys Hindmarch, *A Birth Account* (Vancouver, 1976), reprinted in Laura Chester, ed., *Cradle and All: Women Writers on Pregnancy and Birth* (Boston, 1989), 63.

2. Linda A. Pollock, "Embarking on a Rough Passage: The Experience of Pregnancy

in Early-Modern Society," in Valerie Fildes, ed., *Women as Mothers in Pre-Industrial England* (London, 1990), 46.

3. Constance Classen, *Worlds of Sense: Exploring the Senses in History and Across Cultures* (London, 1993), 2.

4. Robert Latham and William Matthews, eds., *The Diary of Samuel Pepys*, 11 vols. (Berkeley, 1970–1983), iv, 1, Jan. 1, 1663 ("undone").

5. See Barbara Duden, *Disembodying Women, Perspectives on Pregnancy and the Unborn* (1991, Cambridge, MA, trans. 1993), esp. 79–82; and Karen Newman, *Fetal Positions: Individualism, Science, Visuality* (Stanford, 1996).

6. For these details, see Liza Picard, *Restoration London* (New York, 1998), 8 (signs), 13 (smog).

7. For this 1662 portrait see Catharine MacLeod and Julia Marciari Alexander, eds., *Painted Ladies: Women at the Court of Charles II* (London, 2001), 118–22; *Diary of Samuel Pepys*, iii, 230, Oct. 20, 1662 ("copy").

8. *Diary of Samuel Pepys*, iii, 87, May 21, 1662 ("look").

9. See, for example, Anna McGrail and Daphne Metland, *Expecting: Everything You Need to Know About Pregnancy, Labour and Birth* (London, 2004), 104.

10. MacLeod and Alexander, eds., *Painted Ladies*, 124–25 (Madonna and Child); Horace Walpole, *Aedes Walpolianae: or, A Description of the Collection of Pictures at Houghton-Hall in Norfolk . . .* (London, 1747), xvi (French convent); *Diary of Samuel Pepys*, iii, 87, May 21, 1662 ("scales").

11. William A. Pettigrew, *Freedom's Debt: The Royal African Company and the Politics of the Atlantic Slave Trade, 1672–1752* (Chapel Hill, NC, 2013); on Castlemaine's black boy, see *Diary of Samuel Pepys*, viii, 33, Jan. 27, 1667.

12. The re-creation of South Carolinian plantation life in the next few paragraphs draws especially on Charles W. Joyner, *Down by the Riverside: A South Carolina Slave Community* (1984, repr. Urbana, IL, 2009); Marli F. Weiner, *Mistresses and Slaves: Plantation Women in South Carolina, 1830–1880* (Chicago, 1998); Jacqueline Jones, *Labor of Love, Labor of Sorrow: Black Women, Work, and the Family, from Slavery to the Present* (New York, 2009), ch. 1; Emily West, *Chains of Love: Slave Couples in Antebellum South Carolina* (Urbana, IL, 2004); and Cheryll Ann Cody, "Cycles of Work and of Childbearing: Seasonality in Women's Lives on Lowcountry Plantations," in David Barry Gaspar and Darlene Gaspar Hine, eds., *More Than Chattel: Black Women and Slavery in the Americas* (Bloomington, IN, 1996), 61–78. On the plantation hoe, see Chris Evans, "The Plantation Hoe: The Rise and Fall of an Atlantic Commodity, 1650–1850," *William and Mary Quarterly* 69 (2012), 71–100.

13. On South Carolina basketry, see John Michael Vlach, *The Afro-American Tradition in Decorative Arts* (Cleveland, 1977), 4–5.

14. Marie Jenkins Schwartz, *Birthing a Slave: Motherhood and Medicine in the Antebellum South* (Cambridge, MA, 2006), 19–20 (Douglass).

15. George P. Rawick, *The American Slave: A Composite Autobiography* (1941, repr. Westport, CT, 1972) ii, 2, 114 (Gibson); Richard H. Steckel, "Women, Work, and Health Under Plantation Slavery in the United States," in Gaspar and Hine, eds., *More Than Chattel*, 51–55 (timing of "privileges"); L. E. Simpson and M. Weir, *The Weaver's Craft*, 8th ed. (Leicester, UK, 1957), 43–44 (carding).

16. Jones, *Labor of Love, Labor of Sorrow*, 13.

17. V. Lynn Kennedy, *Born Southern: Childbirth, Motherhood, and Social Networks in the Old South* (Baltimore, 2010), 46 (Roach); Sally G. McMillen, *Motherhood in the Old South: Pregnancy, Childbirth and Infant Rearing* (Baton Rouge, LA, 1990), 52 (Allston's sister).

18. Kennedy, *Born Southern*, 55 ("favored"); Henry McMillan, giving an interview to the American Freedman's Inquiry Commission, 1863, quoted in John W. Blassingame, *Slave Testimony: Two Centuries of Letters, Speeches, Interviews, and Autobiographies* (Baton Rouge, 1977), 380 ("cut down").

19. Stephanie M. H. Camp, *Closer to Freedom: Enslaved Women and Everyday Resistance in the Plantation South* (Chapel Hill, NC, 2004), 121.

20. For the proverb, see Mark M. Smith, *Sensing the Past: Seeing, Hearing, Smelling, Tasting, and Touching in History* (Berkeley, 2007), 93.

6. The Rising of the Apron

1. Sarah Jinner, "A Prognostication," in *An Almanack and Prognostication for the Year of Our Lord 1659* (London, 1659), n.p.

2. Carol F. Karlsen and Laurie Crumpacker, eds., *The Journal of Esther Edwards Burr, 1754–1757* (New Haven, CT, 1984), 287 ("Fleshy and Fresh"); Nanci Langford, "Childbirth on the Canadian Prairies, 1880–1930," in Catherine A. Cavanaugh and Randi R. Warne, eds., *Telling Tales: Essays in Western Women's History* (Vancouver, 2000), 149 ("fighting bird"); Phillis Cunnington and Catherine Lucas, *Costumes for Births, Marriages and Deaths* (New York, 1972), 15 ("prodigiously," quoting Sarah Churchill); Verna Mae Slone, *How We Talked and Common Folks* (1978, repr. Lexington, KY, 2009), 161 ("get down"); Linda Pollock, *Forgotten Children: Parent-Child Relations from 1500 to 1900* (Cambridge, UK, 1983), 25 ("Trojan Horse," quoting Sydney Smith); Patricia Crawford, "The Construction and Experience of Maternity in Seventeenth-Century England," in Valerie Fildes, ed., *Women as Mothers in Pre-Industrial England: Essays in Memory of Dorothy McLaren* (London, 1990), 20 ("breeding," quoting Elizabeth Turner).

3. *OED*; Catherine M. Scholten, *Childbearing in American Society, 1650–1850* (New York, 1985), 15; Susan E. Klepp, *Revolutionary Conceptions: Women, Fertility and*

the Family Limitation in America, 1760–1820 (Chapel Hill, NC, 2009); Mary E. Fissell, *Vernacular Bodies: The Politics of Reproduction in Early Modern England* (Oxford, UK, 2004).

4. Judith Schneid Lewis, *In the Family Way: Childbearing in the British Aristocracy, 1760–1860* (New Brunswick, NJ, 1986), 72; Stella M. Drumm, ed., *Down the Santa Fe Trail and Into Mexico: The Diary of Susan Shelby Magoffin, 1846–1847* (New Haven, CT, 1926), 245, 287.

5. Jacob R. Marcus, ed., *The American Jewish Woman: A Documentary History* (New York, 1981), 267 (Cohen); Sylvia D. Hoffert, *Private Matters: American Attitudes to Childbearing and Infant Nurture in the Urban North, 1800–1860* (Urbana, IL, 1989), 38 (Cabot).

6. Joanne Begiato, "'Breeding' a 'Little Stranger': Managing Uncertainty in Pregnancy in Later Georgian England," in Jennifer Evans and Ciara Meehan, eds., *Perceptions of Pregnancy from the Seventeenth to the Twentieth Century* (Cham, Switzerland, 2017), 21, 25; Countess of Ilchester and Lord Stavordale, eds., *The Life and Letters of Lady Sarah Lennox, 1745–1826*, 2 vols. (London, 1901), ii, 292 ("indelicate"); *Gentleman's Magazine* LXI Dec. 1791, 1100, quoted in Maurice J. Quinlan, *Victorian Prelude: A History of English Manners, 1700–1830* (London, 1965), 67.

7. For the slang in this and the next paragraph, see Albert Barrère and Charles G. Leland, *Dictionary of Slang, Jargon and Cant*, 2 vols. (London, 1889–90), i, x (for the assessment of slang), 165 (boozed), 297 (drunk as a lord or a fish), 345 (drunk as an emperor), 377 (flying high, paralyzed), 417 (love), 522 (kisky); ii, 155 (pudding). For these examples of working-class communities, see Ellen Ross, *Love and Toil: Motherhood in Outcast London, 1870–1918* (London, 1993), esp. 107; Deborah Fink, *Agrarian Women: Wives and Mothers in Rural Nebraska, 1880–1940* (Chapel Hill, NC, 1992), esp. 84.

8. Alice Domurut Dreger, *Hermaphrodites and the Medical Invention of Sex* (Cambridge, MA, 1998); Angus McLaren, *Reproductive Rituals: The Perception of Fertility in England from the Sixteenth to the Nineteenth Century* (London, 1984), 46; Stephen Wilson, *Magical Universe: Everyday Ritual and Magic in Pre-Modern Europe* (London, 2004), 161–63.

9. For a synopsis, see Frank Newport, "Americans Prefer Boys to Girls, Just as They Did in 1941," Gallup, June 23, 2011. Reported at https://news.gallup.com/poll/148187/americans-prefer-boys-girls-1941.aspx. A late-twentieth-century review of the academic literature is N. E. Williamson, "Sex Preferences, Sex Control and the Status of Women," *SIGNS: Journal of Women in Culture and Society* 1 (1976), 847–62.

10. On feminist and mainstream "gender," see especially Deborah Cameron, "Gender: The Unsettling Adventures of a Feminist Keyword" (annual lecture of the

Raymond Williams Society, Oxford, UK, 2016); Joanne Meyerowitz, "A History of 'Gender,'" *American Historical Review* 113 (2008), 1346–56.

11. Newport, "Americans Prefer Boys to Girls."
12. On diet, see, for example, Lewis, *In the Family Way* (aristocrats); Sally G. McMillen, *Motherhood in the Old South: Pregnancy, Childbirth and Infant Rearing* (Baton Rouge, LA, 1990), 37.
13. M. Inez Hilger, *Chippewa Child Life and Its Cultural Background* (Washington, DC, 1951), 7–9 (Nett Lake).
14. Laura Gowing, *Common Bodies: Women, Touch and Power in Seventeenth-Century England* (New Haven, CT, 2003), 127 (ruffs), 128 ("foul impressions"), quoting A. M., *A Rich Closet of Physical Secrets* (London, 1652), ch. 1.
15. Laura Gowing, "'The Manner of Submission': Gender and Demeanour in Seventeenth-Century London," *Cultural and Social History* 10 (2013), 37 (Lord Mayor's court); McLaren, *Reproductive Rituals*, 50, citing a story in G. J. Witkowski, *Histoire des Accouchements Chez Tous Les Peuples* (Paris, n.d.), 170 (botanist).
16. Marie Jenkins Schwartz, *Birthing a Slave: Motherhood and Medicine in the Antebellum South* (Cambridge, MA, 2006), 132–34 (Foster); "A Question of Legitimacy," *Western Journal of Medicine and Surgery* (1845), 457, discussed in Schwartz, *Birthing a Slave*, 133; Henry Fielding, *The History of the Adventures of Joseph Andrews, and His Friend Mr. Abraham Adams*, 2nd ed., 2 vols. (London, 1742), ii, 73 (strawberry).
17. For this and the following four paragraphs, see *A Declaration of a Strange and Wonderfull Monster: Born in Kirkham Parish in Lancashire* (1646), quoted in Gowing, *Common Bodies*, 127 (round head); Stephen Wilson, *Magical Universe*, 158 (Shakespeare); Ellen Ross, *Love and Toil: Motherhood in Outcast London, 1870–1918* (London, 1993), 111 (London's lying-in hospital); Leslie J. Reagan, *Dangerous Pregnancies: Mothers, Disabilities, and Abortion in Modern America* (Berkeley, 2010), 19 ("disfigured arm," "deformed"); Indiana University Archives, IU Folklore Institute student papers, 70/149, Barbara J. Stanley, "Superstitions of Pregnancy and Childbirth" (1970), 12, 15, 18, 19, 22 (Midwestern examples, "freaks").

7. This Giving Birth

1. Sharon Olds, *The Sign of Saturn Poems 1980–1987* (London, 1991), 8–9.
2. The history of childbirth has made for a massive body of scholarship. This chapter focuses on four main figures: a seventeenth-century East Anglian minister's wife, an eighteenth-century Cherokee woman, a white tenant farmer of the 1930s U.S. Southeast, and 1940s Manhattanite Otis Burger. A powerful, now-standard

narrative of the leading edge of change is Judith Walzer Leavitt, *Brought to Bed: Childbearing in America, 1750–1950* (1986, repr. New York, 2016).

3. For these birthing metaphors, see Peggy Vincent, *Baby Catcher: Chronicles of a Modern Midwife* (New York, 2002), 134, 135 (Stinson Beach, wind); Lia Purpura, *Increase* (Athens, GA, 2000), 43 (map contours); Steve Humphries and Pamela Gordon, *A Labour of Love: Experience of Parenthood in Britain, 1900–1950* (London, 1993), 15 (poker, milliner); social scientist Margaret Mead, "On Having a Baby" (1972), extracted in Wendy Martin, ed., *The Beacon Book of Essays by Contemporary American Women* (Boston, 1996), 215; Laura Gowing, *Common Bodies: Women, Touch, and Power in Seventeenth-Century England* (New Haven, CT, 2003), 169 (the rack, Alice Thornton).

4. Early modern childbirth has gained unusual interest among English historians. For an overview, see my "Early Modern Birth and the Story of Gender Relations," *History Workshop Journal* 78 (2014), 287–94. The details for the composite account about Earls Colne's Jane Josselin in this section, and the recent past, emerge from Linda A. Pollock, "Childbearing and Female Bonding in Early Modern England," *Social History* 22 (1997), 286–306; Gowing, *Common Bodies* and her "Giving Birth at the Magistrate's Gate: Single Mothers in the Early Modern City," in Stephanie Tarbin and Susan Broomhall, eds., *Women, Identities and Communities in Early Modern Europe* (Aldershot, UK, 2008), 137–52; Adrian Wilson, *The Making of Man-Midwifery: Childbirth in England 1660–1770* (London, 1995), and his *Ritual and Conflict: The Social Relations of Childbirth in Early Modern England* (London, 2013); Mary E. Fissell, *Vernacular Bodies: The Politics of Reproduction in Early Modern England* (Oxford, UK, 2004). For Jane Josselin specifically, see Alan Macfarlane, *The Family Life of Ralph Josselin, a Seventeenth-Century Clergyman: An Essay in Historical Anthropology* (Cambridge, UK, 1970); Alan Macfarlane, *The Diary of Ralph Josselin, 1616–1683* (London, 1976). For the domestic scene, I also drew on Catherine Richardson, *Domestic Life and Domestic Tragedy in Early Modern England: The Material Life of the Household* (Manchester, UK, 2006).

5. To describe eighteenth-century Cherokee birth and its recent past, I consulted James Mooney, "The Sacred Formulas of the Cherokees," *Seventh Annual Report of the Bureau of American Ethnology to the Secretary of the Smithsonian Institution, 1885–1886* (Washington, DC, 1891), 387, 363; Lee Irwin, "Cherokee Healing: Myths, Dreams and Medicine," *American Indian Quarterly* 16 (1992), 239–42; Carol Neithammer, *Daughters of the Earth: The Lives and Legends of American Indian Women* (New York, 1977), 1–22; Katy Simpson Smith, *We Have Raised All of You: Motherhood in the South, 1750–1835* (Baton Rouge, LA, 2013). Additional detail comes from Sarah H. Hill, *Weaving New Worlds: Southeastern*

Cherokee Women and Their Basketry (Chapel Hill, NC, 1997); Theda Perdue, *Cherokee Women: Gender and Cultural Change, 1700–1835* (Lincoln, NE, 1998); Carolyn Ross Johnston, *Cherokee Women in Crisis: Trail of Tears, Civil War, and Allotment, 1838–1907* (Tuscaloosa, AL, 2003), esp. 18–22.

6. For the white tenant farmers of the 1930s U.S. Southeast, and their recent past, I drew on the fine visual writing and insights of the contemporary sociologist Margaret Jarman Hagood, *Mothers of the South: Portraiture of the White Tenant Farm Woman* (1939, repr. New York, 1972), supplemented, about granny midwives, with Linda Holmes and Margaret Charles Smith, *Listen to Me Good: The Life Story of an Alabama Midwife* (Columbus, OH, 1996), 96 (afterbirth); Onnie Lee Logan, as told to Katherine Clark, *Motherwit: An Alabama Midwife's Story* (New York, 1989), 147 (God, easy), and Molly Ladd-Taylor, *Mother-Work: Women, Child Welfare and the State, 1890–1930* (Chicago, 1994), 23–26 ("misery," "hands").

7. For Otis Burger's world, and the changes to birth immediately before and after, I consulted Abigail Lewis [Otis Burger], *An Interesting Condition: The Diary of a Pregnant Woman* (Garden City, NY, 1950), which was commissioned by the publishers (correspondence with author), esp. 190–200 (birth), further details at 117 (doctors), 34 (zoology class), 61 ($750), 101–102, 140, 203 (Dick-Read), 120 (specimen), 171 (Scotch), 173 (stopping a contraction), as well as, for the discussion below, 69–70, 75 (nineteenth-century novels), 98 (science). Grantly Dick-Read, *Childbirth Without Fear: The Principles and Practice of Natural Childbirth* (New York, 1944); as well as, in particular, Jacqueline H. Wolf, *Deliver Me from Pain: Anesthesia and Birth in America* (Baltimore, 2009); Ann Oakley et al., "Becoming a Mother: Continuities and Discontinuities Over Three Decades," in Fatemeh Ebtehaj et al., eds., *Birth Rites and Rights* (Oxford, UK, 2011), 9–27; Paula A. Michaels, *Lamaze: An International History* (New York, 2014); Wendy Kline, "Communicating a New Consciousness: Countercultural Print and the Home Birth Movement of the 1970s," *Bulletin of the History of Medicine* 89 (2015), 527–56; Leavitt, *Brought to Bed*.

8. For the next four paragraphs, see the citations above for each set of protagonist(s).

8. Hello, You

1. Abigail Lewis [Otis Burger], *An Interesting Condition: The Diary of a Pregnant Woman* (Garden City, NY, 1950), 203–204; Ann Oakley, *Taking It Like a Woman* (London, 1987), 62.

2. Theda Perdue, *Cherokee Women: Gender and Cultural Change, 1700–1835* (Lincoln, NE, 1998), 25 (ballsticks), 43; Carolyn Ross Johnston, *Cherokee Women in Crisis: Trail of Tears, Civil War, and Allotment, 1838–1907* (Tuscaloosa, AL, 2003),

19 (fontanel); and see Kim Anderson, *Life Stages and Native Women: Memory, Teachings, and Story Medicine* (Winnipeg, 2011), 57.

3. For details of free black Philadelphia naming practices in these three paragraphs, see Gary B. Nash, *Forging Freedom: The Formation of Philadelphia's Black Community, 1720–1840* (Cambridge, MA, 1998), esp. 79–88; Julie Winch, *A Gentleman of Color: The Life of James Forten* (New York, 2002), esp. 113; Susan Klepp, *Revolutionary Conceptions* (Chapel Hill, NC, 2009), 118 (Dinah).

4. Nancy C. Dorian, "A Substitute Name System in the Scottish Highlands," *American Anthropologist* 72 (1970), 303–19; Nancy C. Dorian, *The Tyranny of Tide: An Oral History of the East Sutherland Fisherfolk* (Ann Arbor, MI, 1985), 83 (John Sutherland), 66 (address them in person).

5. Shirley Boteler Mock, *Dreaming with the Ancestors: Black Seminole Women in Texas and Mexico* (Norman, OK, 2010), 219, 223.

6. Buchi Emecheta recounts her experience in novel and memoir form in *Second-Class Citizen* (London, 1974, repr. Oxford, UK, 1994), 135–38, and *Head Above Water* (1986, repr. Oxford, UK, 1994), 104.

9. Tears and Anecdotes

1. Anne Enright, *Making Babies: Stumbling into Motherhood* (London, 2005), 127–30.

2. Milicent Washburn Shinn, *The Biography of a Baby* (Boston, 1900), 20 (bagpipes); Abigail Lewis (Otis Burger), *An Interesting Condition: The Diary of a Pregnant Woman* (Garden City, NY, 1950), 153 (penny horn); M. Inez Hilger, *Chippewa Child Life and Its Cultural Background* (Washington, DC, 1951), 7 ("pitiful hard moan").

3. Leah Astbury, "'Ordering the Infant': Caring for Newborns in Early Modern England," in Sandra Cavallo and Tessa Storey, eds., *Conserving Health in Early Modern Culture: Bodies and Environments in Italy and England* (Manchester, UK, 2017), 83–86; John and Elizabeth Newson, *Patterns of Infant Care in an Urban Community* (London, 1963), 89–92, quotation at 89 ("crafty").

4. Joanna Bourke, "The Sentience of Infants," in *The Story of Pain: From Prayer to Painkillers* (New York, 2014), 214–18.

5. Lewis, *An Interesting Condition*, 23 (spine-destroying).

6. Katy Simpson Smith, *We Have Raised All of You: Motherhood in the South, 1750–1835* (Baton Rouge, LA, 2013), 90 (Cox); Shirley Marchalonis, *The Worlds of Lucy Larcom, 1824–1893* (Athens, GA, 1989), 70–71.

7. Emily Cockayne, *Hubbub: Filth, Noise and Stench in England, 1600–1770* (New Haven, CT, 2007), 116 ("offence"); Stephanie J. Shaw, "Mothering Under Slavery in the Antebellum South," in Evelyn Nakano Glenn, Grace Chang, and Linda Rennine Forcey, eds., *Mothering: Ideology, Experience, and Agency* (New York, 1994),

245 ("bottle"); Mark M. Smith, ed., *Hearing History: A Reader* (Athens, GA, 2004), 37 (Clark); Work Projects Administration, "Angie Boyce" [formerly Angie King], *Slave Narratives: A Folk History of Slavery in the United States. From Interviews with Former Slaves: Indiana Narratives* (Washington, DC, 1941).

8. Marla N. Powers, *Oglala Women: Myth, Ritual and Reality* (Chicago, 1986), 56 ("frighten"); and also see, for a similar Ojibwe habit, Thomas Peacock and Marlene Wisuri, *The Four Hills of Life: Ojibwe Wisdom* (Afton, MN, 2006), 38.

9. Amanda Vickery, *The Gentleman's Daughter: Women's Lives in Georgian England* (New Haven, CT, 1998), 110.

10. Ann Oakley, *From Here to Maternity: Becoming a Mother* (Harmondsworth, UK, 1979), 252 ("good baby").

11. American Indian Studies Research Institute, Indiana University, Dictionary Database.

10. Staying the Month

1. For the term, see *OED*, quoting the *Magazine of Poetry* of 1892, and *Our Bodies, Ourselves* (Boston, 1978); Ann Oakley, *From Here to Maternity: Becoming a Mother* (Harmondsworth, UK, 1979), 145.

2. Patricia Crawford, *Blood, Bodies and Families in Early Modern England* (2004, repr. London, 2014), ch. 5, quotation at 147 ("curdy"); F. Truby King, *The Expectant Mother, and Baby's First Months: For Parents and Nurses* (Wellington, NZ, 1925), 59; Oakley, *From Here to Maternity*, 181 ("good thing").

3. Alexander Longe, "A Small Postscript on the Ways and Manners of the Indians Called Cherokees," ed. David H. Corkran, *Southern Indian Studies* 11 (1969), 34; and see Julie L. Reed, "Family and Nation: Cherokee Orphan Care, 1835-1903," *American Indian Quarterly* 34 (2010), 312.

4. Oakley, *From Here to Maternity*, 48 ("disease"), 124 ("fishing wire"), 163 ("world war").

5. Irma Honigmann and John Honigmann, "Child Rearing Patterns Among the Great Whale River Eskimo," *University of Alaska Anthropological Papers* 2 (1953), 33; Wendy Mitchinson, *Giving Birth in Canada, 1900-1950* (Toronto, 2002), 89 ("tea"); 286-88.

6. M. Inez Hilger, *Chippewa Child Life and Its Cultural Background* (Washington, DC, 1951), 15-16.

7. Margaret Charles Smith and Linda Holmes, *Listen to Me Good: The Life Story of an Alabama Midwife* (Columbus, OH, 1996), 51.

8. For this paragraph and the next: Mrs. William Parkes, *Domestic Duties or, Instructions to Young Married Ladies*, 2nd ed. (London, 1825), 319-32; Elizabeth Cady Stanton, *Eighty Years and More* (New York, 1898), 118 ("Mother Monroe");

Fanny Fern [pseud.], *Ruth Hall: A Domestic Tale of the Present Time* (New York, 1855), 43.

9. Patrick Minges, *Far More Terrible for Women: Personal Accounts of Women in Slavery* (Winston-Salem, NC, 2006), 148–50.

10. Harold Nicolson to Vita Sackville-West, Aug. 15, 1914, Nigel Nicolson, ed., *Vita and Harold: The Letters of Vita Sackville-West and Harold Nicolson* (New York, 1992), 53.

11. Ji-Yeon Yuh, *Beyond the Shadow of Camptown: Korean Military Brides in America* (New York, 2002), quotation at 100.

12. For this paragraph and the next: Margaret Llewelyn Davies, ed., *Maternity: Letters from Working Women* (1915, repr. London, 1978), 46 ("luxury"), 49 ("get up"), 187 ("first night"), 189 ("pits"), 190 ("harder").

13. Carole Itter, "Cry Baby" (1976), in Laura Chester, ed., *Cradle and All: Women Writers on Pregnancy and Birth* (Boston, 1989), 213.

14. Mary Chamberlain, *Growing Up in Lambeth* (London, 1989), 94 ("wasn't allowed"); Michael Young and Peter Willmott, *Family and Kinship in East London* (Glencoe, IL, 1957), 39–40 (churching).

15. For this paragraph and the next: Helen Sekaquaptewa, *Me and Mine: The Life Story of Helen Sekaquaptewa as Told to Louise Udall* (Tucson, AZ, 1969), 180–81.

16. Oakley, *From Here to Maternity*, 119–20, 215–16.

17. Emily Rathbone Greg, ed., *Reynolds-Rathbone Diaries and Letters 1753–1839* (privately printed, 1905), 76–77.

18. Margaret Jarman Hagood, *Mothers of the South: Portraiture of the White Tenant Farm Woman* (1939, repr. New York, 1972), 137.

19. Connie Young Fu, "The World of Our Grandmothers," in Asian Women United of California, eds., *Making Waves: An Anthology of Writings by and About Asian American Women* (Boston, 1989), 37–39.

20. Helen M. Dart, *Maternity and Child Care in Selected Rural Areas of Mississippi* (Washington, DC, 1921), 4, 30, 40–41.

21. *England's Merry Jester* (1694), quoted in Laura Gowing, "'The Manner of Submission': Gender and Demeanour in Seventeenth-Century London," *Cultural and Social History* 10 (2013), 33.

22. For this example from the history of emotion, see Joel Pfister, "On Conceptualizing the Cultural History of Emotional and Psychological Life in America," in Pfister and Nancy Schnog, eds., *Inventing the Psychological: Toward a Cultural History of Emotional Life in America* (New Haven, CT, 1997), 31–32.

23. Tim Reinke-Williams, *Women, Work and Sociability in Early Modern London* (Houndsmills, UK, 2014), 33.

24. Louise Erdrich, *The Blue Jay's Dance: A Memoir of Early Motherhood* (New York, 1995), 146.

25. Polly Clarke (Lexington) to Mrs. Mary Cotton (Hopkinton), Dec. 11, 1782, Allen-Ware Papers, 1782–1866, Box 1, Folder 1782–1800, Massachusetts Historical Society.

26. Nathan Sellers to [Mrs. Ann Gibson Sellers], (Philadelphia?), Dec. 12, 1785, Sellers Family Papers, American Philosophical Society.

27. Katharine C. Balderston, ed., *Thraliana: The Diary of Mrs. Hester Lynch Thrale (later Mrs. Piozzi), 1776–1809*, 2 vols., 2nd ed. (Oxford, UK, 1951), i, 158.

28. Jean Radford, "My Pride and Joy," in Katherine Gieve, ed., *Balancing Acts, On Being a Mother* (London, 1989), 138.

29. James C. Mohr and Richard E. Winslow, eds., *Cormany Diaries: A Northern Family in the Civil War* (Pittsburgh, 1982), 597.

30. Amanda Vickery, *The Gentleman's Daughter: Women's Lives in Georgian England* (New Haven, CT, 1998), 15–16 (quotations); Adrian Wilson, *Ritual and Conflict: The Social Relations of Childbirth in Early Modern England* (London, 2013), 179.

31. Hannah Woolley, *The Gentlewomans Companion; Or a Guide to the Female Sex: Containing Directions of Behaviour, in All Places, Companies, Relations and Conditions, from Their Childhood Down to Old Age* (London, 1673), quotation at 208.

32. Hagood, *Mothers of the South*, 55.

33. Susannah Shaw Romney, *New Netherland Connections: Intimate Networks and Atlantic Ties in Seventeenth-Century America* (Chapel Hill, NC, 2014), 66.

34. For these three paragraphs, see Cherríe Moraga, *Waiting in the Wings: Portrait of a Queer Motherhood* (Ithaca, NY, 1997), quotations at 85–87.

11. Damp Cloth

1. Li-Young Lee, "The Waiting," *The City in Which I Love You* (Rochester, NY, 1990), 64.

2. For the composite Victorian figure and scene in this section, I drew on Annemarie Adams, *Architecture in the Family Way: Doctors, Houses and Women, 1870–1900* (London, 1996), esp. 131 (kitchen), 136 (parlor), 140–43 (nursery); Jane Hamlett, *Material Relations: Domestic Interiors and Middle-Class Families in England, 1850–1910* (Manchester, UK, 2010), esp. 47, 50, 78, 87 (parlor), 118–19 (servant), 112, 120–24 (nursery, sampler), 130 (Dutch picture); Ruth Goodman, *How to Be a Victorian: A Dawn-to-Dusk Guide to Victorian Life* (New York, 2014), 11–15, 123–27 (smell, cloth), 17, 133–34 (soap, perfume), 214–15 (diapers), 255–70 (laundry); and, illuminating Glasgow in particular, Eleanor Gordon and Gwyneth Nair, *Public Lives: Women, Family and Society in Victorian Britain* (New Haven, CT, 2003), esp. 6, 123–25 (parlor), 45, 150–51 (servants), 96 (*Waverley Journal*).

3. Patricia E. Malcolmson, *English Laundresses: A Social History, 1850–1930* (Urbana, IL, 1986), 23, 34, quotation at 34.

4. The evidence for Perryman, Bowers, and Mobile in this section is drawn from Laurie A. Wilkie, *The Archaeology of Mothering: An African-American Midwife's Tale* (New York, 2003), esp. 25, 28, 104–106 (house and land), 33 (Willie), 83 (Hansberry), 87–88 (status), 91, 96, 97 (food and food objects), 127, 215 (antiseptics, remedies), 214 (cherub vases); Marilyn Culpepper, *Mobile: Photographs from the William E. Wilson Collection* (Charleston, SC, 2001), esp. 9, 55. On the post-emancipation preference for seclusion from whites, see Paula Giddings, *When and Where I Enter: The Impact of Black Women on Race and Sex in America* (New York, 1984), and Jacqueline Jones, *Labor of Love, Labor of Sorrow: Black Women, Work, and the Family, from Slavery to the Present* (New York, 2010).

5. Ann Oakley, *From Here to Maternity: Becoming a Mother* (Harmondsworth, UK, 1979), 163.

6. For Ellie Mae Burroughs, see James Agee and Walker Evans, *Let Us Now Praise Famous Men: Three Tenant Families* (1939, repr. Boston, 1988), in which she is retitled Annie Mae Gudger, esp. liii–liv, 127–89, details at 139 (yard); 151 (soap); 152, 155, 206 (hallway); 154–55 (smells); 165, 173, 259, 272, 275, 279 (wardrobe, clothing); 173 (mantle); 177–82 (kitchen); 441 (nursing). For her neighbor Elizabeth Tingle, retitled Sadie Ricketts, see ibid., xvii, details at 191, 199–200, 364. On the nostalgic odor see ibid., 154, and on the smell of diapers, Margaret Jarman Hagood, *Mothers of the South: Portraiture of the White Tenant Farm Woman* (1939, repr. New York, 1972), 105.

7. The *longue durée* narrative here is especially influenced by Kathleen Brown, *Foul Bodies: Cleanliness in Early America* (New Haven, CT, 2009). For this and the next five paragraphs: For Bascom in particular, see ibid., 221, 237 ("more nice"). For the eighteenth-century servant, see Carolyn Steedman, *Labours Lost: Domestic Service and the Making of Modern England* (Cambridge, UK, 2009), 14. On the tactile language of cloth, see also Amanda Vickery, *The Gentleman's Daughter: Women's Lives in Georgian England* (New Haven, CT, 1998), 149; *OED*, "diaper," "nappy"; Elizabeth Roberts, *A Woman's Place: An Oral History of Working-Class Women, 1890–1940* (Oxford, UK, 1984), 161 (the Lancaster "wiper"); Ellen Ross, *Love and Toil: Motherhood in Outcast London, 1870–1918* (London, 1993), 138 (smelly, loops and ties); M. Inez Hilger, *Chippewa Child Life and Its Cultural Background* (Washington, DC, 1951), 15 ("sweet moss"); and see Kim Anderson, *Life Stages and Native Women: Memory, Teachings, and Story Medicine* (Winnipeg, 2011), 58–61.

8. Martha Vicinus, "The Perfect Victorian Lady," in Martha Vicinus, ed., *Suffer and Be Still: Women in the Victorian Age* (Bloomington, IN, 1972). The classic text of the emergence of this domestic womanhood is Leonore Davidoff and Catherine

Hall, *Family Fortunes: Men and Women of the English Middle Class, 1780-1850* (Chicago, 1987).

9. Adrienne Rich, *Of Woman Born: Motherhood as Experience and Institution* (1976, repr. New York, 1986), 27.

10. Eunice Murray, *Frances Murray: A Memoir* (Glasgow, 1920), 113 (dullness), 117 (babydom).

11. For Mobile's Civil War memorial, see Culpepper, *Mobile*, 48.

12. Lucille Clifton, *Generations: A Memoir* (New York, 1976), esp. 11-12, 34, 79.

12. Time, Interrupted

1. Lisa Baraitser, *Maternal Encounters: The Ethics of Interruption* (Hove, UK, 2009).

2. Amanda Vickery, *The Gentleman's Daughter: Women's Lives in Georgian England* (New Haven, CT, 1988), 114-15.

3. Rebecca Allmon to her aunts, Halifax, Mar. 29, 1787, Byles Family Papers, Box 2, Massachusetts Historical Society.

4. Vickery, *The Gentleman's Daughter*, 115.

5. Ethel Armes, ed., *Nancy Shippen, Her Journal Book* (New York, 1968), 144 (Livingston); Vickery, *The Gentleman's Daughter*, 115-16 (Parker); Frances Marvin Smith Webster to Lucien Bonaparte, Fort Pickens, Sept. 18, 1846, in Van R. Baker, ed., *The Websters: Letters of an Army Family in Peace and War, 1836-1853* (Kent, Ohio, 2000), 109; Louisa Wylie Boisen to Herman Boisen, Bloomington, IN, Aug. 4, 1878, and Rebecca Wylie to Louisa Boisen, Bloomington, IN, Jan. 1875, Wylie House Museum.

6. For these four paragraphs, see Ann Oakley, *From Here to Maternity: Becoming a Mother* (Harmondsworth, UK, 1979), 31, 253-54, quotations at 142 (Wright), 253 (Mitchell).

7. Eleanor Gordon and Gwyneth Nair, *Public Lives: Women, Family and Society in Victorian Britain* (New Haven, CT, 2003), 143.

8. For this and the following two paragraphs, see Margery Spring Rice, "The Day's Work," in *Working-Class Wives: Their Health and Conditions* (Harmondsworth, UK, 1939), 94-127; Selina Todd, *Young Women, Work, and Family in England, 1918-1950* (Oxford, UK, 2005).

9. For these two paragraphs: Mass Observation, "The Housewife's Day," *New Series Bulletin* 42 (May/June 1951), 2, quoted in Claire Langhamer, *Women's Leisure in England, 1920-60* (Manchester, UK, 2000), 31-32.

10. *Manchester Evening News*, Oct. 20, 1955.

11. Mass Observation: DR1831, reply to March/April 1948 Directive, quoted in Langhamer, *Women's Leisure*, 30.

12. For this paragraph and the next: Maria Campbell, "Preface," in Kim Anderson,

Life Stages and Native Women: Memory, Teachings, and Story Medicine (Winnipeg, 2011), xv (stories), and interviewed in Anderson, ibid., 112–14.

13. For this paragraph and the next: Oakley, *From Here to Maternity*, 252–54, quotations at 253 (factory workers), 254 (Mitchell, "going on for years").

14. Margaret Mead, "On Having a Baby" (1972), extracted in Wendy Martin, ed., *The Beacon Book of Essays by Contemporary American Women* (Boston, 1996), 216.

15. Oakley, *From Here to Maternity*, 241.

13. The Middle of the Night

1. For this paragraph and the next, see A. Roger Ekirch, *At Day's Close: Night in Times Past* (New York, 2005), 267–68 (Boswell and his times); Alicia Ostriker, "Postscript to Propaganda," *The Mother/Child Papers* (1980, repr. Pittsburgh, 2009), 47.

2. On early modern beds, I draw here and in the following four paragraphs on John Crowley, *The Invention of Comfort: Sensibilities and Design in Early Modern Britain and Early America* (Baltimore, 2003), esp. 74 ("dagswain"), 81 (Maryland), 91 (Igbo); Jean-Louis Flandrin, *Families in Former Times: Kinship, Household and Sexuality*, trans. Richard Southern (Cambridge, UK, 1979), 90–102; Laura Gowing, "'The Twinkling of a Bedstaff': Recovering the Social Life of English Beds 1500–1700," *Home Cultures* 11 (2014), 275–304; Ferdinand Baynard de la Vingtrie, *Travels of a Frenchman in Maryland and Virginia*, ed. Ben C. McCary (Williamsburg, VA, 1950), 13 ("box-like frame"); Philip D. Morgan, *Slave Counterpoint: Black Culture in the Eighteenth-Century Chesapeake and Lowcountry* (Chapel Hill, NC, 1998), 114; Raffaella Sarti, *Europe at Home: Family and Material Culture, 1500–1800* (New Haven, CT, 2002), 103 (Chesapeake immigrants), 119–31; John Styles, "Lodging at the Old Bailey: Lodgings and Their Furnishings in Eighteenth-Century London," in John Styles and Amanda Vickery, eds., *Gender, Taste and Material Culture in Britain and North America, 1700–1830* (New Haven, CT, 2006), 71–75.

3. On more modern beds, I draw here and in the following three paragraphs on Tom Crook, "Norms, Forms and Beds: Spatializing Sleep in Victorian Britain," *Body & Society* 14 (2008), 15–35; Judith Flanders, *Inside the Victorian Home: A Portrait of Domestic Life in Victorian England* (New York, 2003), 42–47; Hilary Hinds, "Together and Apart: Twin Beds, Domestic Hygiene and Modern Marriage, 1890–1945," *Journal of Design History* 23 (2010), 275–304; Reader-Editors of Woman's Home Companion, *Bedtime Story: Reports on Sleeping Equipment* (New York, 1942).

4. Flandrin, *Families in Former Times*, 100 ("big beds").

5. Crowley, *The Invention of Comfort*, 167 ("mean mats").

6. On the Kentuckian practices explored here, see Verna Mae Slone, *How We Talked* and *Common Folks* (1978, repr. Lexington, KY, 2009), esp. 259 (bed sharing), 251–52 (cabin), 266 and 279 (chickens), 254 (animals), 28 ("scrouging"), 32 ("puncheon"), 61 (old enough), 125 (staying overnight); William Lynwood Montell, *Killings: Folk Justice in the Upper South* (Lexington, KY, 1986), 29 ("you'll crave it"); and, from the perspective of government reformers, Lydia J. Roberts, *The Nutrition and Care of Children in a Mountain County of Kentucky, United States Children's Bureau Publication 110* (Washington, DC, 1922). As an object of later anthropology, see Susan Abbott, "Holding On and Pushing Away: Comparative Perspectives on an Eastern Kentucky Child-Rearing Practice," *Ethos* 20 (1992), 33–65, quotation at 58 (schoolteacher).

7. For *Ammenschlaf*, see Lodewijk Brunt and Brigitte Steger, eds., *Worlds of Sleep: New Perspectives* (Berlin, 2008), 18.

8. The key account of early modern first night and second night is Ekirch, *At Day's Close*, ch. 12.

9. William Gouge, "The Duties of Parents," in *Of Domesticall Duties* (London, 1622), 515 ("wrangle"); and see Elizabeth Lincoln, *The Countesse of Lincolnes Nurserie* (Oxford, 1628).

10. A. Marsh, *The Ten Pleasures of Marriage Relating to All the Delights and Contentments That Are Mask'd Under the Bands of Matrimony* (Oxford, 1682), 122 ("tossing and tumbling"), attributed to Aphra Behn; Alan Macfarlane, *The Family Life of Ralph Josselin, a Seventeenth-Century Clergyman: An Essay in Historical Anthropology* (Cambridge, UK, 1970), 89 ("cryings out"); Mary Collier, *The Woman's Labour: An Epistle to Mr. Stephen Duck* (London, 1739), quotations at 11.

11. Narcissa Prentiss Whitman, Mar. 30, 1837, in Clifford Merrill Drury, ed., *Where Wagons Could Go: Narcissa Whitman and Eliza Spalding* (1963, repr. Lincoln, NE, 1997), 126.

12. The interpretation here and in the following four paragraphs draws on Anne Bradstreet, *The Tenth Muse Lately Sprung Up in America, or, Severall Poems Compiled with Great Variety of Wit and Learning, Full of Delight* (London, 1650), quotation at 43 ("wayward cries"); David H. Flaherty, *Privacy in Colonial New England* (Charlottesville, VA, 1972), 76–79 (bed sharing); Robert S. Cox, "The Suburbs of Eternity: On Visionaries and Miraculous Sleepers," in Brunt and Steger, *Worlds of Sleep*, 53–73; Alec Ryrie, "Sleeping, Waking and Dreaming in Protestant Piety," in Jessica Martin and Alec Ryrie, eds., *Private and Domestic Devotion in Early Modern Britain* (Farnham, UK, 2012), 73–92; Sasha Handley, "From the Sacral to the Moral: Sleeping Practices, Household Worship and Confessional Cultures in Late Seventeenth-Century England," *Cultural and Social History* 9 (2012), 27–46.

13. For these paragraphs, on modern sleep, see: Benjamin Reiss, "Sleeping at Walden Pond: Thoreau, Abnormal Temporality, and the Modern Body," *American Literature* 85 (2013), 5–31; A. Roger Ekirch, "The Modernization of Western Sleep: Or, Does Insomnia Have a History?," *Past & Present* 226 (2015), 149–92. Sasha Handley, "Sociable Sleeping in Early Modern England, 1660–1760," *History* 98 (2013), 79–104, quotation at 84 (*Tatler*).

14. Brenda Shaughnessy, "Liquid Flesh," *Our Andromeda* (Port Townsend, WA, 2012), 22–27, quotation at 26.

15. Steve Humphries and Pamela Gordon, eds., *A Labour of Love: The Experience of Parenthood in Britain, 1900–1950* (London, 1993), 72–73 ("settee").

16. Elizabeth Roberts, *Women and Families: An Oral History, 1940–1970* (Oxford, UK, 1995), 155.

17. The nighttime interpretation here and in the next seven paragraphs draws on Mabel Loomis Todd Papers (MS496C), Manuscripts and Archives, Yale University Library, Series III: Diaries 1879–1881; Journal Volume III; and "Millicent's Journal" Volume I. Todd is best known for her subsequent relationship with Austin Dickinson, brother to the poet Emily Dickinson; see Polly Longsworth, ed., *Austin and Mabel: The Amherst Affair & Love Letters of Austin Dickinson and Mabel Loomis Todd* (New York, 1983). Her voluminous personal writings served as a rich episode in the history of Victorian sexuality for Peter Gay, *The Bourgeois Experience: Victoria to Freud. Volume 1: The Education of the Senses* (New York, 1984), 71–108. Identification of Molly Peyton in *Boyd's Directory of the District of Columbia* (Alexandria, VA, 1880), 711.

18. On bedfellow, see Gowing, "'The Twinkling of a Bedstaff.'"

19. Jacqueline H. Wolf, *Don't Kill Your Baby: Public Health and the Decline of Breastfeeding in the Nineteenth and Twentieth Centuries* (Columbus, OH, 2001), 188 ("American babies").

20. Mrs. W.D. to Mrs. West, May 9, 1918, Pennsylvania, in Molly Ladd-Taylor, ed., *Raising a Baby the Government Way: Mothers' Letters to the Children's Bureau, 1915–1932* (New Brunswick, NJ, 1986), 108; Adrienne Rich, *Of Woman Born: Motherhood as Experience and Institution* (1976, repr. New York, 1986), 31–32.

21. The evidence used here derives from scientific sleep research: William Caudill and Helen Weinstein, "Maternal Care and Infant Behavior in Japan and America," *Psychiatry* 32 (1969), 12–43; Caudill and David W. Plath, "Who Sleeps by Whom? Parent-Child Involvement in Urban Japanese Families," *Psychiatry* 29 (1966), 344–66; M. Gantley, D. P. Davies, and A. Murcott, "Sudden Infant Death Syndrome: Links with Infant Care Practices," *British Medical Journal* 306, no. 6869 (Jane Z, 1993), 16–20 (on Cardiff).

22. Abigail Lewis (Otis Burger), *An Interesting Condition: The Diary of a Pregnant Woman* (Garden City, NY, 1950), 245.

14. Pent Milk

1. For the first two sections: John Donne's poem is "The Extasie," quotations from lines 4, 7–8. On oxytocin, see Sarah Blaffer Hrdy, *Mother Nature: Maternal Instincts and How They Shape the Human Species* (New York, 1999), 137–39; C. Sue Carter and Stephen W. Porges, "The Biochemistry of Love: An Oxytocin Hypothesis," *EMBO Reports* 14 (2013), 12–16. For eros and nursing, see Adrienne Rich, *Of Woman Born: Motherhood as Experience and Institution* (1976, repr. New York, 1986), 37; Maggie Nelson, *The Argonauts* (Minneapolis, 2015), 44.

2. Like birthing, breastfeeding and wet-nursing have made for their own histories. The key works drawn on here and immediately below include Emily West and R. J. Knight, "Mother's Milk: Slavery, Wet-nursing and Black and White Women in the Antebellum South," *Journal of Southern History* 83 (2017), 37–68; Marissa C. Rhodes, "Domestic Vulnerabilities: Reading Families and Bodies into Eighteenth-Century Anglo-Atlantic Wet Nurse Advertisements," *Journal of Family History* 40 (2015), 39–63; Janet Golden, *A Social History of Wet Nursing in America: From Breast to Bottle* (Cambridge, UK, 1996), esp. 22–23 (Boston); Marie Jenkins Schwartz, "'At Noon, Oh How I Ran': Breastfeeding and Weaning on Plantation and Farm in Antebellum Virginia and Alabama," in Patricia Morton, ed., *Discovering the Women in Slavery: Emancipating Perspectives on the American Past* (Athens, GA, 1996), 241–59; Valerie A. Fildes, *Wet Nursing: A History from Antiquity to the Present* (Oxford, UK, 1988); Valerie A. Fildes, *Breasts, Bottles and Babies: A History of Infant Feeding* (Edinburgh, 1986).

3. On wet-nursing for the hospital and on Margaret Collier in particular throughout this section, see Alysa Levene, *Childcare, Health and Mortality at the London Foundling Hospital, 1741–1800* (Manchester, UK, 2007), esp. 111, 132–33, 136 (Collier); 96, 122 (Chertsey); 106–14 (weaning); 134–35 (wages); Gillian Clark, ed., *Correspondence of the Foundling Hospital Inspectors in Berkshire, 1759–1768* (Reading, UK, 1997), xxxvi (inspectors); and, on the foundling's clothing, Gillian Clark, "Infant Clothing in the Eighteenth Century: A New Insight," *Costume* 28 (1994), 47–59. For the particular threat of poverty with a first child, see Barry Stapleton, "Inherited Poverty and Life-Cycle Poverty: Odiham, Hampshire, 1650–1850," *Social History* 18 (1993), 339–55; Patricia Crawford, *Parents of Poor Children in England, 1580–1800* (Oxford, UK, 2010), 9.

4. For Margaret Morris and mid-eighteenth-century Philadelphia in this section, see John Jay Smith, ed., *Letters of Doctor Richard Hill and His Children, Or, The History of a Family as Told by Themselves* (Philadelphia, 1854), 173–74, 178, 183; Catherine La Courreye Blecki and Karin A. Wulf, eds., *Milcah Martha Moore's Book: A Commonplace Book from Revolutionary America* (University Park, PA, 1997), 5, 19.

5. Patricia Crawford, *Blood, Bodies and Families in Early Modern England* (Harlow, UK, 2004), ch. 5, 146 ("suckling").

6. A. Marsh, *The Ten Pleasures of Marriage Relating All the Delights and Contentments That Are Mask'd Under the Bands of Matrimony* (Oxford, UK, 1682), 134.

7. On the gesture of chastity, see Laura Gowing, "'The Manner of Submission': Gender and Demeanour in Seventeenth-Century London," *Cultural and Social History* 10 (2013), 25–45, 34; Lorena S. Walsh, "'Till Death Us Do Part': Marriage and Family in Seventeenth-Century Maryland," in Thad W. Tate and David L. Ammerman, eds., *Chesapeake in the Seventeenth Century: Essays on Anglo-American Studies* (Chapel Hill, NC, 1979), 141 ("good Store").

8. Katy Simpson Smith, *We Have Raised All of You: Motherhood in the South, 1750–1835* (Baton Rouge, LA, 2013), 96 (Cox); Fildes, *Wet Nursing*, 102 (Ramazzini); Angus McLaren, *Reproductive Rituals: The Perception of Fertility in England from the Sixteenth to the Seventeenth Century* (London, 1984), 34 (rampion).

9. Rhodes, "Domestic Vulnerabilities," 44–45 (ads); and more generally on this literature of the servant class, see David M. Katzman, *Seven Days a Week: Women and Domestic Service in Industrializing America* (New York, 1978), 99.

10. Marsh, *The Ten Pleasures of Marriage*, 141 ("estranged"); Amanda Vickery, *The Gentleman's Daughter: Women's Lives in Georgian England* (New Haven, CT, 1998), 107–10, quotation at 108 (Scrimshire).

11. Fildes, *Wet Nursing*, 85 (wills), 87 ("unborrowed").

12. Hrdy, *Mother Nature*, 35 ("elixirs of contentment").

13. Patricia Crawford, "Women's Dreams in Early Modern England," *History Workshop Journal* 49 (2000), 130–31 ("word divine," "fountain").

14. Mary Richardson Walker, *First White Women Over the Rockies*, vol. 2: *On to Oregon: The Diaries of Mary Walker and Myra Eells* (1966, repr. Nebraska, 1998), 331.

15. Judith Schneid Lewis, *In the Family Way: Childbearing in the British Aristocracy, 1760–1860* (New Brunswick, NJ, 1986), 210 (Devonshire); Nora Doyle, "'The Highest Pleasure of Which Woman's Nature Is Capable': Breastfeeding and the Sentimental Maternal Ideal in America, 1750–1860," *Journal of American History* 97 (2011), 958–73, quotations at 961 (Buchan), 958 (Watkins), 962 (Allen).

16. Sally McMillen, "Mothers' Sacred Duty: Breastfeeding Patterns Among Middle- and Upper-Class Women in the Antebellum South," *Journal of Southern History* 51 (1985), 333–56, quotations at 333.

17. Doyle, "'The Highest Pleasure,'" 969 (Lewis).

18. Ibid., 967 ("enchanting").

19. Rhodes, "Domestic Vulnerabilities," 51 ("Wants," "Wanted").

20. For these three paragraphs, see Fanny B. Workman, "The Wet-Nurse in the

Household," *Babyhood* 2 (1886), 142–44; Golden, *A Social History of Wet Nursing in America*, 141, 159–66.

21. Thomas E. Cone, Jr., *History of the Care and Feeding of the Premature Infant* (Boston, 1985), esp. 46.

22. Gerda Lerner, "Dreaming," *Women's Studies Quarterly* 11 (193), 26; Marilyn Chin, "We Are Americans Now, We Live in the Tundra," *The Iowa Review* 17 (1987), 84.

23. Marylynn Salmon, "The Cultural Significance of Breastfeeding and Infant Care in Early Modern England and America," *Journal of Social History* 28 (1994), 247–69, 250 ("White Vitriol").

24. Isabella Beeton, *Mrs. Beeton's Book of Household Management*, ed. Nicola Humble (Oxford, UK, 2000), 1022–24.

25. Margaret B. Blackman, *Sadie Brower Neakok: An Inupiaq Woman* (Seattle, 1989), 128.

26. Mrs. Abby Fisher, *What Mrs. Fisher Knows About Southern Cooking* (San Francisco, 1881), 72.

27. Ann Oakley, *From Here to Maternity: Becoming a Mother* (Harmondsworth, UK, 1979), 187 (mixing powder).

28. Margaret Jarman Hagood, *Mothers of the South: Portraiture of the White Tenant Farm Woman* (1939, repr. New York, 1972), 55.

29. Philippa Mein Smith, "Mothers, Babies and the Mothers and Babies Movement: Australia Through Depression and War," *Social History of Medicine* 6 (1993), 51–83.

30. Jacquelyn S. Litt, *Medicalized Motherhood: Perspectives from the Lives of African-American and Jewish Women* (New Brunswick, NJ, 1999), 58–59, 101 (Selma Cohen), 108.

31. John and Elizabeth Newson, *Patterns of Infant Care in an Urban Community* (London, 1963), esp. 38 ("swill"), 44 ("get rid"), 50, 54 (statistics), 55. All the interviewees' names were changed.

32. Ibid., 37 ("cry," "napkin").

33. Ibid., 36 ("birthright"), 42 ("left arms"), 43 ("idle," "shirking").

34. Ibid., 40 ("nicer"), 41 ("lips," "closeness"), 43 ("job").

35. Ibid., 36 (too watery, etc.), 37 ("wet through").

36. Ibid., 38 (all quotations).

37. Oakley, *From Here to Maternity*, 42–43 (Hilary Jackson), 167 ("leaked"), 186 ("cowsheds").

38. Ibid., 168.

39. Ibid., 182 ("relaxed"), 177 (pain then liking, "nothing"), 178 ("nice").

40. Jackie Kay, "Big Milk," *Granta* 63 (London, 1998), 99–109.

15. Uncertainty, or a Thought Experiment

1. For how-to guides, see especially Angela Davis, *Modern Motherhood: Women and Family in England, c. 1945–2000* (Manchester, UK, 2012), ch. 5; Rima D. Apple, *Perfect Motherhood: Science and Childrearing in America* (New Brunswick, NJ, 2006); Julia Grant, *Raising Baby by the Book: The Education of American Mothers* (New Haven, CT, 1998); Christina Hardyment, *Dream Babies: Childcare Advice from John Locke to Gina Ford* (1983, repr. London, 2007).

2. The notes here and below mainly concern direct quotations from the sources. For this paragraph and the next, see Richard Allestree, *The Ladies Calling, in Two Parts*, 4th ed. (Oxford, UK, 1676), 49–52, quotation at 49, copy held in Lilly Library, Bloomington, IN; Jane Sharp, *The Midwives Book, Or, The Whole Art of Midwifry Discovered*, ed. Elaine Hobby (Oxford, UK, 1999), quotation at 374.

3. Eminent Physician, *The Nurse's Guide: Or, the Right Method of Bringing up Young Children* (London, 1729); William Cadogan, *An Essay upon Nursing and Management of Children from Their Birth to Three Years of Age* (London, 1748); James Nelson, *Essay on the Government of Children Under Three General Heads, viz, Health, Manners, and Education* (London, 1753); William Buchan, *Domestic Medicine* (Edinburgh, 1769).

4. Michael Underwood, *A Treatise on the Diseases of Children, with Directions for the Management of Infants from the Birth; Especially Such as Are Brought Up by Hand* (London, 1784), and many further editions.

5. A Lady, *The Ladies Library, Volume 1* (London, 1714).

6. Lydia Maria Child, *The Mother's Book* (Boston, 1831); L. H. Sigourney, *Letters to Mothers* (Hartford, CT, 1838), vii ("you are sitting"); Mrs. William Parkes, *Domestic Duties, or, Instructions to Young Married Ladies*, 3rd ed. (London, 1828), 184, 186; Eliza Warren, *How I Managed My Children from Infancy to Marriage* (London, 1865); Milicent Washburn Shinn, *The Biography of a Baby* (Boston, 1900); Sidonie Matsner Gruenberg, *Your Child Today and Tomorrow: Some Practical Counsel for Parents* (Philadelphia, 1912); Sophia Jex-Blake, *The Care of Infants, A Manual for Mothers and Nurses* (London, 1898).

7. L. Emmett Holt, *Care and Feeding of Children*, 6th ed. (New York, 1894), 15–16.

8. For example, Sir Frederic Truby King, *Feeding and Care of Baby* (London, 1913); Benjamin Spock, *The Common Sense Book of Baby and Child Care* (New York, 1946, and further editions published until 1998); Penelope Leach, *Babyhood: Stage by Stage, from Birth to Age Two; How Your Baby Develops Physically, Emotionally, Mentally* (Harmondsworth, UK, 1974); Mabel Liddiard, *Mothercraft Manual, or The Expectant and Nursing Mother and Baby's First Two Years* (London, 1948), diagram reprinted in Hardyment, *Dream Babies*, 153.

9. Eminent Physician, *The Nurse's Guide*, 46 ("keel"); Sigourney, *Letters to Mothers*, vii ("tendrils"); Eric Pritchard, *Infant Education* (London, 1907), 94 (telephone); Shinn, *The Biography of a Baby*, 6 (monkeys).

10. Henry Newcome, *The Compleat Mother, or, An Earnest Perswasive to All Mothers* (London, 1695), 6–7; William Moss, *Essay on the Management and Nursing of Children* (London, 1781), title-page (comprehension); John D. West, *Maidenhood and Motherhood; or The Ten Phases of a Woman's Life* (Detroit, 1888), 25–29. The BMA is quoted in Ann Oakley, "Normal Motherhood: An Exercise in Self-Control?" in Bridget Hutter and Gillian Williams, eds., *Controlling Women: The Normal and the Deviant* (London, 1981), 80 (worry), 82 (pram).

11. John Locke, *Some Thoughts on Education* (London, 1693), 2 (cockering).

12. Mrs. Childs, *The Mother's Book*, 2nd ed. (Boston, 1831), dedication; Benjamin Spock and Michael B. Rothenberg, *Dr. Spock's Baby and Child Care*, 6th ed. (New York, 1992), xvi–xvii.

13. James N. Green, librarian, Library Company of Philadelphia, correspondence with the author; Spock, *The Common Sense Book*, 1 ("Trust yourself").

14. Mary R. Melendy, *Perfect Womanhood for Maidens-Wives-Mothers* (Chicago, 1903), 5; Charlotte Perkins Gilman, *Concerning Children* (Boston, 1900); Gillian E. Hanscombe and Jackie Forster, *Rocking the Cradle: A Challenge in Family Living* (London, 1981); and see Kristin G. Esterberg, "Planned Parenthood: The Construction of Motherhood in Lesbian Mother Advice Books," in Andrea O'Reilly, ed., *Feminist Mothering* (Albany, NY, 2008), 75–88.

15. Apple, *Perfect Motherhood*, 19 (literacy), 47 (Carlin); Elizabeth Roberts, *Women and Families: An Oral History, 1940–1970* (Oxford, 1995), 142; Lucinda McCray Beier, "Expertise and Control: Childbearing in Three Twentieth-Century Working-Class Lancashire Communities," *Bulletin of the History of Medicine* 78 (2004), 379–409.

16. Sharp, *The Midwives Book*, 376; Underwood, *A Treatise on the Diseases of Children*; Edith Buxbaum, *Your Child Makes Sense: A Guidebook for Parents* (New York, 1949).

17. Mary Truby King, *Mothercraft*, 15th printing (London, 1944), 4 ("happiest"), 66 (timetable), 164 ("21 hours").

18. C. Anderson Aldrich and Mary M. Aldrich, *Babies Are Human Beings* (New York, 1942), 60–61 (quotation, marginalia), 75 (kick), 76 (appetite), copy belonging to Indiana University South Bend. Electronic cataloguing of Indiana University libraries in 1990 entailed loss of the original card catalogue and checkout records.

16. Queer Ideas at the Clinic

1. Rivka Galchen, *Little Labors* (New York, 2016); Trevor MacDonald, *Where's the Mother? Stories from a Transgender Dad* (Dugald, Canada, 2016); Sarah Manguso, *Ongoingness: The End of a Diary* (Minneapolis, 2015); Maggie Nelson, *The Argonauts* (Minneapolis, 2015); Lia Purpura, *Increase* (Athens, GA, 2015); Eula Biss, *On Immunity: An Innoculation* (Minneapolis, 2014); Rachel Zucker, *the pedestrians* (Seattle, 2014); Rachel Zucker, *MOTHERs* (Denver, 2014); Lisa Baraitser, *Maternal Encounters: The Ethics of Interruption* (Hove, UK, 2009); Lonnae O'Neal Parker, *I'm Every Woman: Remixed Stories of Marriage, Motherhood, and Work* (New York, 2005); Anne Enright, *Making Babies: Stumbling into Motherhood* (London, 2004); Rachel Cusk, *A Life's Work: On Becoming a Mother* (London, 2001).

2. For Burger and Logan, see Abigail Lewis (Otis Burger), *An Interesting Condition: The Diary of a Pregnant Woman* (Garden City, NY, 1950), 123–25; Onnie Lee Logan, as told to Katherine Clark, *Motherwit: An Alabama Midwife's Story* (New York, 1989), 98 ("understand"), 90 ("wisdom"); Clarebeth Loprinzi-Kassell, "Onnie Lee Logan / Matilda Mitchell: Grand Midwives," *Birth Gazette* 12 (1996), 26–28.

3. For this paragraph and the next, see: C. Anderson Aldrich and Mary M. Aldrich, *Babies Are Human Beings* (New York, 1942), 102 ("crackers"); Lewis, *An Interesting Condition*, 241 (restless cousin), 133 ("tomboy"), 255 (cartoon). My interpretation of Burger and her world also draws on Benjamin Spock, *The Common Sense Book of Baby and Child Care* (New York, 1946); Rima D. Apple, *Perfect Motherhood: Science and Childrearing in America* (New Brunswick, NJ, 2006), esp. 107–34, quotation at 83 ("too much emphasis").

4. For this paragraph and the next, see: Logan and Clark, *Motherwit*, 62 (bitterweed), 64 (teething remedies). My interpretation of Onnie Lee Logan and her world also draws on Christa Craven and Mara Glatzel, "Downplaying Difference: Historical Accounts of African American Midwives and Contemporary Struggles for Midwifery," *Feminist Studies* 36 (2010), 330–58; Gertrude Jacinta Fraser, *African American Midwifery in the South: Dialogues of Birth, Race and Memory* (Cambridge, MA, 1998), esp. 240, 242–44; Margaret Charles Smith and Linda Holmes, *Listen to Me Good: The Life Story of an Alabama Midwife* (Columbus, OH, 1996), quotation at 155 ("raised"); Jacqueline S. Litt, *Medicalized Motherhood: Perspectives from the Lives of African-American and Jewish Women* (New Brunswick, NJ, 2000), 63–81; Debra Anne Susie, *In the Way of Our Grandmothers: A Cultural View of Twentieth-Century Midwifery in Florida* (Athens, GA, 1988).

5. Nancy Oestreich Lurie, ed., *Mountain Wolf Woman, Sister of Crashing Thunder: The Autobiography of a Winnebago Indian* (Ann Arbor, MI, 1961), 1, 84.

6. Harriet Connor Brown, *Grandmother Brown's Hundred Years, 1827–1927* (Boston, 1929), 24, 33, 40, 95–96.

7. Eleanor Gordon and Gwyneth Nair, *Public Lives: Women, Family and Society in Victorian Britain* (New Haven, CT, 2003), 146.

8. Anne Megna Dunst, "How I Fought for My Schooling with a Baby in My Arms," *Italian Americana* 5 (1979), 249–53; Elizabeth Roberts, *A Woman's Place: An Oral History of Working-Class Women, 1890–1940* (Oxford, UK, 1984), 23–25 (Mrs. Phillips, a pseudonym).

9. For this paragraph and the next, see Elizabeth Keckley, *Behind the Scenes, Or, Thirty Years a Slave and Four Years in the White House* (New York, 1868), 19–21; Stephanie J. Shaw, "Mothering Under Slavery in the Antebellum South," in Evelyn Nakano Glenn et al., eds., *Mothering: Ideology, Experience and Agency* (New York, 1994), quotations at 244.

10. Cathy Cade, *A Lesbian Photo Album: The Lives of Seven Lesbian Feminists* (Oakland, CA, 1987), 86.

11. For these four paragraphs, see Lewis, *An Interesting Condition*, 111 (suburbs), 227 (crisis), 123 ("engrossed"), 92 ("psychology"), 242 ("attention"), 111 ("knitted suits"); Philip Wylie, *Generation of Vipers* (New York, 1942); Rebecca Jo Plant, *Mom: The Transformation of Motherhood in Modern America* (Chicago, 2010), ch. 1.

12. Litt, *Medicalized Motherhood*, 80 ("watching," "pattern").

13. For this paragraph and the next, see Logan and Clark, *Motherwit*, 89 ("progressing"), 95–96 (bed); Smith and Holmes, *Listen to Me Good*, 42 ("tread sash," moles' feet), 155 ("big old girl"), 93 ("cardboard box," "usually put"); 99 ("comb," "titties").

14. Bartlett Jere Whiting, *Early American Proverbs and Proverbial Phrases* (Cambridge, MA, 1977), 323 ("motherwit"); *OED* ("mothersome").

15. Karen Ritts Benally, "Thinking Good: The Teachings of Navajo Grandmothers," in Marjorie M. Schweitzer, ed., *American Indian Grandmothers: Traditions and Transitions* (Albuquerque, NM, 1999), 25–52, quotations at 38.

16. Michael Young and Peter Willmott, *Family and Kinship in East London* (Glencoe, IL, 1957), 28–43, quotation at 28.

17. Linda W. Rosenzweig, *The Anchor of My Life: Middle-Class American Mothers and Daughters, 1880–1920* (New York, 1993), 117–21, quotations at 118 (Tuttle), 120–21 (Winsor Allen).

18. For cunning intelligence as the hallmark of these several occupations, see Mary E. Fissell, "Sarah Stone: Artisan of the Body" (unpublished paper); Jane Sharp, *The Midwives Book, Or the Whole Art of Midwifry Discovered*, ed. Elaine Hobby (Oxford, UK, 1999), 273.

19. Ellen Ross, *Love and Toil: Motherhood in Outcast London, 1870–1918* (New York,

1993), 120–21; Lucinda McCray Beier, "Expertise and Control: Childbearing in Three Twentieth-Century Working-Class Lancashire Communities," *Bulletin of the History of Medicine* 78 (2004), esp. 397–98, 400; Elizabeth Ewen, *Immigrant Women in the Land of Dollars: Life and Culture on the Lower East Side, 1890–1925* (New York, 1995), 130–36, quotation at 132 (Serpe).

20. Mrs. Layton, "Memories of Seventy Years," in Margaret Llewelyn Davies, ed., *Life As We Have Known It by Cooperative Women* (1931, repr. New York, 1975), 43–46; Susan L. Smith, *Japanese American Midwives: Culture, Community, and Health Politics, 1880–1950* (Urbana, IL, 2005), 60–103, esp. 78–79, 86.

21. Fran Leeper Buss, *La Partera: Story of a Midwife* (Ann Arbor, MI, 1980), esp. 45 ("move and stay out"); 64–65 (swaddling); 50 (other midwives); 66 (beans); 67 (nursing); 79 (chamomile); 52, 68 (nails).

22. Lewis, *An Interesting Condition*, 16 ("too complicated"), 24 ("patronising"), 160 ("whoops"), 231 ("social-worker"), 252 ("lost").

23. Apple, *Perfect Motherhood*, 25 (Stanton, Combe), 22 (constant reading); Litt, *Medicalized Motherhood*, 127 (Marion Marks).

24. Angela Davis, *Modern Motherhood: Women and Family in England, c. 1945–2000* (Manchester, UK, 2012), 128–32, quotations at 129 (Spock); Apple, *Perfect Motherhood*, 124 (army wife).

25. Molly Ladd-Taylor, ed., *Raising a Baby the Government Way: Mothers' Letters to the Children's Bureau, 1915–1932* (New Brunswick, NJ, 1986), 89 (Mrs. N. F.), 81–83 (Mrs. C. S.), 103–104 (Mrs. H. S.).

26. Logan and Clark, *Motherwit*, 102; Smith and Holmes, *Listen to Me Good*, 114; and on medical experimentation, see Deidre Benia Cooper Owens, *Medical Bondage: Race, Gender, and the Origins of American Gynecology* (Athens, GA, 2017).

27. Young and Willmott, *Family and Kinship in East London*, 37.

28. Logan and Clark, *Motherwit*, 129–30 (white clientele); 174–75 (complaining doctors).

29. Richard A. Meckel, "Educating a Ministry of Mothers: Evangelical Maternal Associations, 1815–1860," *Journal of the Early Republic* 2 (1982), 403–23, quotation at 413.

30. F. Prochaska, "A Mother's Country: Mothers' Meetings and Family Welfare in Britain, 1850–1950," *History* 74 (1989), 379–99, quotation at 397.

31. Litt, *Medicalized Motherhood*, 129–30 (Tot Club); Apple, *Perfect Motherhood*, 98 (Better Babies).

32. Lynn Y. Weiner, "Reconstructing Motherhood: The La Leche League in Postwar America," *Journal of American History* 80 (1994), 1357–81; Terry Slater, "Why I Decided to Have a Baby," *Spare Rib* 63 (1977), 10–12.

17. Back and Forth

1. For babysitting, see Miriam Forman-Brunell, *Babysitter: An American History* (New York, 2009), esp. 14.

2. These relationships are revealed through Lucy's words. For this and the next five paragraphs, see: Daniel Dulany Addison, *Lucy Larcom: Life, Letters, and Diary* (Boston, 1894), esp. 29–31 (the cabin), 42 ("French leave"); Lucy Larcom, *A New England Childhood, Outlined from Memory* (Boston, 1889), esp. 190 (Dickens), 226 ("half-live creature"); 261 (sardines); 258–64; supplemented by a modern biography based on further manuscripts: Shirley Marchalonis, *The Worlds of Lucy Larcom, 1824–1893* (Athens, GA, 1989), chs. 2–3, esp. 32–33, 53 ("domestic happiness"), and 257 ("affection"). Caroline Matilda Kirkland, *A New Home—Who'll Follow? Or, Glimpses of Western Life* (New York, 1839, repr. 1855), 115. Lydia Maria Child, *The Mother's Book*, 2nd ed. (Boston, 1831), 4.

3. For this and the next six paragraphs, the key source is the field research written up by Madeline Kerr: *The People of Ship Street* (London, 1958), esp. 15 ("mother-dominated," unlikeliness of break); 50–51 (cooking, mother/mum); 192–95 (details of everyday life); 196–97 (Mrs. U); 104, 198 (Eunice). All names, including the street's title, were falsified by Kerr.

4. My key sources for Minde and her relatives, throughout this section, are two sets of interviews conducted by a younger Cree, Freda Ahenakew, in the late 1980s: Freda Ahenakew and H. C. Wolfart, ed. and trans., *Their Example Showed Me the Way: A Cree Woman's Life Shaped by Two Cultures, Told by Emma Minde* (Edmonton, Canada, 1997), esp. xi (*nisikos*), 59 (Justine), 67 ("difficult time"), 79–83 (work), 91 (raising granddaughter), 131–35 (diapers, laundry, "picnic"); and Ahenakew and Wolfart, ed. and trans., *Our Grandmothers' Lives, As Told in Their Own Words* (Saskatoon, Canada, 1992), 26 (Cree values), 97 (seaplanes, canoes), 241 ("babysitter"), 224 ("suckling"), 325–27 (moss). See also David G. Mandelbaum, *The Plains Cree: An Ethnographic, Historical, and Comparative Study* (1940, repr. Regina, Saskatchewan, 1979), based on fieldwork from 1934 and 1935, 140 (moss), 142–43 (weaning); Jane Willis, *Geniesh: An Indian Girlhood* (Toronto, 1973) (adoption); Regina Flannery, *Ellen Smallboy: Glimpses of a Cree Woman's Life* (Montreal, 1995), 32 (cross-feeding). For seventeenth-century speakers of Miami and Montagnais, see Sarah M. S. Pearsall, "Native American Men—and Women—at Home in Plural Marriages in Seventeenth-Century New France," *Gender and History* 27 (2015), 591–610, quotations at 596.

5. Patricia Hill Collins, *Black Feminist Thought* (New York, 1990, repr. 2000), 131–32; and her "The Meaning of Motherhood in Black Culture and Black Mother–Daughter Relationships," in Patricia Bell-Scott et al., eds., *Double Stitch: Black Women Write About Mothers and Daughters* (Boston, 1991).

6. For the world of Winney Jackson explored in this and the following four paragraphs, I am indebted to Richard S. Dunn, *A Tale of Two Plantations: Slave Life and Labor in Jamaica and Virginia* (Cambridge, MA, 2014), esp. 46, 51, 53, 107–12, 209–14; supplemented by Dell Upton, "White and Black Landscapes in Eighteenth-Century Virginia," in Robert Blair St. George, ed., *Material Life in America, 1600–1860* (Boston, 1988), 357–69, esp. 360, 367; Laura Croghan Kamoie, *Irons in the Fire: The Business History of the Tayloe Family and Virginia's Gentry, 1700–1860* (Charlottesville, VA, 2007), esp. 95, 99–100.

7. Frederick Douglass, *My Bondage and My Freedom* (1855, repr. New Haven, CT, 2014), 46–47, 61, quotation at 47; Katy Simpson Smith, "Black Aunts," in *We Have Raised All of You: Motherhood in the South, 1750–1835* (Baton Rouge, LA, 2013), 231–41, esp. 233–34; Stephanie J. Shaw, "Mothering Under Slavery in the Antebellum South," in Evelyn Nakano Glenn et al., eds., *Mothering: Ideology, Experience and Agency* (New York, 1994), esp. 250 (Aunt Mandy).

8. Collins, "Meaning of Motherhood," 47 (Brooks).

9. Virginia Woolf, *A Room of One's Own* (London, 1929).

10. For the discussion of Woolf in these paragraphs, see Alison Light, *Mrs. Woolf and the Servants* (London, 2007).

11. For the unmarried Alice Fisher in these three paragraphs, see the interview with Alice Field (as she refers to herself), "Interview with Mrs. Field," SN2000 The Edwardians, 1870–1913, accessed online Aug. 22, 2016; P. Thompson and T. Lummis, *Family Life and Work Experience Before 1918, 1870–1973*, 7th ed. (UK Data Service, 2009).

12. For these five paragraphs, see Martha Haygood Hall, "The Nursemaid: A Socio-Psychological Study of an Occupational Group" (MA thesis, University of Chicago, 1931), esp. iii, 123 (Haygood Hall), 8, 32 (meals), 25–27 (European origins), 36–42 (conditions and turnover), 171 (marcelling); quotations at 60, 68 (Kathie), 103 ("wanderers"), 110 ("get along," "good feelings," "grudge," "likes me"), 153 (Lisa), 182–83 (Anna).

13. For this paragraph and the next, see Mrs. William Parkes, *Domestic Duties or, Instructions to Young Married Ladies*, 2nd ed. (London, 1825), esp. 155; Eliza Warren, *How I Managed My Children from Infancy to Marriage* (London, 1865), 25–26 (Hester).

14. Mary Ann Ashford, *Life of a Licensed Victualler's Daughter. Written by Herself* (London, 1844), reprinted in Claudia Nelson and Susan B. Egenoff, eds., *British Family Life, 1780–1914*, 5 vols. (London, 2013), iv, 159–77, quotations at 162.

15. On the history of fathering of infants in particular, explored in this section, see Shawn Johansen, *Family Men: Middle-Class Fatherhood in Early Industrializing America* (New York, 2001), 73–79, quotations at 75–76 (Lincoln Clark, John Wesley, and Ann North); Lynn Abrams, "'There Was Nobody Like My Daddy':

Fathers, the Family and the Marginalisation of Men in Modern Scotland," *Scottish Historical Review* 78 (1999), 219–42, esp. 233 ("change a nappy"); Laura King, "'Now You See a Great Many Men Pushing Their Pram Proudly': Family-Oriented Masculinity Represented and Experienced in Twentieth-Century Britain," *Cultural and Social History* 10 (2013), 599–617, quotations at 607 ("Jessie," "thumb"), 608 (Rochford, pub); Julie Smith, "The First Intruder: Fatherhood, A Historical Perspective," in Peter Moss, ed., *Father Figures: Fathers in the Families of the 1990s* (Edinburgh, 1995), 17–26, esp. Figure 1 (Avon), 19 (Woman's Hour). Further details in Lynn Jamieson and Claire Toynbee, *Country Bairns: Growing Up, 1900–1930* (Edinburgh, 1992), 110 (Mrs. West on her father). Lincoln Steffens, "Becoming a Father at 60 is a Liberal Education," *American Magazine* 106 (Aug. 1928), 48. Johan de Brune, *Emblemata of zinne-werck* (Amsterdam, 1661).

18. Paper Flowers

1. Viola Paradise, *Maternity Care and the Welfare of Young Children in a Homesteading County in Montana* (Washington, DC, 1918), chapter title.

2. For the early modern English scenes, I draw especially on Barry Stapleton, "Inherited Poverty and Life-Cycle Poverty: Odiham, Hampshire, 1650–1850," *Social History* 18 (1993), 339–55; Amanda Flather, *Gender and Space in Early Modern England* (Woodbridge, UK, 2007), ch. 3; Patricia Crawford, *Parents of Poor Children in England, 1580–1800* (Oxford, UK, 2010); supplemented by Linda Oja, "Childcare and Gender in Sweden c. 1600–1800," *Gender and History* 27 (2015), 77–111.

3. For the twentieth-century homesteading examples in these two paragraphs, see Paradise, *Maternity Care and the Welfare of Young Children*; Deborah Fink, *Agrarian Women: Wives and Mothers in Rural Nebraska, 1880–1940* (Chapel Hill, NC, 1992); Julie Jones-Eddy, *Homesteading Women: An Oral History of Colorado, 1890–1950* (New York, 1992).

4. Betty Sutherland is her real name. Evidence comes from interviews with her son and daughter-in-law undertaken by an anthropologist in 1976–78: Nancy C. Dorian, *The Tyranny of Tide: An Oral History of the East Sutherland Fisherfolk* (Ann Arbor, MI, 1985), esp. 7 (foot-rocking), 15 (flagstone floor), 30–31 (widows, carrying), 34 (shoes), 35 (barter), 49 (kinds of fish), 51 (shopping), 80 (relatives).

5. For these four paragraphs: On the Italian tenement homeworkers in New York, see Mary Van Kleeck, *Artificial Flower Makers* (New York, 1913), esp. 86–87 (how income is spent), 90 (relative numbers of factory and home workers), 95 (the process of manufacture), 97–98 (anonymous case of skilled homeworker, the

working "half the night"), 110 (violet), photograph facing p. 143; Elizabeth Ewen, *Immigrant Women in the Land of Dollars: Life and Culture on the Lower East Side, 1890–1925* (New York, 1985), esp. ch. 1 (southern Italy), photographs at 105–106 (nursing, white box); Eileen Boris, *Home to Work: Motherhood and the Politics of Industrial Homework in the United States* (New York, 1994), esp. 104 (income), 106 (Italian trade). Beyond this setting, see Boris, *Home to Work*, esp. 191; Shelley Pennington and Belinda Westover, *A Hidden Workforce: Women Homeworkers in England, 1850–1985* (New York, 1989).

6. For this and the next three paragraphs, see Xialoan Bao, *Holding Up More Than Half the Sky: Chinese Garment Workers in New York City, 1948–1992* (Urbana, IL, 2001), 122 (slang), 125–27 (quotations, the case of Mrs. Lee, a pseudonym).

7. Mary H. Blewett, *Men, Women, and Work: Class, Gender, and Protest in the New England Shoe Industry, 1780–1910* (Urbana, IL, 1988), and for the details here, see esp. 6–9 (kitchen shoemaking), 12 (shoes for enslaved people), 14–15, 30–31 (shoebinding), 51–53 (Guilford and McIntire), 144, 156 (kinds of shoes), 150 (factory description), 209, 213 (wives in 1870s); quotation at 17 (Gilmans).

8. On the emergence and history of day care, a neglected topic, see Patricia E. Malcolmson, *English Laundresses: A Social History, 1850–1930* (Chicago, 1986), 34–35 (the London evidence), quotation at 35; Elizabeth Roberts, *A Woman's Place: An Oral History of Working-Class Women, 1890–1940* (Oxford, UK, 1984), 144 (bush telegraph); Elizabeth Rose, *A Mother's Job: The History of Day Care, 1890–1960* (New York, 1999).

9. Sherna Berger Gluck, *Rosie the Riveter Revisited: Women, the War and Social Change* (Boston, 1987), 128–50, esp. 143–44, 146–47 (Loveless).

10. Sheila Patterson, *Dark Strangers: A Sociological Study of the Absorption of a Recent West Indian Group in Brixton, South London* (Bloomington, IN, 1964), 310–11 ("Miss Thelma L"), with other quotations at 316 (U.S. color bar); Elyse Dodgson, *Motherland: West Indian Women to Britain in the 1950s* (London, 1984), quotation at 31 (giving out); Nancy Foner, *Jamaica Farewell: Jamaican Migrants in London* (Berkeley, 1978), esp. 60 (education), 80–83 (work and childcare), quotation at 82 ("grandmother or aunties").

11. For Mrs. Burrell (a pseudonym) and the multigenerational history of Northern Lancashire, see Elizabeth Roberts, *Women and Families: An Oral History, 1940–1970* (Oxford, UK, 1995), esp. 135 (quotations); Roberts, *A Woman's Place*.

12. Rachel Thomson, "Making Motherhood Work?," *Studies in the Maternal* 2 (2011), 1; Jodi Vandenberg-Daves, *Modern Motherhood: An American History* (New Brunswick, NJ, 2014), 249; Boris, *Home to Work*, 347, suggesting that half of all mothers with babies under a year old worked for wages in 1987.

19. An Oak Dolly Tub

1. Jane Lazarre, *The Mother Knot* (Boston, 1976), 109–10.
2. Daniel Thomas Cook, *The Commodification of Childhood: The Children's Clothing Industry and the Rise of the Child Consumer* (Durham, NC, 2004), 100–104 (pink and blue).
3. Ann Oakley, *From Here to Maternity: Becoming a Mother* (Harmondsworth, UK, 1979), 250 (Diggery).
4. For this paragraph and the next: Colette A. Hyman, *Dakota Women's Work: Creativity, Culture, and Exile* (St. Paul, MN, 2012), esp. 17–18 (cradleboard), 27 (painting); John C. Ewers, *Plains Indian History and Culture: Essays on Continuity and Change* (Norman, OK, 1997), 76, fig. 4.7.
5. Frances Densmore, *Chippewa Customs* (1929, repr. St. Paul, MN, 1979), 48–49, plate 22.
6. James S. Chisholm, *Navajo Infancy: An Ethological Study of Child Development* (New York, 1983), esp. 78 (diaper, cliffrose).
7. Robert Holt, "Extract from an Account of a Charity, for Assisting the Female Poor, at the Period of Their Lying In," *Reports of the Society for Bettering the Condition and Increasing the Comforts of the Poor* (London, 1798), i, 120–21; Mary Chamberlain, *Growing Up in Lambeth* (London, 1989), 95 (binders and flannelette).
8. Stuart Campbell, "Work and Play: The Material Culture of Childhood in Early Modern Scotland," in Janay Nugent and Elizabeth Ewan, eds., *Children and Youth in Premodern Scotland* (Woodbridge, UK, 2015), 67–68.
9. Christian August Struve, *A Familiar Treatise on the Physical Education of Children During the Early Period of Their Lives*, trans. A.F.M. Willich (London, 1800) ("sucking bags"); Albertine de Saussure, *Progressive Education Commencing with the Infant* (Boston, 1835), 335 (sugar rag, discussed by translator Almira Phelps); John and Elizabeth Newson, *Patterns of Infant Care in an Urban Community* (London, 1963), 57–60 (terminology for dummies).
10. Laurie A. Wilkie, *Creating Freedom: Material Culture and African American Identity at Oakley Plantation, Louisiana, 1840–1950* (Baton Rouge, LA, 2000), esp. 189–92; Newbell Niles Puckett, *Folk Beliefs of the Southern Negro* (Chapel Hill, NC, 1926).
11. The two key histories of cradles, cribs, and cots, used across this section, and both focused on the white middle and upper classes, are Karin Calvert, *Children in the House: The Material Culture of Early Childhood, 1600–1900* (Boston, 1992), esp. 27–29, 65–69, 132–35; and Sally Kevill-Davies, *Yesterday's Children: The Antiques and History of Childcare* (Woodbridge, UK, 1991), esp. 106–24.
12. John Henry Mole, *Minding Baby* (1852).

13. Kevill-Davies, *Yesterday's Children*, 106 ("kept rocking").

14. Isabella Beeton, *Mrs. Beeton's Book of Household Management*, ed. Nicola Humble (Oxford, UK, 2000), 496 ("squaws," "mummying").

15. Anne Winters, "Night Light," *The Key to the City* (Chicago, 1986), 25.

16. George Frederic Still, *The History of Paediatrics; The Progress of the Study of Diseases of Children up to the End of the XVIIIth Century* (London, 1931), 265 ("wax candle"); Harriet Connor Brown, *Grandmother Brown's Hundred Years, 1827–1927: Settling the Midwest* (Boston, 1929), 97 (feathers, "poppies"); Oakley, *From Here to Maternity*, 170 (Brady).

17. Steve Humphries and Pamela Gordon, *A Labour of Love: The Experience of Parenthood in Britain 1900–1950* (London, 1993), 58 (Siddall); Michele Felice Corne, *Hanging Out the Wash* (1800), reprinted in Kathleen M. Brown, *Foul Bodies: Cleanliness in Early America* (New Haven, CT, 2009), 219.

18. Amanda Vickery, *The Gentleman's Daughter: Women's Lives in Georgian England* (New Haven, CT, 1998), 117 (Parker); John Spargo, *The Bitter Cry of Children* (New York, 1909), 28 (clothes basket); Charles A. Le Guin, ed., *A Home-Concealed Woman: The Diaries of Magnolia Wynn Le Guin, 1901–1913* (Athens, GA, 1990), 71 ("cracker-box," pallet); Elizabeth Roberts, *A Woman's Place: An Oral History of Working-Class Women, 1890–1940* (Oxford, UK, 1984); 150–51 (banana box); Chamberlain, *Growing Up in Lambeth*, 96 (flour bags and old drawers); Margaret Jarman Hagood, *Mothers of the South: Portraiture of the White Tenant Farm Woman* (1939, repr. New York, 1972), 97 (kiddie-coop); Regina Flannery, *The Gros Ventres of Montana: Part 1, Social Life* (Washington, DC, 1953), 141 (stiffened leather).

19. Chisholm, *Navajo Infancy*, 79 (baby bottles).

20. Margaret Mead, "On Having a Baby" (1972), extracted in Wendy Martin, ed., *The Beacon Book of Essays by Contemporary American Women* (Boston, 1996), 207.

20. Yard Baby, Lap Baby

1. Sylvia D. Hoffert, *Private Matters: American Attitudes Toward Childbearing and Infant Nurture in the Urban North, 1800–1860* (Urbana, IL, 1989), 132 (Cabot).

2. American Indian Studies Research Institute, Indiana University, Assiniboine Dictionary.

3. *OED*, "weanling"; George Thornton Emmons, *The Tlingit Indians*, ed. Frederica de Laguna (Seattle, 1991), 257, 260.

4. Margaret Jarman Hagood, *Mothers of the South: Portraiture of the White Tenant Farm Woman* (1939, repr. New York, 1972), 68, 139.

5. For this paragraph and the next: Marie Campbell, *Folks Do Get Born* (New York, 1946), 192–203, quotations at 202–203.

6. Isaac Williams, *Aunt Sally, Or, They Cross the Way to Freedom. The Narrative of the Slave-Life and Purchase of the Mother of Rev. Isaac Williams, of Detroit, Michigan* (Cincinnati, 1858), 10 and 63–64 (carrying the infants), further details at 31, 35, 59, 60, 61.

7. Shepard Knapp, ed., *Gideon Lee Knapp and Augusta Murray Spring, His Wife* (privately printed, 1909), 66.

8. Charles A. Le Guin, ed., *A Home-Concealed Woman: The Diaries of Magnolia Wynn Le Guin, 1901–1913* (Athens, GA, 1990), quotations at 7–8, 16 (Askew), 11, 28 (Fred), 44–45 (Jane Miller), 53 ("no time").

9. Viola Bankes and Pamela Watkin, *A Kingston Lacy Childhood: Reminiscences of Viola Bankes* (Wimborne, UK, 1986), 7–9.

10. Mary Chamberlain, *Growing Up in Lambeth* (London, 1989), 94.

11. John and Elizabeth Newson, *Patterns of Infant Care in an Urban Community* (London, 1963), 52; Philippa Mein Smith, "Mothers, Babies, and the Mothers and Babies Movement: Australia through Depression and War," *Social History of Medicine* 6 (1993), 70–71.

12. Jean Radford, "My Pride and Joy," in Katherine Gieve, ed., *Balancing Acts, On Being a Mother* (London, 1989), 137–44, quotations at 137 ("English mother"), 141 ("miracle").

13. Susan Abbott, "Holding On and Pushing Away: Comparative Perspectives on an Eastern Kentucky Child-Rearing Practice," *Ethos* 20 (1992), 33–65, esp. 55–58 (quotations); and also see Deborah Madansky and Craig Edelbrock, "Cosleeping in a Community Sample of 2- and 3-Year-Old Children," *Pediatrics* 86 (1990), 197–280, on Worcester, MA, in the same decade.

14. Philippa Maddern and Stephanie Tarbin, "Life-Cycle," in Sandra Cavallo and Silvia Evangelisti, *A Cultural History of Childhood and Family in the Early Modern Age* (Oxford, UK, 2010), 114–15.

15. Ibid., 124 (Shepard); Nancy C. Dorian, *The Tyranny of Tide: An Oral History of the East Sutherland Fisherfolk* (Ann Arbor, MI, 1985), 6, 10–11, 50, 54.

16. Maddern and Tarbin, "Life-Cycle," 130 (Le Jeune).

17. Laurie A. Wilkie, *The Archaeology of Mothering: An African-American Midwife's Tale* (New York, 2003), 66–69.

18. M. Inez Hilger, *Chippewa Child Life and Its Cultural Background* (Washington, DC, 1951), ix ("just old," "sense"), 39.

19. Peter Wheeler, *Chains and Freedom: Or, The Life and Adventures of Peter Wheeler* (New York, 1839), 21; Katy Simpson Smith, *We Have Raised All of You: Motherhood in the South, 1750–1835* (Baton Rouge, LA, 2013), 46 (Catawba).

20. Linda Pollock, *Forgotten Children: Parent–Child Relations from 1500 to 1900* (Cambridge, UK, 1983), 107 (rope); Carolyn Steedman, *Labours Lost: Domestic Service and the Making of Modern England* (Cambridge, UK, 2009), 48; and, here

and in the next paragraph, Martha Haygood Hall, "The Nursemaid: A Socio-Psychological Study of an Occupational Group" (MA thesis, University of Chicago, 1931), 143 ("happy," "read," "maid"), 145 ("nothing," "tell"), 147 ("tricks").

21. Navigating the Times

1. Sara Ruddick, *Maternal Thinking: Toward a Politics of Peace* (Boston, 1989), 75.
2. For these dynamics, see Gerda Lerner, *The Grimké Sisters from South Carolina* (New York, 1971), and Lois W. Banner, "Elizabeth Cady Stanton: Early Marriage and Feminist Rebellion," in Linda K. Kerber and Jane De Hart-Mathews, eds., *Women's America: Refocusing the Past* (New York, 1987), 201–12; Adrienne Rich, *Of Woman Born: Motherhood as Experience and Institution* (New York, 1976).
3. For this and the following three paragraphs, see Annelise Orleck, *Common Sense and a Little Fire: Women and Working-Class Politics in the United States, 1900–1965* (Chapel Hill, NC, 1995), 215–40, quotations at 218 ("in the home"), 220 (Gerson); Julie Guard, "A Mighty Power Against the Cost of Living: Canadian Housewives Organize in the 1930s," *International Labor and Working-Class History* 77 (2010), 27–47.
4. The discussion in this and the following two paragraphs draws on Katherine M. B. Osburn, *Southern Ute Women: Autonomy and Assimilation on the Reservation, 1887–1934* (Albuquerque, NM, 1998), 3–7, and ch. 4, esp. 73–75; Emily K. Abel and Nancy Reifel, "Interactions Between Public Health Nurses and Clients on American Indian Reservations During the 1930s," *Social History of Medicine* 9 (1996), 89–108.
5. For this paragraph and the next: Daniel W. Rivers, *Radical Relations: Lesbian Mothers, Gay Fathers, and Their Children in the United States since World War II* (Chapel Hill, NC, 2013), 176–78, quotation at 178.

A Note on Method

1. Annabel Patterson, "Anecdotes," *Early Modern Liberalism* (Cambridge, UK, 1997), 153–82; Michael McKeon, *The Secret History of Domesticity: Public, Private, and the Division of Knowledge* (Baltimore, 2005), quotation of Antoine Varillas at 470–71 ("Men in Public"). Most recently and sustainedly, the anecdote surfaced as the archetypal framing device or opening scene in cultural historical analysis.
2. Ruth H. Bloch, "American Feminine Ideals in Transition: The Rise of Moral Mother, 1785–1815," *Feminist Studies* 4 (1978), 111; Amanda Vickery, *The Gentleman's Daughter: Women's Lives in Georgian England* (New Haven, CT, 1998), 110; Anthony Fletcher, *Growing Up in England: The Experience of Childhood,*

1600–1914 (New Haven, CT, 2008), 106; Linda Oja, "Childcare and Gender in Sweden c. 1600–1800," *Gender and History* 27 (2015), 78, 82. See also the discussion in ch. 9 above.

3. Lisa Baraitser, *Maternal Encounters: The Ethics of Interruption* (Hove, UK, 2009), 12 ("constant attack," "punctured").

4. Eve Kosofsky Sedgwick, *Tendencies* (Durham, NC, 1993), 25.

5. Linda A. Pollock, *Forgotten Children: Parent–Child Relations from 1500 to 1900* (Cambridge, UK, 1983), 98.

6. Joan W. Scott, "Rewriting History," in Margaret Higonnet et al., eds., *Behind the Lines: Gender and the Two World Wars* (New Haven, CT, 1987), 19–30, quotations at 22.

7. Ellen Ross, *Love and Toil: Motherhood in Outcast London* (New York, 1993); Judith Walzer Leavitt, *Brought to Bed: Childbearing in America, 1750–1950* (New York, 1986, repr. 2016).

A Note About the Author

Sarah Knott grew up in England. Educated at Oxford University and the University of Pennsylvania, she is now a professor of history at Indiana University and the mother of two small children. She is the author of *Sensibility and the American Revolution* and numerous articles on the histories of women, gender, and emotion. Knott has served as an editor of *The American Historical Review*, the American Historical Association's flagship journal, and sits on the editorial board of *Past and Present*. She is a fellow of the Kinsey Institute for Research in Sex, Gender, and Reproduction.